To the love of my
life .

Hugs & Kisses

Cathy

August 2008

THE BLACK GRIZZLY OF WHISKEY CREEK

BOOKS BY SID MARTY

Non-fiction
Men for the Mountains
A Grand and Fabulous Notion
Leaning on the Wind
Switchbacks

Poetry
Headwaters
Nobody Danced with Miss Rodeo
Sky Humour

SID MARTY

For Wes

THE
BLACK GRIZZLY
OF WHISKEY
CREEK

Sid Marty

2008

McCLELLAND & STEWART

LIBRARY AND ARCHIVES CANADA CATALOGUING IN PUBLICATION

Marty, Sid, 1944–
The black grizzly of Whiskey Creek / Sid Marty.

ISBN 978-0-7710-5699-4 (bound)

1. Bear attacks – Alberta – Banff region – History – 20th century.
2. Grizzly bears – Alberta – Banff region.   I. Title.

QL737.C27M37 2008   599.784   C2007-906188-5

We acknowledge the financial support of the Government of Canada through the Book Publishing Industry Development Program and that of the Government of Ontario through the Ontario Media Development Corporation's Ontario Book Initiative. We further acknowledge the support of the Canada Council for the Arts and the Ontario Arts Council for our publishing program.

Typeset in Van Dijck MT by M&S, Toronto
Printed and bound in Canada

Illustrations on pages ii and v by Paul Marty.

Excerpt on page 55 from "The Bear" is from *New and Selected Poems, 1957–1994* by Ted Hughes. Copyright 1995 by Ted Hughes. Reprinted by permission of Faber and Faber Ltd, London.

Excerpt on page 201 from "To the Unseeable Animal" is from *The Selected Poems of Wendell Berry* by Wendell Berry, p. 80. Copyright 1998 by Wendell Berry. Reprinted by permission of Counterpoint.

Excerpt on page 243 from "God Bless the Bear" by John Newlove reprinted by permission of the Estate of John Newlove. "God Bless the Bear" originally appeared in *Apology for Absence: Selected Poems 1962–1992*, The Porcupine's Quill, 1993.

This book is printed on acid-free paper that is 100% recycled, ancient-forest friendly (100% post-consumer recycled).

McClelland & Stewart Ltd.
75 Sherborne Street
Toronto, Ontario
M5A 2P9
www.mcclelland.com

1 2 3 4 5   12 11 10 09 08

TO WILDERNESS

CONTENTS

AUTHOR'S NOTE

In 1980 we thought we knew something about bears, but the bears in Whiskey Creek eluded us, outwitted us, and humbled us for a while. In the course of this book, I have tried to tell part of the story from a bear's point of view. This is obviously an imaginative exercise, rather than reportage. I have based this interpretation on my personal knowledge of and experiences with bears, first as a park warden and later as a journalist who has covered bear stories and conservation issues. I have tethered my imagination also to the evidence uncovered in Whiskey Creek and vicinity, and to the experiences shared with me by the victims and their families and friends, and by those involved as hunters, biologists, police officers, dispatchers, reporters, and interested observers. No one can say with any certainty what goes on in the mind of a bear (hell, on some days, some of us barely know what goes on in our own minds), but I, for one, never get tired of wondering what the answer to that question might be. So here goes my best guess.

"The earth is the bear's ear."

JOHN STEVENS
Elder, Bearspaw Band, Stoney Nakoda Nation

"Speak to this bear
for he may know you"

SID MARTY
from the poem "Three Bears," *Headwaters*

WHISKEY CREEK AND SURROUNDING AREA

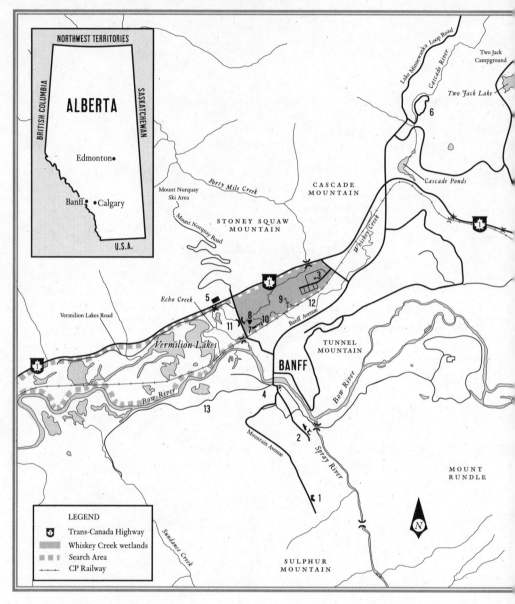

Inset map:
NORTHWEST TERRITORIES
BRITISH COLUMBIA
SASKATCHEWAN
ALBERTA
Edmonton•
Banff• •Calgary
U.S.A.

Map labels:
Lake Minnewanka Loop Road
Cascade River
Two Jack Campground
Two Jack Lake
Cascade Ponds
Forty Mile Creek
CASCADE MOUNTAIN
Mount Norquay Ski Area
STONEY SQUAW MOUNTAIN
Mount Norquay Road
Whiskey Creek
Echo Creek
Vermilion Lakes Road
Vermilion Lakes
Banff Avenue
TUNNEL MOUNTAIN
BANFF
Bow River
Mountain Avenue
Spray River
MOUNT RUNDLE
Sundance Creek
SULPHUR MOUNTAIN

LEGEND
⚜ Trans-Canada Highway
▨ Whiskey Creek wetlands
▰▰ Search Area
⊢⊣ CP Railway

1) RIMROCK HOTEL
2) BANFF SPRINGS HOTEL
3) PARK WARDEN HEADQUARTERS
4) BANFF NATIONAL PARK ADMINISTRATION
   BUILDING
5) TIMBERLINE INN
6) SANITARY LANDFILL

7) CP RAILWAY DEPOT AND CABOOSE RESTAURANT
8) BANFF RECREATION CENTRE
9) RAILROAD "Y"
10) SHEDS AND STORAGE TANKS
11) FENLAND AREA
12) WHISKEY CREEK SUBDIVISION
13) CAVE AND BASIN HOTSPRINGS

THE BEAR IN MY HEAD

Stoney tribal elder the late John Stevens was part of the Bearspaw band at Morley, Alberta, in the foothills of the Rockies. I was fortunate to spend a few hours talking to John and Nora Stevens in September of 2005, while their son Virgil translated. Historically, bears were important to native people for both food and medicine, and they remain so today. The elders told me that they did not approve of the way Parks Canada interfered with the bears in Banff National Park. They told me that the earth is the bear's ear, that when we talk about the bear it hears us, so we have to be careful and speak respectfully. "We use them in our ceremonies; we ask for guidance from them," said John. "When one is tranquilized or trapped, it affects all the bears."

John Stevens was suggesting, if I understood him correctly, that when we upset the community of bears, the effect is to unbalance, in a sense, the people who are spiritually connected to them. There appears to be what we might call an "ecology of spirituality," a spiritual inter-connectedness between animals and between people and animals that mirrors the physical ecology in which all life forms are connected. When we mess with the bear, we mess with the bear's medicine. The bear cannot help us anymore, and it might elect to hurt us instead.

Our ancient ancestors faced the bear on its own terms, armed with stone-tipped weapons and sympathetic magic, and with awe, reverence, and courage. But the old Cult of the Bear was founded on hunting. The life of a bear could be taken, its flesh and its sacred paw could be used for food and spiritual succour, but the bear had to be treated with deference, praised and honoured by enshrined rituals and secret paintings down in the torch-lit depths of the cave, down in the earth that was its home.

Replacing awe with scientific knowledge, today we have a new Cult of the Bear. Many North Americans no longer hold hunting in esteem. We are trying to save the bear from itself and trying to save it from us. We never think to simply leave it be, to allow it to be a mystery. In the end, will it remain the largest and most dangerous predator in the Rockies, or will it adapt to our constant concern and tinkering and morph into a different kind of bear? Perhaps a more timid and crepuscular version like the European brown bears that still survive in the Old World in isolated pockets. Then, will we expect it to learn to love us, like other domesticated beasts? Will that be the final price of our acceptance of its right to exist? And when it refuses our solicitude, which is inevitable, what then?

Today, the anti-hunting lobby demands the bear must live by its terms: be a teddy bear, a cartoon bear or even a wild bear – just not too wild – and give us a hug. Meanwhile the hunting lobby sees the brown bear in particular mainly as a trophy animal, not as a source of meat and medicine. No wonder the grizzly has a humped back: he's staggering under the weight of our impossible agendas.

Did the great preservationists like John Muir, "Guardian of Yosemite," realize what it was they were saving when they advocated to save the apex predators? They thought they were saving the beautiful places of the earth and the wild animals that lived there, but in fact what we may eventually wind up saving is one of humanity's most redeeming and most diminished virtues – humility. Alas, humility, in this era of burning rainforests and climate change, may not be enough. But it's a beginning.

My wife, Myrna, married into the bear business when she married me. Wildlife management, including the live trapping, tranquilizing and relocation of black and grizzly bears, was one of several functions I performed first as a seasonal and later as a full-time national park warden, from 1966 to 1978. Having lived in grizzly and black bear country in Yoho, Jasper, and Banff national parks, my wife had this to say one day in 1981, after we had moved our household and our two sons to an old ranch headquarters at the foot of the Livingstone Range, in southwestern Alberta: "It is so nice to be able to step out the door without worrying about tripping over a bear."

She was speaking only five months after the sensational bear maulings near Banff in 1980 that are the subject of this book. Left to her own devices in bear country far too often, my wife has had her own ursine encounters. She has shooed black bears away from her screen door late at night, and had grizzly bears press their noses against her picture window. (Note to Parks Canada contractors: Never install a picture window lower than 12 feet off the ground in grizzly country – but that's another story.) So I didn't want to shatter her illusion by pointing out that although we had moved hundreds of miles from Banff, we were still in "fringe habitat" for grizzly bears, and that the better habitat, the forest reserve on the Livingstone Range, was only a mile or so west.

Although they were once rarely seen in our valley, black and grizzly bears have become more frequent visitors since the late 1990s. In 2006, bears came down from the mountain to feast on a neighbour's winter-killed steer 400 yards from our door. Earlier, a grizzly had raided another neighbour's chicken coop and it ate every chicken she had. There are two grizzly bears on a prairie butte just a half-mile east of the house as I write this, feeding on saskatoon berries. A lot of things have changed in bear country since 1980, when the main events in this book transpired.

As many readers know, a bear's footprint has an uncanny resemblance to a human's footprint. One morning a few years back, a black bear passed by close to my writing shack on the hill above our home. Later, I came down to the house and found the back door wide open, which was not like Myrna. I was thinking of that black bear; he reminded me of one that once crept into our bedroom in Jasper National

Park when Myrna, pregnant, was having a nap, and left again without waking her up. Having a bear in your head sometimes makes you jump to conclusions. I jumped to one that day when I saw the muddy, five-toed tracks on the deck, going right onto the back porch. I didn't stop to take a closer look at those smeared prints (hint: a bear's big toe is on the outside of its foot); I just grabbed a stout walking stick from among those stored in an old milk can by the door and crept inside, prepared to drive the intruder out of the house. I followed the muddy prints into our kitchen. I peered around the corner of the fridge and there was the bear – talking on our telephone! That's when I remembered that Myrna likes to garden bearfoot, or rather barefoot, in hot weather. She had not had time to wipe her feet when the phone rang. She gave me a quizzical look. I felt as if I were in a Monty Python sketch.

The numbers of grizzly bears in southern Alberta, including Banff National Park, are currently declining, and yet the trend in bear–human conflict shows an increase over time. Writing in *Ursus* magazine (June 2003), Stephen Herrero and Andrew Higgins have demonstrated that bear attacks in Alberta since 1960 have risen in proportion to the increase in the human population: "Between 1960 and 1998, bears caused 42 serious or fatal human injuries in the Province of Alberta – 29 (69%) by grizzly (brown) bears (*Ursus arctos*) and 13 (31%) by American black bears (*U. americanus*). Considering Alberta's estimated bear population – about 1,000 grizzly bears and 38,000–39,000 black bears – these numbers suggest that the grizzly bears are the more dangerous of the 2 species. Serious and fatal bear-inflicted injuries increased in number in Alberta, including its national parks, each decade, from 7 during the 1960s to 13 during the 1990s, an increase proportional to the province's human population growth during that period." The Herrero–Higgins study is the most recent I know of, and there have been a number of other attacks since it was written.[*]

[*] In 1981 the population of Alberta was 2,237,724. Alberta is currently Canada's fourth most populated province at 3,435,511 (Statistics Canada estimate). Its growth since October 1, 2004 is estimated to have been 65,400 people per year, the highest in the country.

Aside from in national parks, we are tripping over bears in Alberta because Alberta's antique doctrine of "multiple use" allows road building for subdivisions on provincial park lands and logging, mining, cattle grazing, and natural gas well-drilling in the forestry reserve – the doctrine of "multiple abuse" conservationists call it. In Alberta's hyper-drive fossil fuel economy, fragmentation of bear habitat caused by roads and by thousands of miles of old seismic access trails means the big mammals are constantly hounded by thousands of all-terrain vehicles, nitwit 4 x 4 mud boggers, dirt bikes, hunters, hikers, anglers, loggers, helicopters, seismic blasters and thumpers, Ski-Doos, RVs – you name it. In 2005–2006, 45 grizzlies, including 14 females are known to have died, most of them violently, in Alberta including in national parks (eight in 2005, zero in 2006). The loss of the females is particularly disturbing due to the species low reproductive rate. Eleven bears were killed in legal hunts, six were killed illegally, and eight were killed in self defence. Highways, railroads, management and research action, mistaken identity (shot by accident), and unknown causes took the rest. Authorities drastically downgraded the population estimate to 500 or less, and Alberta suspended its spring hunt until 2008 pending a more thorough population study.[1] So people are seeing fewer bears, more often. Not surprisingly, most bears that die by human hand die within 1,640 feet of a road or trail. In recent years, grizzly bears have been pushed by this pressure out onto the private ranchlands where there are fewer people, fewer machines and fewer dogs to harass them.

Grizzly bears are coming to the ranchlands and making forays out on to the plains (their old homeland before we confined them to the mountains) to find peace and quiet. There are grizzlies in the Porcupine Hills south of Calgary once again, and there are bears on prairie stretches of the Wateron River, spooking the hell out of the fly fishermen. In 2004, bear biologist Gordon Stenhouse collared a grizzly near Milk River, Alberta, 100 or so miles by air east of the mountains of Waterton National Park, halfway to Saskatchewan. Incidentally that bear came from the Blackfoot Indian reservation at

Browning, Montana, without clearing customs. Bears don't read maps; grizzlies belong to the mountain and to the prairie, not to us. Speaking of Montana, from January 1 to October 31, 2007, five people, all of them hunters, were mauled by grizzlies there. The strangest case was that of Brian Grand, mauled by a grizzly bear October 15 in a prairie habitat while pheasant hunting four miles east of Dupuyer. His friends were firing at pheasants, and one bird dog was wearing a bear bell when the bear rushed out of its hidden bed in some willow bush and attacked. A cow carcass, on which the bear had been feeding, was found in the vicinity.[2] If we want the bears to survive, we are going to have to adjust the way we live, keeping human food and garbage and dead steers out of their reach – or stashing the dead steers in some remote valley for their dining enjoyment – and peering out the window before we go barging outside.

There are not just rural bears, there are urban bears, too. All over North America, as bear habitat is compromised by development, there have been incidents of the black bear species foraging in urban areas. In 2005, the northern Ontario town of Marathon (pop. 4,000), where teachers routinely record bear sightings at the elementary school, found itself under siege by roving black bears that took over the local dump and backyard gardens, or roamed through town, breaking into a home in one case and sunbathing at the Canadian Tire store parking lot in another. Northern Ontarians in this and a dozen other communities blamed the incursions on the closing of the spring bear hunt in 1999, which they said gave rise to more numerous and bolder bears.[3]

In Calgary, along with cougars, coyotes, white-tailed deer, and the odd moose, occasional black bears (but not grizzly bears – not yet), mostly subadults that are trying to find a home range for themselves, will take a notion to go berry picking in subdivisions on the banks of the Elbow River – in a city of a million people. It makes for a lot of excitement and a great story as cops and conservation officers chase the bear through the city slickers' backyards.

Bears are roaming out on the prairies and wandering in urban subdivisions for the same reason they came to the back alleys of the Banff townsite in 1980; these places were all part of their ancient home, and we have not left them enough wild land to live without our company, which they would much prefer to do. (Approximately 3 percent of the land in Banff National Park's 2,650 square miles is prime habitat for bears and other wildlife and that is the same habitat where we have built townsites, roads, and campgrounds.)

Even though I have not baited a live trap for a bear, or darted one with a tranquilizer for many years, the bears, in a way, have not forgotten me. When I don't go to see them, in my occupation as a journalist writing on conservation issues, they come to see me. One bear in particular haunts my memory. I have a picture of him taken in death, looking forlorn and beaten, betrayed by his own appetite for flesh, by his overpowering need to fatten for winter hibernation. It is as if he demands that I answer a very simple question: "Why?"

It is a question also asked in 1980 by bear-mauling victims and their friends and families in Banff, when five people were attacked during an 11-day rampage, a question that I don't think was answered fully at the time. I have long wanted to give a full account of that summer, of the victims' suffering and of the hard work and dedication of those who hunted the Whiskey Creek bears. I hope the account will help in some way to prevent such tragedies happening in the future. And I wanted to try to tell part of the story from the perspectives of a black bear and a grizzly bear. I wrote this book both as a minor participant in some of the events, and as someone who, as a former warden, had access at the time and afterwards to those involved in the hunt.

A lawsuit, as we shall see, was launched against Parks Canada in the wake of the Whiskey Creek maulings. Most of the officials named in the suit have long since retired, but Parks Canada is still determined to keep a veil of secrecy over the incident. After applying to Library and Archives Canada for access to a long list of files, and after waiting with increasing desperation for more than 10 months, I finally received the last documents, copies I paid for under the so-called Access to Information Act. Time and again, vital text was

blacked out by a censoring pen. Many documents contained newspaper clippings. I'm surprised the censor didn't black out the news
items as well.

When it gets right down to it, I have serious doubts about fixing
blame on particular individuals involved in park operations. First,
despite exhaustive research, I don't pretend to know all the answers
about the maulings of 1980. Second, there is so much blame to go
around, it's a shame to share it out parsimoniously. I'd like to see it
shared out the way park warden Ernie Stenton used to do it, back in
the day when the wardens had to cull the ballooning elk population
in Banff National Park. The elk were breeding like rats and eating
themselves out of browse, due to a lack of natural predators caused
by the government's misguided war on wolves and cougars. The
wardens had not signed on to be professional hunters or butchers,
but they had perforce to act as both. After shooting a truckload of
elk they would butcher their kills in the abattoir set up in Banff
townsite and truck the meat to the local old folks' homes. It was
excellent meat and I'm told the oldtimers really enjoyed it. No doubt
it reminded them of life back on the ranch, when they could not
afford to eat the beef they raised, and lived on venison instead. (I
have rancher neighbours who live the same way today, and for the
same reason.)

There would always be some white-shirted manager hanging
around the abattoir supervising, but when Ernie accidentally started
missing the gut bins and splashing offal on their shirtfronts, they left
and didn't come back. "Heads up!" he'd cry, but always a second or
two late, as a loop of flying intestine or other innard came snaking
through the air. So this is where I say "Heads up!" to whoever those
mental midgets are that the government employs to underestimate
folks like me to death: Heads up, boys and girls! Watch out for the
flying shitloops. Don't get any on your BlackBerrys.

The defendants, my former peers and supervisors, were judged
by what they knew about bears at the time of the lawsuit, in 1990,
not by what they knew a decade earlier in 1980, which was much

less, after advances in biological sciences and wildlife management. They took the rap, buttoned their lips, and kept their jobs. I understand why they needed to keep those jobs, incidentally, from personal experience, having published a book in 1978 (*Men for the Mountains*), which, ironically, got me into hot water with those very same supervisors.

In essence, I wrote myself right out of a job and I resigned later that year to become a full-time writer. I cashed in my pension and swapped the Freedom 55 plan for what I call the Freedom 85 plan, a.k.a. the Work Till You Die plan. In 1980, I found myself on the outside looking in when the first mauling in Whiskey Creek occurred. Instead of wading through a swamp looking for the bear, I was sitting in my basement in Canmore, Alberta, chasing interview subjects on the telephone, or pitching ideas for assignments at magazine editors, a race of irritable skeptics not unlike bears in some ways – except that they tend to hibernate in the summer rather than in the winter.

The crazy thing is, after all these years, I still have that forlorn-looking bear in my head and he refuses to fade away. So I am writing this also on behalf of the beast with many names that cannot speak for itself: *Wahtonga* ("Biggest Bear") to the Stoneys, the Real Bear or *Pah'-ksi-kwo-yi* ("Sticky Mouth") to the southern Blackfoot, but known at one time to another mountain-dwelling tribe as *Mustahyah* ("Our-Brother-Across-the-River"). He is the "white bear" of Lewis and Clark, and the silvertip of our Canadian Rockies. My former colleagues named him 757. Scientists know him in my part of his range as *Ursus arctos horribilis*, the grizzly bear, part of the tribe of Holarctic-ranging brown bears. (There are as many names for the sacred as there are for the profane.) This book is also for those he eluded for awhile, old friends and some old adversaries; skilled and brave for the most part, most of them retired, some of them now "gone west." I have done my best to be fair in what I write here. This book is to assuage my memory of the wounded and the dead of this and other bear stories over the years, for the hapless human victims and those who loved them. And this is for what came winging out of the wetlands under a Jet Ranger helicopter, hanging on the end of a steel cable, the terror and the glory reduced to a hi-tech freak show.

Heads up, it's bleeding!

Don't get any on you.

— ONE —

BUSHWHACKER'S SOLILOQUY
A FEW THOUGHTS WHILE WAITING IN AMBUSH

All his movements were furtive and cautious, as if he expected to
meet an enemy at every step.

WILLIAM H. WRIGHT

The Grizzly Bear: The Narrative of a Hunter-Naturalist (1909)

YOU CAN FEEL GRAVITY leaning on the night when you live in the
mountains; you can feel the trend of the earth, how it shifts under
your feet, not in the sudden way that rocks in a mountain torrent will
shift: massively, suddenly, dangerously, and either trap your foot and
drown you, or send you tumbling into swimming water. It is more
subtle than that, in this stony ground where thrust faults have been
at work for millions of years. It is more a sense of your foot not con-
tacting the ground at the exact place where you meant to put it down
a split second earlier. Learning to climb is the easy part; learning how
to descend where it's too steep to see what's under your feet, learning
how to arrest the inevitable slide, that's the real test. The coming
down is harder on your body, and your soul, than the going up. But
each mountain is its own country, each mountain touches you to the
heart and bone.

Save your knees for the mountains, that is my advice. Not much
else is worth bending them for, or worth wearing them out for, except

the people you love and the earth that carries you, which for me is this mountain earth along the Great Divide where the American black bear, the grey wolf, and the mountain lion live on in the little fringes of Rocky Mountains sublimity that we have allowed them, and where the Real Bear, as the Blackfoot call the grizzly bear, still acts as if it were the Emperor of Pristine, acts sometimes as if our human flesh is just another tithe that is its due.

It was an unseasonably cool late summer's evening in September 1980, and I was sitting on top of a rusty CPR boxcar with a rifle in my hands staring into the black trees on the edge of the Whiskey Creek Swamp. Few people even know the place by that name anymore; the name initially morphed into Whiskey Creek wetlands, but as climate change continued the creek's flow declined, so with a nod to nominative nuances, it became known as the Whiskey Creek Wild Area and then, as its wildness continued to decrease, as the Whiskey Creek Area.

A cool rain (turning to snow high above me on the grey peaks ringing the valley) pattered on my shoulders as I gazed down on the siding, where several sets of rails merged into two silver bands that narrowed to a vanishing point in the forest westward, adjacent to the Vermilion Lakes. The smudged lights of the town of Banff, Alberta, could be glimpsed faintly through the trees behind me when I turned that way. I was waiting for a rough beast to emerge from the darkness, a shape occluded by shadow but dense with muscle and rolling with fat; something rounded, rangy, and vaguely asymmetrical – from living on steep angles perhaps, from finding no rest on the angle of repose. Its claws were blunted at the tips from digging into rock slides for hoary marmots and ground squirrels. They were also, or so we suspected, stained with the blood of man, and its loins were streaked with pond slime. Like haunted Grendel come calling again at Heorot's "motley-treasured hall" (or update that rather to "many-treasured shopping mall"), it was at once a thing shaggy with hidden threat and lurking doubt: something you could smell coming if the wind was right, before you saw, at the edge of the station's yard light, a certain kind of shadow suddenly grow legs, claws, and teeth.

Funny how the railroad gets into so many Canadian epics. The Canadian Pacific Railway has been described as Canada's National Dream. But westerners have been selling cheap and buying dear for generations via this steel tentacle of colonization, and regular railroad passenger service on this original main line ended years ago – except for rich tourists.

A railway is moved by fact, not myth, and money greases its wheels. Money and blood. It is true that the CPR opened the rude frontier of western Canada to tourism (as well as sodbusters) in 1883 and made our first national park possible, because the railway was in desperate need of revenue from tourist (and sodbuster) traffic to justify the costs of construction, a justification needed to keep the government of Sir John A. Macdonald in office.

Our national parks, these islands of wilderness whose rocky shores are gnawed relentlessly by the tides of development, were not fledged from the transcendental philosophy of some Canadian Thoreau. Our first national park, founded to protect the Cave and Basin Hot Springs, was set aside "for the sanitary advantage of the public" (according to Order-in-Council No. 2197, November 28, 1885), hot water being a luxury in those days, and it was serenaded into existence by the jingle of cash registers. It was gazetted to "recoup the treasury" (as prime minister John A. Macdonald famously put it) emptied by railroad construction, not to preserve wilderness, which was then thought to be in limitless abundance in the vast Dominion of Canada. Only later was it repositioned as a national park meant to preserve nature, including wild predators, "unimpaired for future generations," and indeed to this day there are big tracts of wild lands in the national parks system worthy of that ideal. That is the good news, though the cash register rides herd on idealism in our first national park.

As a former park warden, I had found myself on this stretch of track several times over the years, looking for big game that had been struck by locomotives. Blood on the tracks of progress is not the kind of red ink that makes it into the annual report of the shareholders. The railroad, like the highway that followed it, is a double-edged sword, giving access to millions but bringing tragedy, too. Locomotives have, during the last two centuries, sparked forest fires, slaughtered a herd of bighorn sheep, and killed untold numbers of other beasts from deer to moose to grizzly bears. Over the years and up to the present, black and grizzly bears in Banff and other mountain areas of North America, attracted to the rail bed to feed on spilled grain or on train-killed animals, have been run down and mangled by the big steel wheels.

The moon that night, waning gibbous, was cloud-wracked as it rose over the peaks. I felt the cold hardwood and steel of the rifle biting into my hands, and fished through my slicker pockets for my leather riding gloves. I was 36 years old but the cold night made me feel older. I had a lot to learn about "older" (and now that I've learned it I feel younger all the time).

When I ducked my head, the rain rolled off my hat brim and spilled down my slicker; it ran down the barrel of my .308 pump-action carbine and dripped from the muzzle as if it were a tiny drain-pipe. The shiny barrel gave back the light from the station lamppost, and I wiped the water off with a corner of my bandana. It was a saddle gun, built to be carried in a scabbard. A bush gun, but it was a solid weapon at a more moderate range. I had set my kill zone – just in case I needed it – out at about 50 yards in front of me, to the north. Any bullet I sent that way would be backstopped by the timber. There were no people in those woods that night, so we had been told, but I knew enough about transient campers in that stretch of bush to be cautious of assumptions like that.

The whole Whiskey Creek Area was surrounded by a cordon of armed wardens and mounted police officers. They had parked vehicles along the roads, left them running with headlights on to illuminate the ditches. There were perhaps 25 people watching the forest, some of whom had not had a full night's sleep for over a week. There was still room for the bear to slip past them unseen. It could ease out of the bush and crawl under the boxcars between me and park warden Clair Israelson, a hundred or so paces to the east of me, or warden Don Mickle, 300 feet to the west. There was a good chance for it to go shuffling behind the restaurants of Banff, looking for some discarded burgers and takeout chicken, looking to chugalug a draught from the many 45-gallon drums of used cooking fat cached in the alleys.

When I turned toward the east, I could just make Clair out. I must have looked the same to him, a vague scarecrow backlit by the glow of the town. If the bear comes out, I thought, I will wait until he steps fully into the light. If he faces me, I'll have to compensate for the downward angle. I won't get a brisket shot unless he lifts his head to look at me. And I can't shoot him through the head – we have to preserve the brain for a rabies test. So I'd better wait until he turns sideways, try to take out the shoulder or place the bullet just behind the shoulder, depending on the light. I will keep shooting until he stops moving. In fact, the opportunities that I would have to make that shot at all were few. I was glad of that.

Rabies! This notion was a joke to the wardens who rendezvoused in the local coffee shop between midnight shifts. We'd been chasing – or maybe *harassing* is a better term – these latter-day dinosaurs for years. Rabies would explain this bear's behaviour very neatly, and other embarrassing questions would not be asked of Parks Canada later, in the ensuing rabies scare. I was betting a thousand to one against it. I was betting this would be a perfectly healthy predator just doing what comes naturally. I grinned, thinking somebody's butt was going to be roasted over the fire when the smoky fog of doublespeak cleared.

Just contemplating shooting this magnificent beast made me feel sick. Such a brutal action represented a failure of everything I valued about the national parks ideal, one of the most grand and fabulous notions western civilization has ever originated. But if I choked up and merely wounded him, if he made it back into that shintangle of dog-hair pines and sand willows, well, picturing that outcome made me break into a cold sweat. I knew they wouldn't send me in there after him because, having resigned from the service two years earlier I was a mere civilian now, a volunteer. It was my former workmates who would be sent in, and if he did not bleed out fast and die, the wounded bear would morph into quite a different nightmare.

I watched for the bear to come out of the bush while other bears moved through my memory. A few could easily pass for the one that was lying in wait, if they were still alive, if their hides were not hanging on a wall in some museum, or rotting at the bottom of the former Banff sanitary landfill, or lining ravens' nests in the wild timber. I could picture all my bears, all my ambushed wilderness kings and defeated contenders. I recalled one huge grizzly glaring out through the bars of a culvert trap, his eyes full of indomitable hatred. A culvert trap, from a bear's point of view, is like a dead-end cave. Built from a length of highway culvert, it is equipped with a bait trigger that, when pulled on by a bear – or a stray dog! – closes the entry gate, which locks in place, trapping the animal without injuring it.

I remembered other bears: one sat on his haunches unable to use his legs, moaning like a beaten old man, trying to bite the chrome splinters from an automobile bumper out of his flank; one lay broken and bleeding to death by the side of the railroad line; another, the biggest bear I ever encountered, moved off the trail to let me and my horse go past and stood there as if he were going to ask a question (I have been wondering what that question might have been for a very long time). My bears wait for me and they will wait for me until the day I die.

Something moved out into the woods, moved like an eel sliding through a pond of ink. I eased the carbine out from under the slicker onto my lap, and with my right hand on the weapon's forearm, I stared into the dark until I felt the darkness pouring into my brain, until I saw myself staring back from the darkness, my scarecrow shape outlined against the glow of the constellations.

I saw the enemy: I am the enemy.

— TWO —

FACTS AND MYTHS

Many of the hunters never molested a grizzly, the bear being regarded as a sort of medicine or sacred animal, many believing that it was really a human being. It was commonly called Kyai'-yo [bear], but the medicine-pipe men were obliged when speaking of it to call it Pah'-ksi-kwoi-yi, sticky mouth.

J.W. SCHULTZ

My Life as an Indian (1907)

SOMETIMES I WONDER WHY the Whiskey Creek bear didn't finish what he started. I don't think he meant to kill anyone, though I'm not suggesting for one moment that it mattered to him, one way or the other. A grizzly bear typically kills its prey with a crushing bite to the head or spine. This includes animals the size of beef cows that may weigh more than half a ton. The power of the bear's bite is chastening indeed. On the cow's withers there may be only the puncture marks of its teeth. But if you were to take a knife and skin the hide down to the flesh, you would see that the spine has been pulverized as if the cow had been shot with a high-calibre rifle. As for the strength in the bear's front legs and massive humped shoulders, we are talking about a beast that can turn a small car over on its roof. With its jaws for gripping and its clawed feet for traction, an adult grizzly can drag a dead moose halfway up a mountain through alder bush and over fallen logs and tumbled boulders.

Endowed with such physical power, a grizzly does not necessarily know its own strength in encounters with humans. Taking a pat from a grizzly's paw is like taking a pat from a backhoe bucket. But a grizzly bear's paw is a kinetic marvel when compared with a machine. The bear can manipulate its four-inch non-retractable claws independently and with great finesse. Author Enos A. Mills raised two grizzly cub orphans. In *The Spell of the Rockies* (1911), he relates how the male cub, using one claw only, "could slide a coin back and forth on the floor more rapidly and lightly than I could."

A grizzly bear is a hard-working animal, a beast of great endurance, one that, when wounded, will turn and hunt the man who injured it. Bear expert James Gary Shelton has compared the grizzly to a professional athlete who must deal with a lot of aches and pains. Certainly it wears its claws down with hard use (they grow out again during hibernation), wears the hair off its forearms, bears the scars of mating fights (in the case of males), loses a toe occasionally to a trap or suffers wear and tear from pinching its feet among the loose boulders in rock slides. Resident bears often wander onto provincial land and run afoul of hunters and stockmen, and as a park warden I sometimes encountered bears scarred by bullet wounds, bears that had been crippled by vehicle strikes, and on one occasion I saw a bear carrying a bow hunter's broken arrow in its hindquarters. Like us, the grizzly bear has a body that will wear out, a life that will end (its life expectancy is about 15 to 20 years in the wild, 30 or more in captivity). Knowledge of morality is one pain that he is spared, but he feels its message in his joints, in the roots of his teeth, in the pads of his feet, the message that he cannot ignore. What effect such aches and pains have on his general irritability is anybody's guess.

Bears are omnivores, as are humans, and they are famous for their gluttony. Their motto is, after devouring an Everest of grub, "I ate it because it was there." When we are really hungry we say, "I'm as hungry as a bear," but the opportunistic appetite of nature's biggest omnivore pales in comparison with our level of consumption. Filling the stomach is the least of humanity's appetites. Not only do we consume water, flesh, grain, and fruit in great quantity, we reach into the earth to gnaw out valuable ores and minerals, to feed an insatiable appetite for iron ore and coal, or to pump out fossil fuels to feed other machines that slave away to sate our greed for endless variety in plastic gimcracks, and to feed our need for bigger houses, faster cars, and wider-screen TVs. What is a car, or an ATV, or a motor home, if not a device for eating up space and time by displacing the natural world from out of our path as we speed from A to B? We are not savouring our time on this earth, we are cramming it down our craws at a ravenous pace. Our days vanish in the wake of our furious assault on our own bodies and spirits. "Where did the time go?" we ask each other. I suppose the easiest response to that question would be a belch. We North Americans have the appetites of gods. Hungry as a bear? We are far, far too modest.

It is this failure to acknowledge humankind's disproportionate appetite for everything from food to new highways to second homes built in bear habitat that leads to conflict with the bear. It's what we will not admit to and what the bear cannot understand about us that leads to tragedy. Pound for pound, the bear is far stronger than we are, so it doesn't realize that humans, not bears, are the gods of eating and occasionally it decides to eat one of us either literally, which is rare, or figuratively in the form of a bear mauling. Then the fires of hell open, and the bear is cast down into them as a lesson to the rest of its tribe. "Put the fear of God into him," we say, as if the beast were capable of committing the same moral errors as ourselves.

Our flesh is not for the eating; the very possibility terrifies us and that terror goes all the way back to the bones of the cave bear, ritually buried in a stone chest at the back of the neolithic hunter's cave. When we hear of a bear attack, it is as if in our subconscious mind the bones have metamorphosed into a living predator once more; the bear is risen, it has dragged us back down out of the clouds, back down into our basic mammalian reality. It is a reality we keep on denying, a reality we need to remind ourselves of because our big brains keep forgetting what sustains and nurtures us.

Men and brown bears have been living together and living at odds since the era of the Neanderthals. Although the date of man's arrival in North America, from 12,000 to 14,000 years ago, is currently a subject of debate, the brown bear, which originated either in Asia or in Europe, may have confronted the first men to appear in the lee of the great ice sheets. A fossil of a brown bear found in a gravel pit near Edmonton, Alberta, is believed to be 26,000 years old, and it is genetically related to present-day grizzly bears.[4] Scholars suggest that ancient men probably learned the uses of some plant foods by following the tracks of the great bear and observing his digs, his foraging habits, and his feces. No doubt they learned from observing other omnivores and herbivores as well. But here was a beast unlike the others, whose footprint was eerily similar to our own, a beast that suddenly stood up on its hind legs in the middle of the berry patch, mimicking our human posture, and examined us as if expecting a password; one who, stripped of its hide by a flint blade or a Buck knife, looks weirdly man-shaped, as if a man had taken refuge in the skin of a beast. Little wonder that neolithic man attributed supernatural wisdom and occult powers to the bear.

At the time of European contact, brown bears ranged from British Columbia all the way east to what is now Manitoba, and south all the way to Mexico, and their Holarctic range was global.

As far as I have been able to discover, the European experience with grizzly bears in Canada begins on August 20, 1690, in the parkland prairies west of what is now Saskatoon, Saskatchewan. Henry Kelsey, a 20-year-old explorer travelling with a party of "Stone Indians" (Assiniboine) from York Factory on Hudson Bay, became the first European to see a grizzly bear, which he described in his diary as "a great sort of a Bear wch is bigger then any white Bear [polar bear]; is Neither White nor Black But silver hair'd like our English Rabbit."[5] Kelsey noted the grizzled (white-tipped) guard hairs that have given the bear its eponymous name.

Kelsey was also the first white man (in what is now Canada) to see a plains bison and he set the template for the white tribe that followed, which was to duly note the Indians' religious reverence for the Great Bear and then try to kill one for a trophy. Kelsey, however, killed two bears in self-defence when they attacked one of his party, earning the Assiniboine name Little Giant for his prowess, but the Indians would not let him keep the carcasses as trophies. The shots he fired signalled the beginning of the end for the uneasy balance that prevailed between brown bears and neolithic hunters, due to the then primitive nature of the hunters' weapons.

I don't know of any research that has put a number on the aboriginal people killed by grizzly bears, but certainly there are many anecdotes that point to the shift of power in conflicts with bears after the First Nations obtained new weapons from the whites. In 1809, Kootenae Appee of the Peigan exhorted his people, then in a vengeful mood against the whites, not to destroy a North West Company fort at Rocky Mountain House. "Before the white men came to us," he reminded them, "we were weak; every year the grizzled bears . . . destroyed many of us; our arrows were headed with stone, which broke on them; now we have guns, balls, and powder. Our arrows are headed with iron, we are masters of all the animals."[6]

Early firearms gradually took a toll on the bear population, but the first repeating rifle, which would decimate both the buffalo and the bears, was still a century away.

Henry Kelsey also wrote one of the earliest literary efforts set in western Canada, a verse introduction to his 1690 journal. I do not claim that Kelsey was a literary genius, but I'm captivated by the notion that poetic expression in western Canada starts out with the grizzly bear as one of its central images. A few of his lines echo with Chaucerian energy. Of his arrival on the parkland prairies of central Saskatchewan he wrote:

Thus it continues till you leave ye woods behind
And then you have beast of severall kind

The one is a black a Buffillo great
Another is an outgrown Bear wch. is good meat
His skin to gett I have used all ye ways I can
He is mans food & he makes food of man
His hide they would not me it preserve
But said it was a god & they should Starve.[7]

And what are we to make now of that ancient arrangement, those days when men and bears shared the same home? They both roamed the open plateaus between the great ice sheets and both species lived mainly in their own skins for a long time. Except for caves, humans had no hard-sided shelter to keep the bear away, but likewise the bear had learned that man's primitive weapons could be dangerous, even fatal. Men avoided the bear whenever they could, killing one occasionally when they needed its flesh for food, and its body parts for "medicine," as the Stoneys, who claim the mountains and foothills of Alberta as their ancient home, still do to this day. The great bear returned the compliment, defending his berry patches, his rich salmon streams, and his buried carrion, and eating the odd human in the process.

"He is mans food & he makes food of man."

Men spoke of the bear in hushed tones and refrained from using its real (meaning its sacred) name, in everyday parlance, similar to the Christian admonition against taking the Lord's name in vain. They feared such disrespect might trigger a hostile interest on the bear's part. Our-Brother-Across-the-River was a particularly apt euphemism. The river was a border between the sacred beast and the profane world of everyday material need. Men and gods go together like matches and dynamite: when the god crossed the river and entered man's world, friction began and chaos ensued. When a man killed a bear, he had to be extremely observant of elaborate rituals to propitiate its proud and vengeful spirit. If treated without proper honours, it might counsel the other animal spirits to deny their flesh to such ungrateful hunters for a time. Its hide, head, claws, and flesh must all be used or consumed with great respect and with prayers of thanks. The bear's talons might be worn as a necklace to show a hunter's prowess, or kept as part of a medicine bundle that would be opened only with elaborate ceremony. In some cultures, the bear's head would be set in a place of honour, and offerings made to it, sometimes consisting of its own flesh and blood. Bears, then, were big medicine.

"But said it was a god & they should starve."

Science, not religion, has been the lens by which mainstream society views the grizzly bear, but science alone is no guarantee of bear conservation. We have never, in our history, had so much factual knowledge of the natural world available to us, and had so little time, or if not time then inclination, to absorb it. Meanwhile wild nature is hounded before us, constantly retreating into shadow, sometimes disappearing, sometimes reappearing but diminished in size and variety, or it presents us, like a three-legged frog in a polluted pond, with some freakish mutation, from sipping at our poisoned cups. For example, in Alberta, the speed at which the prevailing right-wing political attitude toward natural phenomena like grizzly bears and global warming changes in favour of conservation is very slow. In our era, glaciers change faster than the right-wing mind, and glaciers, unlike right-wing politicians, are shrinking, with alarming impacts on water supply. I no longer recognize the remnants of the glaciers that I traversed with skis and climbing boots a mere 40 years ago, which is not even a millisecond in geological time. I have been watching glaciers melt and "progressive conservatives" (now there's an oxymoron) refusing to blink at climate change for many years.

We can see that the brown bear has an ancient claim to the mountains and plains of Alberta. Yet, in defending that right, our adversary in Whiskey Creek that summer kept trying to pull his punches; that was the way most wardens thought of it back then. In the resulting mess, we pictured him looking puzzled and confused by the fragility of the two-legged creatures who kept insisting on getting in his way. We stood around the Whiskey Creek Swamp all night, backlit by the headlights of the patrol trucks and police cars, or we sat on boxcars of the CPR line, armed to the teeth and stared into the darkness where he lived unseen.

Straining our eyes against the night, each of us was alone with our thoughts and memories in the space we had set between our guns. In the bush, his story was written in the grass bending under his footpads; we could not have read it in the dark had we dared to venture in after him. For us, the stars were but bright periods in a light-polluted sky, not the blazing torches that opened up ancestral nights. The wild places that we love to death are cowed by human tumult by day but return to their true nature after sundown. Darkness has become our last wilderness.

THREE

"THE MOST DANGEROUS PLACE
IN BANFF NATIONAL PARK"

"We continue to bear up with the greatest forbearance despite the unbearable pressures in times of a bare till but fortunately have access to Bayer products for relief of bear problems."

SUPERINTENDENT R.T. FLANAGAN

Jasper National Park, March 1976

ON THE EAST BANK OF Forty Mile Creek in Banff National Park, Alberta, not far from the edge of the town of Banff, there is an unusual depression at the foot of a nondescript spruce tree with a double trunk. Over the years, it has filled with dead spruce needles, with fallen branches and cones, while the creek flowed past, muttering to itself about the snows of yesteryear. There are perhaps a half-dozen men, all of them no longer young, who know about the beast that dug this pit to wait in ambush. None, I think, would look upon it today without some feeling of sadness. Soon enough it will be filled in with forest duff and forgotten, just like those who remember it now will be forgotten. In the scale of human and environmental tragedy, its disappearance would not even measure up as a footnote, and yet I can see it clearly in my mind's eye, one of the countless fading markers of a shrinking wilderness left by the triumphal march of human folly.

Forty Mile Creek lies in the Bow River Valley and is a tributary of that major mountain river. Here, overlooked by a high circle of grey rock peaks and timbered mountainsides, it drains, via Whiskey Creek, a small area of beaver dams and moose marshes, of white spruce, sedges, and willows that most visitors pass by with hardly a second look. Known as the Whiskey Creek Area, it is only one and a half miles long by half a mile wide. It has long been a kind of accidental green belt between the town and the Trans-Canada Highway, Highway 1. It is bounded to the west by the Mount Norquay access road that joins Banff to the highway and the ski resort of that name, and is hemmed to the east by the park maintenance compound, park warden headquarters, and the Banff "industrial park." The Norquay Road has cut it off from an area known as the Fenlands, lying adjacent to Vermilion Lakes. The lake view, typically portrayed with Mount Rundle and Tunnel Mountain as a backdrop, is one of the most photographed, and painted scenes on Earth. Parks Canada lists Whiskey Creek as part of the Vermilion Lakes biophysical unit, "part of a flat, poorly drained, broad valley flood plain with a mosaic of plant communities that varies according to soil conditions and water saturation."[8] Just beyond the railway line, on the south side of the area, are Banff's residential subdivisions of Whiskey Creek and Marmot Marsh, built in the 1970s. The town of Banff numbered 4,200 permanent residents in 1980; another 400 people resided at Lake Louise, a half-hour drive to the west. Several thousand more resided just outside the park boundary in Canmore, Alberta, a former coal-mining town 14 miles east of Banff.

Banff National Park saw 3.6 million visitors pass through its gates in 1980. Banff National Park was then, and is now, an international tourism destination and the most frequently visited national park in Canada. The resort town was administered by Parks Canada until 1990, when it was granted autonomy and incorporated as a municipality under provincial law. The park owes its creation to the discovery of the hot springs on Sulphur Mountain, by three CPR workers in 1883. Banff is a creature of the CPR, which at one time promoted the Rockies as "the Canadian Pacific Mountains." Banff was conceived and destined to be a famous resort from the moment that Sir William Cornelius Van Horne, then president of the CPR, first laid eyes on the cave and basin hot springs. "These springs are worth a million dollars!" cried that venerable tycoon, perhaps the only time in his life that he ever undervalued a piece of real estate. The Banff Springs Hotel, as it was first known, was the premier hotel in Banff and one of the grand hotels of the world. From mom-and-pop motel and sou-venir shop to grand hotel, Banff has always lived and died by tourist dollars. Anything or anyone that interfered with the flow of those dollars in that earlier era was treated like a blockage in a major artery and excised.

The Whiskey Creek Area, including part of Forty Mile Creek and the adjacent area known as the Fenlands, is a small microcosm of the larger national park milieu in North America: such parks are tiny islands of wildness in a sea of human development, though the devel-opment in this case is also an urbanized portion of Banff National Park itself, one of the more urbanized of the larger national parks in the world. As a wildlife reserve, this part of Banff National Park, known to the warden service as Area 1 (the "high visitor use area" near the park highway from the east gate to Castle Mountain Junction) is too developed to be a wilderness area and too dangerous, due to rail and vehicle traffic, to qualify as a zoo, though elk, cougars, grey wolves, and black and grizzly bears all wander through it from time to time, and in some cases, take up residence.

Back in 1887, the Whiskey Creek Swamp was referred to by Park Superintendent George Stewart as the "station bush," because of its proximity to the CPR station. It was notorious as the haunt of whisky peddlers, as bootleggers were then called, hence the name that soon accrued to it. In the 1970s and early 1980s, Whiskey Creek, which flows through the new subdivisions and then out into the wet-lands, was an urbanized trout stream that local boys could fish from their front doors. Banffites who remember those days mourn its decline, for now it is little more than a runoff channel for snow melt and heavy rains, and is dry for most of the year.

In 1980, the locals noted something else about Whiskey Creek, something that might be totally unnerving to citizens anywhere except in a national park: they frequently saw bears travelling along its banks, entering the subdivision, by way of a culvert under the CPR line, to forage in the garbage bins at night. The residents became far too accustomed to this encroachment for their own good. What was undesirable and hazardous now seemed normal, even safe. On July 4, 1980, a local mechanic, Andreas Leuthold, summed up the attitude of some Banff locals toward the resident bears. He was spoken to by Assistant Chief Park Warden Paul Kutzer for running after a black bear to get photographs. Kutzer reported that Leuthold "demonstrated a very arrogant attitude and stated that 'bears don't hurt people.'"[9] Leuthold, whom I interviewed for this book, has his own take on that statement, but the words would come back to haunt the young man before the summer was over.

From the beginning the Whiskey Creek Swamp had its hobo jungles, and in more recent years it was a popular hangout for transients who preferred sleeping rough for free among roaming bears to camping in the official campgrounds. The practice still continues, though it appears to be less frequent these days. I found two illegal huts, or wick-i-ups, as wardens once called them, while hiking there in 2004, but in the early 1970s, as a park warden, I rousted illegal campers every week of the summer. Other wardens did likewise. We were worried, and with good reason, that illegal campers, many of them immature city kids, could trigger a wildfire that might engulf the town. Bear management aside, in the summer our duties in Area 1 ranged from the sublime to the ridiculous, from rescuing stranded mountaineers on glaciated peaks to wrestling teenage drunks in the valley campgrounds. There were wildfires to fight, dangerous mother elk to control, poachers to pursue, and roadkill to remove. We were somewhat less concerned that illegal campsites would attract the attention of black or grizzly bears because there was so much smelly garbage set out everywhere else in the park that transient campsites were hardly worth a bear's attention. That sanguine attitude toward bears, typical of the era, has not stood the test of time. People have died throughout North America because smelly campsites attracted bears or, in the infamous case of teenagers Jane Ammerman and Kim Eberlee, because they camped on a bear trail too close to a garbage dump and became opportune prey (both were killed) for a garbage-habituated grizzly bear.[10]

Bears and garbage go together like junkies and heroin. Why do bears love our trash? Well, for one thing, because it is much easier to chew than their natural foods, which are full of tough plant fibres. For another, it holds in abundance two vital components of a bear's natural diet that are typically available in quantity for only brief periods: meat – which the bear tends to acquire in the spring in the form of winter-killed big game, or on the hoof in the form of fawns – and sugar, which it finds in the annual berry crop, buffalo berries (*Shepherdia canadensis*) being the most abundant in this part of the Rockies.

The bear is a versatile carnivore, eager to feed on meat when it can get it but evolved, like humans and pigs, to thrive on an omnivore diet. The bear's massive jaws contain a surprising array of big grinding teeth for a carnivore. This part of its dentition evolved not for killing steers or biting backpackers, but for grinding up the roots, corms, buds, and other coarse vegetable material loaded with cellulose that make up the bulk of a bear's annual diet. This may be why the brown bear survived in North America when its competitors, the huge short-faced bear and the lion, did not. They got stuck in the meat-eater pattern, unlike this adaptable beast, whose diet can consist of 80 to 90 percent vegetable matter, in more pristine habitat. Yet a brown bear must function with a single-stomach digestive system similar to ours. It has no rumen, like the deer family, to predigest cellulose, and its coarse, gritty diet is hard on teeth and jaws and also on the claws that are worn down every summer from the task of digging up the rock-studded mountain earth while foraging for plant roots or small game. Grizzly bears are hard working predators. They will gouge out a ton of dirt and move stones weighing hundreds of pounds for the chance to kill a fat marmot. Garbage dumps, on the other hand, are loaded with high-calorie processed sugars, fats, and protein, all easily digested by both species of bears. To the bear, it is like tons of carrion meat and berries were all piled up in one convenient location.[11]

When it comes to finding food, grizzly bears have very good memories. The cub learns where the berry patches are by following at its mother's heels. Likewise, it recalls avalanche slopes where winter-killed goats and bighorn sheep may be found melting out of the snow in spring. A bear remembers picnic grounds where it successfully stole a camper's lunch, or garbage dumpsters that were once left open. We wardens found that once a bear was successful in obtaining human food, its memory of that success drew it back to an area again and again.

In Banff National Park, the trash cans were one source of calories for bears, but garbage dumps located near Banff and Lake Louise had been the preferred choice, especially for grizzly bears, for decades. The dumps were semiofficial tourist attractions and people flocked to them every evening, as they did in America's Yellowstone National Park, to watch the bears foraging on human discards. (The old Banff dump was actually sprayed with insecticide to stop biting flies from pestering the spectators.) As society's attitudes toward wildlife became more enlightened, park defenders objected to the degrading spectacle of bears feeding on garbage. In 1965, a park worker, Frederick Sturdy, was mauled while walking, at night, near a garbage dump at Maligne Lake in Jasper National Park. The lawsuit (ultimately unsuccessful) that he launched against Parks Canada set alarm bells ringing, albeit briefly, in Ottawa. By 1970, the Banff dump was closed and a new facility, a sanitary landfill, was opened a few miles north of the town, on the east side of the Cascade River Valley. It was closed to the tourists and fenced to keep out the bears. The fence, though made of steel mesh, offered grizzly bears about as much challenge as a volleyball net.

An electrified fence was eventually installed, but the bears soon defeated that by tunnelling underneath, and their smaller cousins, the black bears, followed discreetly on their heels. Suggestions were made by both wardens and scientists that the solution might be to "install a pollution-free incinerator, or to transport the garbage out of the park by truck or rail."[12] As I recall, park management's response to such suggestions could be summed up as "We have no budget for such improvements." The bear management teams scraped by year after year with outdated tranquilizing agents and rusty, beat-up culvert traps. Nevertheless they performed as well as any other such agency in that era; we were all pioneers in bear management and we all had much to learn.

The Banff landfill was set up to deal with a garbage volume generated by a city of 45,000 people, which is what the population was during the peak tourism season. At the landfill, billions of calories of garbage food and discarded roadkills were centralized in an unintentional, but gargantuan bear banquet prepared by Banff park's general works department operators using front-end loaders as serving spoons. I often patrolled to the landfill while on night shift to "count heads" for the "bear occurrence" forms we were required to fill out each shift. At the dump, the fiery eyes of grizzly bears shone like embers in my headlight beams. At night, the bears ruled the joint, and once they had broken in they were inclined to keep humans out. One night, as I got out of my patrol truck to unlock the gate, a grizzly bear came charging out of the darkness and sent me fleeing back into the vehicle. Other park workers had similar experiences. We watched shaggy behemoths gorging on road-killed elk, saw others roll, moaning with sensuous pleasure, through the garbage piles like cats in a patch of catnip, making the gas-distended garbage bags pop like stinky balloons.

Human beings had created, by default, the number one essential artificial food source for generations of black and grizzly bears in Banff National Park. A similar situation prevailed at Lake Louise at a garbage dump maintained there in the 1970s. In fact, the bear hazard at Lake Louise was greater than it was at Banff. The major hotels shut down for the winter at Lake Louise before the bears went into hibernation, cutting off the grub pile at the local landfill. Hungry bears then moved into the village looking for food, and armed wardens had to escort the school kids home from the bus stop as a result.

In the 1970s, as North America's environmental consciousness began to awaken, park wardens were joined in their protests over this degradation by biologists like Laszlo Retfalvi and Steve Herrero, who were doing research in the park. Having failed to prevent access to the site, we were continuing to encourage bears to feel comfortable feeding in the presence of humans (the operators and local business employees dumping garbage at the pit), thus training them to regard human food as bear food.

In 1973, I was stationed at Lake Minnewanka, a few miles north of the landfill. Grizzly bears migrated literally through my backyard to get to the dump. I often encountered the tall, wiry Californian, Steve Herrero, and his colleague David Hamer, who were doing research in my district. It was an opportunity for me to hear some of the ideas that would later find their way into Herrero's published work. In an early essay on bear–human conflict, Herrero noted a serious increase in human injuries in Glacier National Park (Canada) and Banff National Park. In Banff, Herrero cited the "continuing inability to solve serious garbage management problems, thus allowing grizzlies to forage unnaturally and become habituated to human odour. For instance, in Banff park in 1970–73, four of five injuries were caused by grizzlies with known histories of garbage/campground feeding . . . In Banff National Park, serious and immediate effort is needed to improve management, especially with regard to garbage . . . during 1972–73 wardens in one district alone (District 2, Lake Louise) handled grizzlies 56 times in control incidents, purposely destroying nine and one dying accidentally. During this same period in Glacier Park U.S., one family of bears was handled in a control incident, and one bear was purposely destroyed."[13]

Laszlo Retfalvi of the Canadian Wildlife Service wrote that the waste management systems then in place "seriously affect the ecology of bears and bring about a situation that could lead to the extinction of grizzly bears in the parks." Steve Herrero told me he met with national park superintendents and directors from 1970 on, including Superintendent Paul Lange (Banff National Park), and National Parks Branch Director Stephen Kun, "lobbying for better garbage management . . . I was the squeaky wheel going into Paul and Steve Kun's offices over that, but they were caught; they didn't have the money to do the job. It took the fatal attacks and the other injuries to release some money, sadly."

For me, Herrero's words were dipped, not in ink, but in the blood of both bears and men. One of the casualties of Parks Canada's garbage management policy in Banff park was Retfalvi's assistant, Wilf Etherington. Etherington, a well-regarded Canadian Wildlife Service technician, was killed by a garbage-habituated grizzly bear in 1973, during a relocation operation at the head of Totem Creek. Etherington had made a fatal error; he had underestimated how fast a bear can move upon its recovery from tranquilization, and therefore had come too close to the bear while filming it. The bear charged up a steep slope, caught up to Etherington in seconds, and killed him with massive bites to the head.

Etherington was a gentle soul who loved bears and everybody in the Outfit (as the wardens referred to the Parks Canada Warden Service) liked him. His death demoralized the field wardens, who believed it might have been prevented if proper safety procedures had been implemented by Parks Canada (as I have explained in a previous book).[14] In his role as a CWS technician, Etherington did not carry a gun, and an armed warden should have been sent along to protect him. On the day in question, it appears there was no warden available, due to other operations underway.

We were fully aware of the dangers posed by handling grizzly bears, whether by the use of tranquilizer darts or by live traps, but familiarity with the procedures over time had bred, in some of us, not contempt but perhaps overconfidence. Wilf Etherington's death was a brutal warning of what could happen if you underestimated the powers of a grizzly bear.

The bureaucratic mills grind exceeding slow, but after years of agitation the rusty lever of decision was tripped: in the spring of 1980 Parks Canada announced that henceforth all garbage would be shipped out of the park for disposal at the landfill in Calgary. Parks Canada built a bear-proof transfer station near the warden office to hold the collected trash for shipment by truck. The budget for the new program was $800,000. The generations of bears that had made a ritual of feeding on man's throwaways would feed on them no more – that was the theory. Dry debris and trade waste could still be dumped at the landfill, but no foodstuffs.

The planners' assumption seems to have been that the landfill bears would simply go back to feeding on berries and herbs, that they would become ecologically correct once again, and we would all live happily ever after. There was some basis for the assumption; given a good berry crop, even garbage bears forsook the dump temporarily to harvest the natural sweets. But every few years, the berry crop is hit by early frosts and fails. And in actual fact, bears continued to break into the old landfill site that summer and dig craters to work the garbage mine, since there was still a lot of food buried there. There was also a steady trickle of illegally deposited food matter.

But the main supply of bear heroin had been cut off; Parks Canada deserves great credit for that. However, the bears were not going to go cold turkey; there were still tons of calories in the restaurant bins and campground bins in Area 1, and few of those bins had been bear-proofed. Worse, collections were not frequent enough to keep up with overflowing bins at peak times. Chief wardens in Banff and other parks had complained about this part of the waste cycle, and the hazard it posed, since at least 1972, if not longer. L.H. Robinson, then regional director, noted the problem and wrote a memo to his park superintendents that improvements must be "pursued with vigour," but changes would be a long time in coming. In the spring of 1980, Parks Canada had installed some bins with doorknob-type latches in the campgrounds, which were described by Superintendent Lange as being bear-proof, but this proved to be an inadequate measure; the bins were too often left open by careless campers. Specifications for a truly bear-proof container were still in the works. In the meantime, Lange ordered his wardens to step up their efforts in educating residents and business owners to make their trash facilities bear-proof. On August 20, 1980, Warden Cardinal told the Banff *Crag and Canyon* that this could be accomplished for the sum of $55 per bin, but the newspaper offered no details as to how exactly this should be done. "70% of those approached cooperated fully with the warden's suggestions," reported the *Crag.* "The ones that didn't cooperate can expect warnings followed by charges."

Like many issues in the national parks, the bear-proof bin design was apparently caught up in a turf war, in this case between engineers at the federal Department of Public Works, who formerly did all the engineering design for national parks, and the new planning department set up in Parks Canada's western regional office in Calgary. During an interview for this book, I asked former chief park warden Andy Anderson for his take on the holdup with completing such a relatively simple task in Banff. He said that, for one thing, the engineers and planners didn't communicate with park staff to exchange ideas.

Anderson went down to the regional office to see what was going on and wandered into a boardroom where the experts had covered 12 feet of wall with hieroglyphics representing their latest obsession – Critical Path Planning, or CPM. Through the voodoo organizational magic of CPM, the bear-proof container would spontaneously appear somewhere down the critical path. But CPM, as I understand it, involves a network of "performers" with a task to complete. To Anderson the planning nodes and arcs of CPM were just "little circles with three sticks coming out. This is the start of this," he recalled, waving the imaginary pointer of the CPM evangelist above his head, "and then while this is going on we're at this stage over here, and then we've got to bring this together over here and then go out again over here." He shook his head and chuckled at the memory of this chartboard square dance as we sat over coffee one Banff afternoon. "So that was what took all their time, planning, critical path planning," he told me. "It was a big thing for them down in regional."

So when the transfer station was set up and the landfill was closed, the bear-proof garbage container was still more planned than real.

For a blueprint of how not to do garbage management, Parks Canada had only to look at how Yellowstone National Park had dealt with the issue in 1968. Against the advice of the famed Craighead bear research team, then operating in the park, the authorities had abruptly closed the park garbage dump. Bears were drawn into the campgrounds looking for food; rangers went from dealing with 33 bear problems in 1967 to 84 in 1968.[15] Thirty-three grizzly bears were destroyed between 1968 and 1971.[16] Several people were injured by bears, but in 1972 a young man, Harry Walker, who had an illegal camp in the Old Faithful area, was killed by a "large, toothless grizzly," which "crushed his larynx without even breaking the skin." The bear was captured and destroyed, but one result of this incident was a lawsuit in which the National Parks Service was found to be negligent on several counts. In short, it had failed to warn Walker that there was a grizzly bear in the area, it had failed to take control action on the bear in question, and it had abruptly closed the garbage dumps causing an extra hazard while at the same time discontinuing the bear-monitoring program.[17]

Andy Anderson reminded his superiors in the regional office about the Yellowstone disaster and the need for bear-proof bins. The report went up the food chain to an engineer type (his name forgotten now), then back to Anderson with a note that read, as Anderson recalls: "There's no reason to believe that Canadian bears would act the same way as the American bears."

Andy Anderson knew at that point that his wardens were going to have to kill some bears that summer, and the risk to humans and the ensuing legal implications were an ongoing worry. On July 1, 1977, a grizzly bear in Waterton National Park, Alberta, apparently not realizing it was a polite Canadian bear, had fatally injured a five-year-old child, Allison Tracy Muser, near the Little Prairie picnic site. The female bear, which weighed 214 pounds and was described as being in poor condition, returned to the mauling site on July 12 and was destroyed by warden Keith Brady. She had no previous record of having shown aggression to humans. The site was clean and well maintained, and there was a bear-proof garbage container on hand, according to reports. The family commenced a civil action against Parks Canada, listing several grounds, including an assertion that they had not been adequately warned on the presence of bears in the park. The suit was settled out of court for an amount that still remains confidential.[18]

Given Banff National Park's record of sloppy garbage management, the possibility of human injury, followed by another lawsuit against Parks Canada, should have been obvious. But regional staff in Calgary didn't worry; they would not be the ones standing in the dock. The burden of liability fell on Banff park administrators and, inevitably, on Chief Warden Andy Anderson.

Frustrated at running a system where bears were being treated like feeder hogs in a stockyard, Anderson kept on racking up helicopter time at $380 an hour relocating bears into the bush as if on an airborne assembly line. He told me that the cost of flying the bears out was the only lever he had to pressure his superiors to act. I didn't agree; I thought he should have used the law to enforce action, but that was easier said than done.

Like it or not, the garbage dump and the landfill that followed had become part of the annual food supply for generations of park bears. Now the bears had to find another source of calories. With the berry crop still a few months away, and the supply of winter-killed carrion already cleaned up, the richest source was the bonanza of fat in the restaurant garbage bins in Banff, a fact well known to black bears, at least, for many years. But there was also a long history of grizzly bears doing some bin bashing at outlying restaurants, such as the Rimrock, Timberline, and Caboose. These establishments offered both a food source and good escape cover; they were all built at the forest edge. These garbage-raiding grizzlies were seldom seen by most residents of the town; I met many Banff people in fact, who had never seen a grizzly and who doubted that they ever came that close to town.

The Caboose Restaurant, located in the CP Rail depot, was popular with "Banffites" (Banff residents). Proprietor Louis Kovacik, a well-known resident of Banff, was a retired railroad worker and the depot's former agent. In 1980, Alden Brososky was the Texaco bulk-fuel dealer in Banff townsite, and his depot was across the tracks from the Caboose and next door to the restaurant's garbage enclosure. (Incidentally, the plans for this enclosure had originally been approved by Chief Warden Andy Anderson.) In 2003, Brososky told me, "We had a lot of trouble with bears for a couple of years because of that darn place. The Parks had him [the proprietor] build it, he fenced it, he put barbed wire on it, and it seemed to work for quite a while. But Parks weren't getting around to empty the darn thing. There'd be garbage in there right up, bins were full, and a lot of it was lobster and crab that they served in those days. You could smell it miles away, it stunk so bad. So it attracted bears. And we saw up to eight bears around the bins or up in the trees. Black bears. You had to see them crawling over that fence with the barbed wire. They'd put their hind leg up and over, they'd keep feeling and feeling till they get their claws hooked on to the fence, then they'd lift their other hind leg over."

The situation at the Caboose was not unique. There were similar problems at some of the large hotels and the downtown restaurants, and in the large campgrounds run by Parks Canada Visitor Services Department. That fact hampered the park warden service in its attempts to enforce the garbage-handling regulations when dealing with commercial establishments in the park. Some business owners resented being chivvied by park wardens about mundane garbage handling. Their attitude, not without some justification, was "Clean up your own act before you come around hassling me." Some proprietors were even more critical: "Bears are a warden service problem;

why don't you guys spend less time dunking donuts and more time getting your bears the hell out of here."

In reality, bears, like other large predators, are a fact of life in national parks where all wildlife is protected and allowed to roam freely. The residents of Banff were aware of that fact; many of them took pride in living in a game preserve. Most tourists hoped to see wildlife during their stay, and even the sight of a garbage-loving bear thrilled them. Most locals in my experience did not see the bear situation as a serious threat: Banff bears had been knocking over trash cans and stealing Fido's lunch since 1883. A park report shows that from September of 1929 to June of 1980, only 12 people were injured by black bears in Banff National Park, none of them seriously. The report shows nine people were injured by grizzly bears for the same period: one injury was fatal (that of Wilf Etherington), three were serious, and five were minor.[19]

Black bears in particular were seen as timid creatures that offered little threat to people. The locals tended to forget that most of the bears that displayed real aggression to humans were either destroyed or trapped and relocated by the warden service, before they had a chance to inflict major injuries. Over time, a myth of harmlessness accrued to park bears, particularly black bears. In fact, what we were doing, without realizing it at the time, was selecting genetically for more docile bears by eliminating the more aggressive individuals from the breeding population. Hence the wardens' mystified reaction – "Where the hell did he come from?" – in response to the attacker in Whiskey Creek.

On May 14, 1980, the manager of the Caboose Restaurant was formally warned, in writing, that his garbage management practices were in violation of the *National Parks Act*, and that he must clean up the site. The record shows that he complied.

In addition to restaurant scraps attracting bears to the area that summer, there was a report claiming that persons unknown had been setting out meat, tied to the trees along the railroad line, probably as a means of getting a close-up photo of a bear, but no one was ever brought to book for that offence. Other bins that were raided by bears were within the residential subdivisions themselves, or behind the stores and restaurants in the heart of town. Some operators kept their bins locked, others did not. Every restaurant set out large (up to 45 gallons) containers of old deep-fry fat for collection at some point, and to a bear these were like Winnie the Pooh's pail of honey. Some of the dumpster bins were mounted on large casters. The bears would either climb into them to feed, or grapple them and try to knock them over. More than one local had thrown a bag of empty jars or cans into a bin, only to have a hidden black bear swat it back out again – or jump out of the bin like a gigantic alley cat, which was even scarier.

In 1980 Whiskey Creek was as popular with the locals as it had been in the days when whisky peddlers haunted its forests. Friends of mine had grown up there, building rafts on its beaver ponds and roasting filched potatoes over illegal campfires while playing Cowboys and Indians. Many a budding fisherman had learned the skill with a worm on a bent-pin hook and a line of mother's linen thread, perched on a log over a pool on Forty Mile Creek, or lying prone on a raft on one of Whiskey Creek's beaver ponds.

Adults went jogging or walked their dogs along the margins of the wild area: tour buses dropped off groups of amateur photographers eager to snap the beavers that created these natural trout ponds. So the area became an undeveloped extension of the town's backyard, and yet, all that time, avoiding contact whenever possible, the other residents of the wild land foraged for food, lay down to sleep, and cared for their young, largely unseen as they passed through the thick brush. The wilderness still lived in Whiskey Creek, and refused to be domesticated.

The warden service's report on the Whiskey Creek bear maulings of 1980 draws on information available in 1979 and clearly shows the importance of the area to wildlife such as deer, elk, and moose, as well as "carnivores and avifauna" (birds). Grizzly and black bears were noted as being "present."

Parks Canada, in other words, knew quite clearly that the area was frequented by bears, even though it lay close to town. Considering that black bears ventured into the heart of town at night, it would not be surprising to find them on the edge of town at other times. But the presence of grizzly bears close to town, although not uncommon, was always a cause for concern. Of the two species of bears in the park, the grizzly bear has always been considered the more dangerous. The grizzly bear has been called the most ferocious and dangerous mammal in North America, but I don't agree. As mammals, humans have proven to be more ferocious and more dangerous than any grizzly bear. The most dangerous quadruped is the domestic dog. In the United States, at least 800,000 people report being bitten by dogs every year; 334,000 wind up in emergency wards. Between 1979 and 1996, 304 dog bite victims died, at the rate of 17 per year. Most who died were children, and most serious attacks were directed at the victim's face.[20]

Nonetheless, bear-caused injuries, though rare, can be extremely serious. As for grizzly bear occurrences in Area 1, looking back in time we can see an ominous trend that apparently went unnoticed as the snows melted in the spring of 1980. The Whiskey Creek Report shows that grizzly bear sightings in the Whiskey Creek Area were increasing over a three-year period. There were two sightings of grizzly bears in the Whiskey Creek Area in 1978, and four in 1979. There would be six sightings there by the fall of 1980.

The report notes that on June 30, 1980, Warden Perry Jacobsen observed "a large grizzly near the CPR station at close range." Jacobsen noted that "the bear had a very light-yellowish head and a distinctive yellow band around the hump and girth." The yellow grizzly did not appear to be aggressive, and moved away from the humans to seek cover in the forest. Nowadays, the fact that it appeared "unconcerned" and that it "moved away slowly" into cover would be a red flag to a bear expert. He or she would view this as a bear that had little fear of human beings, that may have been conditioned to feed close to people; in other words, as a potentially dangerous bear in a tourist setting like Banff National Park.

Jacobsen did fill out a bear occurrence report on the sighting, which was passed on to the next shift of wardens by the area manager. This was a warning to keep an eye out for the bear, with a view to trapping and removing it from the area if it came to be a threat to the public.

Up until the evening of August 24, 1980, Whiskey Creek was part of Banff's backyard playground. But by September, the people of Banff would learn to shiver when the little creek was mentioned. And it would be mentioned repeatedly on national radio and television and in many other parts of the world. In September of 1980, Steve Herrero would make a pronouncement that locals would have openly ridiculed only two weeks earlier: "Whiskey Creek," he told the *Calgary Herald*, "is the most dangerous place in Banff National Park."

FOUR

THE YEAR OF ASHES

"Meanwhile in Banff, bear attacks are uncommon since there is plenty
of food available to them, says Andy Anderson, chief park warden."

Calgary Sun, August 21, 1980

IF I WERE AN ELDER of an old montane tribe, creating a picto-
graph for the annual winter count, I would portray the year 1980 as
the year of ashes; I would paint an image on my deerhide palimpsest
of a volcano blowing its top.

For several months vulcanologists and the news media had been
watching Mount St. Helens, in Washington state, after the peak was
rocked by a series of earthquakes and minor explosions starting on
March 15 of that year. By mid April, according to information
posted by the United States Geological Survey (USGS), a crypto-
dome caused by magma intruding upwards into the cone formed on
the north flank of the mountain and began growing at the rate of
eight feet a day. On May 18, a 5.1 magnitude earthquake a mile
below the volcano triggered a massive landslide on the north side of
the peak, which, travelling at from 70 to 150 miles per hour buried
the north fork of the Toutle River under a lake of stone for a distance of 16 miles. Scientists have proposed that this landslide
unloaded the pressure cap of rock on the crypto-dome, after which
subterranean pools of water came into contact with the magma

under the dome and "flashed to steam," triggering a massive lateral blast at 8:32 a.m.

Imagine a mountain losing 1,314 feet of its height in a matter of seconds. The volcano, which was 9,677 feet in altitude before the blast was 8,363 feet high after the eruption subsided. According to the USGS, the blast released 24 megatons of thermal energy and produced a "stone wind" of flying debris travelling at 300 miles per hour, which covered an area of 230 square miles, for 17 miles northwest of the crater. Fifty-seven people were killed or reported missing, 7,000 big-game animals were estimated killed (along with all small birds and mammals), and trees containing four billion board feet of timber were blown down. The blast was followed later that day by lahars (rivers of mud), fed in part by the volcano's melted glaciers, that rushed down the Toutle and other streams, destroying buildings, bridges, and miles of highways, and plugging the shipping channel on the Columbia River with debris. A mushroom cloud of grey ash, played over by chain lightning, reached about 80,000 feet in less than 15 minutes, turning night into day for the residents of Spokane, some 250 air miles northeast of the volcano and Seattle, 100 air miles to the north. The volcanic cloud, containing 1.4 billion cubic yards of ash, circled the earth in 15 days and was detected over an area of 22,000 square miles. It formed a half-inch-deep layer 300 miles downwind.[21]

At the time of the Mount St. Helens explosion, I was living in the mountain community of Canmore, Alberta, with my wife and two sons, where I worked full-time at the writing trade. Canmore was then a small coal-mining town in the Bow River Valley. It is located a few miles east of the Banff National Park boundary and about a 50-minute drive west from Calgary. Canmore Mines closed down the last active underground mine in 1979. The population consisted, for the most part, of retired miners, Parks Canada employees, mountain guides, artists, local business operators, provincial parks employees, and ski bums. It was a delightful, laid-back mountain town; the perfect place to raise kids and not the intrusive investment opportunity for oilmen and serial golfers that it is today.

Canmore is about 465 air miles northeast of Mount St. Helens, and we followed events there with the awed interest of people who were not directly affected by a major disaster – or so we thought. We woke up one morning, amazed to find a shroud of ashes settled on the town, covering the green leaves of spring and coating parked cars like talcum powder. In geological and meteorological measure, Mount St. Helens, it turns out, was just down the road and had made its presence felt. When we looked out the window into the greenish-yellow light of day, it seemed as if the whole world were in a state of mourning. We were still sweeping up the ashes when the cloudy skies, seeded with volcanic dust, burst open on May 23 and dropped over an inch of rain on the valley.

In retrospect, the signals that something was badly askew in the web of life were initially obscured by the seasonal routines of the "bear business," meaning the park's bear management program. As per usual in that era, bruins, lured close to town by the scent of garbage and sizzling barbecues, began raising hell not long after coming out of hibernation. The black bear, which hibernates at lower elevations, such as the slopes of the Bow River Valley, usually made its presence felt first. The annual bear trap-a-thon began on May 18 with the capture of a black bear near the Rimrock Hotel, on the slopes of Sulphur Mountain, which overlooks the town of Banff, one of nine bears (eight black bears and one grizzly) that would be caught at the Rimrock that season. It was frequently a bear hotspot that summer, as it had been during the late 1970s when I worked the area. Bears that raised hell once too often wound up in a bait-triggered culvert trap.

Bears were either trailered out into the backcountry on the old park wildfire access roads (some of which have since been permanently removed) or they were tranquilized and flown out in a helicopter cargo net. Oftentimes bears made their way back overland to their old haunts, and their old bad habits, within 72 hours or less. Repeat offenders, especially grizzly bears, became trap-wise; they were then captured using tranquilizer darts, the method favoured by the more experienced bear control wardens. Habituated bears, as they were known, were usually numbered bears, the number in those days being tattooed in ink on the inside of the upper lip with the help of medieval-looking spiked tattoo pliers. (This practice ended in the early 1990s; park bears these days are identified humanely using DNA analysis of discarded hair collected at bait stations.) However, they were not always given a number on their first bust. The system lacked consistency, and scientific rigour and oversight, in part because professional standards were still being developed, and also because there were no professional biologists on staff.

The management plan for bears in 1980 was pretty straightforward, and I would sum it up as "three strikes and you're out" for habituated bears. If an habituated bear was trapped and relocated three times and the senior wardens felt that its behaviour around people made it an obvious hazard to the public, it didn't get a fourth trip. A few were donated to zoos or wildlife parks, but usually there was no room for more bear exhibits, so they were destroyed. A bear donated to a zoo was as good as a dead bear for our purposes, since it was removed from the breeding population. Wardens prosecuted or warned anyone caught feeding bears by hand, but charges against restaurants proceeded far too slowly. Meanwhile it was a matter of "you feed 'em, we weed 'em."

The warden bear control teams, led by wardens Monte Rose and Perry Jacobsen, pursued black bears around the townsite and the park campgrounds on a daily basis. The record shows that the wardens in Area 1 logged 291 "trap nights" in 1980, compared with 113 trap nights in 1979. Significantly, the number of bears captured actually had decreased from 1979, from one bear per four trap nights to one bear per nine trap nights.[22] Like the grizzly, the black bear has a very strong memory. If you catch him twice in a live trap he tends to be quite cautious on the third try. You can often tree him, however, where he is an easy target for a tranquilizer dart, unlike his grizzled cousin, who would rather knock a tree down any day than climb it. But you had better have a rope handy and be able to climb up after him to lower him to the ground when he conks out, or have a net ready to catch him if he falls.

There were 19 relocations of grizzly bears involving 12 individuals (some were moved more than once) in 1980. More than half of those had been handled in previous years. Only one bear, later listed as the Whiskey Creek bear, was unknown to the Banff warden service.

As the season progressed, the frequency of sightings and escalating encounters with bears began to wear on everyone's nerves. Considering the bizarre nature of some of these encounters, it is amazing that no humans were injured. The 1980 Bear Summary Report provides terse but intriguing anecdotes:

> June 11. Two Jack Campground. Black bear tore down tent and attempted to nip leg of person inside. Bear died due to fall from tree when later being tranquilized.
>
> June 17. Black sow and cub entered Banff Springs Hotel and went to garbage room in basement.
>
> June 27. Orphan cub-of-year "Albert" fell into basement of Admin. Building through window.
>
> June 30. Bear entered garbage room inside Banff Springs Hotel – staff startled.

These reports are maddeningly devoid of detail. What did the staff at the hotel do when they went to empty the garbage and found a bear in the basement? How did Albert get out of the Administration Building – via the window or the front door? Did he lodge a complaint with the superintendent about the quality of basement window glass before leaving?

From Yellowstone to Yukon, the Rocky Mountains frame a wilderness cradle for the ursine species, but as spring gave way to summer, it seemed as if this cradle had been rocked to consternation by the Mount St. Helens explosion. In late April, the media had assured us that this summer would be the hottest and driest on record. Then came the eruption, and the rains.

It has been shown that a volcanic ash coating on plants reduces photosynthesis by 90 percent, until the rains work to wash off the covering. This type of abrasive ash is also lethal to insects such as bees, which are pollinators of berry plants.[23] The falling ash was soon followed by cool wet weather just at the end of the period – late April to mid May – when the buffalo berry sets out its blooms. Environment Canada gives the mean annual precipitation for Banff in May as 39.2 mm, but in 1980, the total rainfall for May was 87.6 mm and 80.7 mm of this fell after May 18, while heavy rains in June produced 92 mm in total. The trend moderated for July (31 mm), then continued on into August (64 mm). Overcast skies robbed the plants of energy. Also, the minimum temperatures measured at the Banff fire hall weather station were close to the freezing point on several days in May (at 4° C for four days and 2° C on May 31), a measurement that may have been higher than it would have been in the forest, due to the urban heat island effect.[24] Furthermore, Banff sits at 1384 metres (4500 feet) in a valley bottom, and temperatures decrease with altitude (2° C per 1000 metres). Buffalo berry is a plant that prefers the forest edge. Compromised by lack of sunlight, the blooms were withered by frosts, with a devastating effect on fruit production.

Just how serious can such a crop failure be? Steve Herrero cites studies that show a bear may continue to lose weight after emerging from the den right up until berry time. Think of trekking across the desert, putting your entire faith in drinking at the one waterhole available, only to find it dry, and you may imagine how a bear feels when the berry patch comes up empty – or crowded with humans. It must find other high-calorie foods – and quickly. For a bear, body fat is everything, from winter survival to sexual gratification and mating success. In *Bear Attacks*, Herrero cites the research of biologist Art Pearson. Pearson was an exemplar of scientific dedication. He wanted to know how many soapberries a grizzly bear can consume in a day. The fact that the soapberry has only one seed is key. Daily Pearson collected the scat left by an adult bear and counted the seeds to get the answer – 200,000. Those of us who have detoured around long red streaks of loose grizzly bear crap on the trail in berry time are content to take Pearson at his word without doing a recount.

In Banff, residents were both irked and amused by the antics of park bears staring through their patio doors as if waiting for an invitation to lunch, or for a chance to steal the dog's dinner, but their complacent outlook was hard to sustain, as the evening news and the morning papers began listing story after story about bear maulings in western North America.

Some of the similarities were positively glaring. In the hamlet of Lodgepole, Alberta, as many as nine bears at a time were wandering down the main street in broad daylight looking for food, freaking out housewives and forcing kids to stay indoors. The town dump where the bears used to feed had been filled in, and the new one was still under construction. Bears camped on people's back steps and ignored the watchdogs that tried to chase them off. Some also attempted to break in, attracted by the smell of cooking food.

Those who lifted an eyebrow at that story, or went out to have a nervous look around the backyard, would have definitely frowned at news of the death of 10-year-old Allan Russell Baines, killed by a black bear while fishing with two friends near Fort St. James, British Columbia, on July 19, 1980, or of the deaths of Jane Ammerman and Kim Eberlee, killed by a grizzly on July 24. After a short respite, the bear stories erupted in a flood. On August 15, Calgary geologist Lee Randall Morris, 44, and oil-rig worker Carol Ann Marshall, 24, of Edmonton, were killed near Zama, Alberta, 450 miles northwest of Edmonton. Again, a black bear was the culprit.

This attack was a very traumatic one and the papers covered it for days. Marshall and another worker, Martin Ellis, had decided to go for a stroll and had run into the bear. What they didn't know at that moment was that the bear had already killed and partially eaten Morris earlier that same day. The pair tried to climb a tree (a mistake when dealing with the predatory type of black bear attack since this species is arboreal, unlike the grizzly). Ellis made it, but the bear dragged Ms. Marshall out of Ellis's grip and, in a moment, snapped

her neck. It shook her body violently like a dog with a ground squirrel, then dragged it back into the bush to lay it next to Morris's
corpse. The bear returned immediately to the tree and climbed up to
try and drag Ellis out. The critter was a real meat-Midas, determined
to add Ellis to its cache, but Ellis did the right thing, which was to
fight it off with all his might, using his feet as weapons. A nine-year-
old boy, Reagan Whiting, next came upon the scene. Ellis yelled for
him to go for help, and distracted the bear by loud shouting while the
youngster escaped. Whiting's father came to the rescue with a
shotgun and wounded the bear, driving it off. It was killed by a helicopter pilot the next day.

But the season of aggressive bears continued in rural Alberta. On
August 17, a woman who was camping with four others in a tent near
Slave Lake was injured by a black bear while she slept. It seems her
head was against the tent wall and Mr. Bear, always curious and ever
ready to exploit a situation, bit her right through the canvas. She
escaped with 15 stitches.

That same week, in Blairmore, Alberta, which sits in a major river
valley like Banff, a Mountie shot a black bear that was walking down
a busy street. In Banff bears walked down the street all the time.
Nobody shot them, though once in a while somebody might bean one
with a beer bottle. (I also know of at least one case, involving one
Myrna Marty, where a bear was hit over the head with a broom when
caught raiding her garden.)

During another incident, a large crowd of tourists treed a black
bear, known by his tattoo number as B953, at the Sundance Mall in
downtown Banff; luckily all escaped without injury when the bear
charged at them. Indeed, the 1980 Bear Summary Report for Area 1
stresses the tolerance bears displayed that year to humans during 29
incidents where they were "closely approached, encircled, chased by
humans or dogs" yet injured no one. "In addition," the account continues, "57 reports of bears ripping into coolers, packs, and tents
were recorded; many of these incidents occurred while people were
close by, again with no human injuries. It must be concluded,

however," the report warns "that sooner or later the odds will catch up with the facts and human injury will result." The document calls for aggressive public education about bears and facility improvements, such as bear-proof food lockers in campgrounds.[25]

Seasonal Warden Alan Westhaver, one of the report's authors, noticed a strange bear-displacement energy around the edges of Whiskey Creek that August, a kind of bubble effect, as if something was pushing the bears out of the forest, pushing them farther into the back alleys closer to downtown. It seemed as if he hardly slept some days; he was chasing bears with Warden Monte Rose day and night. He couldn't even make it to his own birthday party on time. He found the cold beer had been drunk and the guests were already partied out, so he just went back to work. By August 24, Rose's control team alone had logged operations involving 29 black bears and 14 grizzly bears, part of the total of 60 bears the wardens had moved from Area 1 by that date. That didn't include the dozens of other complaints about bear activity that they had also investigated, where no control action proved necessary. There had been 187 "bear occurrences" in Area 1 in 1979; there would be 272 before the bears went to bed in 1980.

Warden Rose specialized in tranquilizer-darting trap-wise bears at night, when they felt it was safe to come out to play. Darting roaming bears at night in the middle of a town is more than merely risky: there are pedestrians, dogs, passing vehicles, and dim lighting conditions to cope with, as well as a moving target to try and hit using a CO_2-powered pistol or a tranquilizer gun powered by a .22 calibre gunpowder charge. Tranquilized bears have to be held overnight in a cage, then tranquilized again for transport. Too much power on the gun could bury the dart too deeply, causing hemorrhaging and infection. Bears have to be monitored to ensure they do not become dehydrated; their eyes must be protected while under the drug; penicillin has to be administered if the bear has an injury. Sometimes the wardens ran out of Sernalyn (known on the street as angel dust, it is no longer used as a tranquilizer) or the preferred Ketamine-Rompun mix, and had to resort to Anectine, a leftover from a more primitive era. If I had to use one word to describe Anectine as a tranquilizing agent on mammals, "barbaric" springs to mind. Anectine works only on the muscular system: bears are completely aware of being manhandled, but powerless to respond.[*]

Some bear control operations went quickly, others stretched on for hours or even days, depending on many factors, including the cleverness of the bear, the location, or the presence of bystanders bumbling into harm's way.

One of the bears trapped early that season was a large male black bear numbered B054. Bear 054 was a traveller, and a determined wannabe resident of the Bow Valley who preferred the high-calorie life of an urban bear to rooting for grubs and scoffing down skunk cabbage out in the sublime wilderness. The record shows this bear was captured four times, contrary to departmental practice. On June 6 he succumbed to the charms of the Rimrock Hotel's garbage bins on the southern edge of town and was caught and relocated to the Dormer River area, which lies around 25 miles by air north of Banff. By July 4 he had followed his nose over three mountain passes to lap up spilled grease and frolic among the garbage bins at his beloved Rimrock hostelry again. This time he was shipped out to Mount Oliver, a mere stroll over the peaks (17 air miles from town), a pit stop from which he returned like a boomerang. En route to the Rimrock no doubt, he was seduced instead by the turf-and-surf aroma at the Caboose Restaurant on the north side of town, where he was captured on July 9.

According to the available records, B054 showed no aggression during his "third strike." Wardens punched his ticket for one last trip, this time to the Clearwater area, on the far north end of the park. Some people would later see this decision as a mistake; others would say that it didn't make any difference. B054 probably felt ill at ease in the pristine wilderness of the Clearwater Area. Just when he began his last journey overland back to Banff is anybody's guess.

---

[*] Ketamine (ketamine hydrochloride) is an anaesthetic; Rompun (xylazine) is an analgesic and sedative.

It is likely he was back in the urban edge forest within a week of his last departure.

At any rate, the fourth and last time B054 encountered the Area 1 wardens was late on the evening of August 27, just behind the Caboose Restaurant. By that time he had put on a considerable amount of fat compared with his condition on June 6.

In fact, B054 was an unusual specimen of a black bear. The black bear has a sharper, more roman-style nose, unlike the flatter, dished-in muzzle and rounder face of the grizzly bear. Bear 054's face was strangely broad for a black bear, and he was more heavyset in the shoulders than the typical black bear, probably due to the weight he was putting on dining at the Rimrock and Caboose. In the right kind of light and on first glance, he looked more like a small adult grizzly, with its typically humped back, than an adult black bear with its sloping shoulders. Yet, strangely, this distinct appearance of the bear was not noted in his first three encounters with the wardens.

This large, dirty-brown male bear would soon cast a long shadow over Whiskey Creek.

The public was confused, as they tried to relate what they had always assumed about the comical black bear to the vicious, predatory behaviour they were hearing about late that summer. But one fact was gradually coming to light as the newspapers turned to biologists and game wardens for explanations. There had been a failure in the blueberry crop in the northern part of the range, and black bears were desperate to replace the calories they would normally get from berries, so they were moving into close proximity to people, looking for castoff food and, when that was not available, preying, as a last resort, on humans.

Trust the pesky *Calgary Sun* and *Calgary Herald* to ask the authorities in Banff about the berry crop. The answers they got from Parks Canada were reassuring, but overly optimistic to say the least. "Meanwhile in Banff," the *Sun* reported on August 21, "bear attacks are uncommon, since there is plenty of food available to them, says Andy Anderson, Chief Park Warden." The *Sun* didn't specify what kind of food he meant, but Ken Preston, Parks Canada's regional information officer, made the situation clearer: "We keep an eye on garbage, that's where the bears head," he said.

The berry crop fluctuated from year to year, but the supply of human food was constant. That supply was so readily available and so obviously desired by bears that I think just about everyone concerned in 1980 discounted the importance of the berry crop in the Bow River Valley. Someone probably asked the question "What happens with these bears if we shut off the flow of trash food and there's a failure in the berry crop at the same time?" Someone must have, but I haven't been able to find out who. I'm sure he or she will come forward eventually, maybe after this book is published.

— FIVE —

STICKY MOUTH AWAKES

In the huge, wide-open, sleeping eye of the mountain
The bear is the gleam in the pupil
Ready to awake
And instantly focus.

TED HUGHES
from his poem "The Bear"

IN HIS WINTER DEN, lying on a bed made of juniper and balsam fir boughs dragged there for the purpose, Sticky Mouth sleeps close to the mountain's heart. For him the mountain must seem like a living thing because it provides both food and drink all summer long from alpine meadow to valley bottom, and it speaks to him with the voice of water, with the voice of wind and the voice of the falling rock and snow. It is May of 1980 and now the mountain speaks with a new voice like distant thunder, and the mountain trembles, every so slightly, as Sticky Mouth rouses to a dazed wakefulness.

For centuries the bear's ability to survive the winter without food or drink was one of the enduring mysteries of a predator that many cultures held to be sacred. How could it vanish during the first big snowstorm of the year, in October or November, as if the snow had buried it alive, yet reappear magically from March to May (depending on the weather) a bit slimmer but otherwise healthy? (It was as if it had been sleeping with the warm sun all winter, leaving men to endure the cold-hearted sun of that long season.) The Siksika ("Real People," or Blackfoot First Nation) have a legend in which the bear captures the warm Chinook wind that brings temporary spring to the mountain-front country. Bear keeps it in a leather bag in his lodge, denying them the pleasure of Sun's warm breath, until a band of supernatural animals raids the lodge and sets the wind free again. People who had suffered through the months of famine often wished they had been able to sleep through the miserable season of cold and hunger, like the bear did. It was as if the warm sun returned with the appearance of the bear in the spring. That miracle could not be taken for granted, and so a supernatural explanation was invented.

Today we know some homely truths about how bears survive the winter, though the seeds of mystery are still contained within them. For example, the bear neither defecates nor urinates during its long sleep but reabsorbs the urine from its bladder to prevent a toxic buildup that could kill it. Its alimentary tract is blocked with a waxy plug containing the last meal of indigestible fibres it swallowed before going to sleep. Its heartbeat slows to 10 beats a minute, but its body temperature stays only a few degrees below normal, so it burns up fat while sleeping, and bears are light sleepers compared with other wintering beasts. The sounds of men moving on the surface above the den is enough to rouse a bear into a dangerous (albeit constipated) wakefulness. If they persist too long after its rumbling threats, the interlopers could find the bear suddenly surfacing among them, snow and claws flying.

There is nothing else there to be seen or heard but the sound of Sticky Mouth's own heart beating in the perfect quiet. Inside his huge head there forms a picture of an avalanche; that kind of spring thunder has awoken him before. (If he had a keeper in the wild, it would be the avalanche that buries the den in insulating snow, and threatens all intruders with its crushing embrace.) His heart is waking up: in his ears he hears a familiar drum beating. Soon the furnace of his stomach will need stoking, but for now it is shrunken, dormant.

The big grizzly is curled up below the tree roots on the uplifted, petrified beach of an ancient sea now lying thousands of feet above the tumult of distant valleys known to humankind. Fossil shells in the stone pressed against his ear still hold the voice of vanished oceans. The footings of the mountains are very deep, so even a slight shifting in the earth's mantle is transmitted to his nerves through the embracing arms of limestone that form the ceiling and floor of the den. He listens, then he feels the whole mountain trembling again; that was what had roused him, though it was a slight movement, as if a pine siskin had rested on his shoulder by mistake, then fanned its alarmed wings to spring clear. Lying with his head close to the stone, Sticky Mouth had heard a sound he had never heard before. It was like the thunder's voice, but muffled by leagues and leagues of stone and hidden caverns full of glacial meltwater where thunder could never go, and where nothing animate had ever been. Blood surges in his ears and he feels his hackles rising in reply.

On the surface, there is a small stand of isolated balsam firs on an avalanche chute. The trees are huddled at the foot of a high cliff band that interrupts the gulley, and the force of winter snow slides hurtling down this gully has allowed a backwash of cascading snow to accumulate on the little grove. It is a place where few humans – perhaps none – have ever stepped. Below the trees is a white page of snow where a wisp of steam wafts from an ice-coated vent, as if there were a hidden hot spring among the tree roots. Otherwise the slope is unprinted by even the track of a red squirrel, for there are hardly enough cones in those gnarled trees to sustain a squirrel in that deadest end of a dead end canyon. If any living thing were there to witness Sticky Mouth announcing the new season, it could only be a corvid, a mere whisky-jack perhaps, making a desultory transit across the floor of the canyon; looking for a half-remembered food cache, a few seeds or a scrap of dried carrion tucked under the ragged edge of bark where the tree has been scarred by falling rock.

And then the white world erupts.

At the base of a fir tree, slabs of old snow suddenly fly up from the surface as if a land mine has exploded. Two huge forepaws, fringed with coal-black fur, thrust from a dark opening in that white expanse. Ten black toe pads tipped with 10 four-inch-long ivory talons, each sharp from a winter's slow growth, are splayed up as if in homage to the narrowing shaft of the sky above the canyon walls. The snow streams away as the front legs follow and out comes the muzzle held low to the front knees, the dread jaws opening, a surprisingly deli-cate-looking tongue showing to taste the fresh air, the lighter brown muzzle pointing out from a dark head round as the bottom of a whisky barrel, the small brown eyes close set above it blinking at the light, snow spilling from above the perched circlets of the ears. The beast risen with the spring: the secret of the winter revealed. Sticky Mouth fills that vast emptiness with a roar that echoes from the canyon walls.

At this altitude and in these northern temperate latitudes, winter is never really defeated, but although the last storm had not yet struck, its grip was broken, for the coming of the new sun is prophesied by this furred troglodyte and sage. He paces slowly to and fro by the den mouth for a few minutes, getting his bearings. The brilliant light hurts his eyes and the steep slope is not comfort-able to balance upon. At length he begins scooping and trampling a day bed near the den, making blocks of snow fly and clatter down the slope, working down to the mountain earth and blackening the snow with his efforts. The blackened snow becomes a sun trap, warming the bear as he rests on this aerie and waits for his stomach to wake up and work its purposes upon his brain. He'll spend the evening hours in the den, still sustained by the fat he has stored in his body the previous year.

A day or two later he rises suddenly from the day bed and points his nose into the wind like a giant bloodhound. He sniffs loudly. In the valley below, the sun has warmed a bubble of air and caused it to rise upslope, carrying the scent of carrion, and this tickles Sticky Mouth's nose. Down the valley, two miles south of his den, the hindquarters of a moose killed in a winter avalanche has melted finally out of the

snow. It is slowly decomposing and giving off gases. He gives himself
a shake, from nose to tail and, prompted by the growling deep inside
his guts, sets off without further ceremony for the forest edge a thousand feet below, which files away in green ranks from the bottom of
the avalanche chute that protected his den all winter. The steepness
of the slope would give a mountaineer pause, but it's trifling to him,
with his built-in crampons. Right now it is too slow-going to suit
him. He takes a few deliberate steps straight down the fall-line, then,
front paws extended, suddenly flops on his belly and slides down at a
great rate, leaving a wide groove like a toboggan track to mark his
passage. The rocks that foot the bottom of the snow slope soon loom
large, with the threat of a bloody crash. But just as a mountaineer
reaches out with the adze of the ice axe to brake his glissade down
such slopes, so Sticky Mouth reaches out and rakes the surface with
his claws, slowing his descent. He continues the run sitting on his
rump, his heels stretched in front of him, his front paws at chest
height. Creatures watching from the forest edge see him hurtle into
view, the Old Man of the Mountain at play, his eyes gleaming, his
mouth open and tongue lolling.

At the edge of the snow, which is six feet thick, the ancient rock
slide has been exposed by winter winds and the early spring sun. He
twists around and stops himself with his front claws again and rises
to all fours as if dismounting from an invisible sled. He peers down on
the rocks from the shelf of snow, then turns around and, holding
himself back with his front paws, steps down, hind foot first, from the
lip of thick snow onto the jumble of boulders piled below. He bal-
ances there on a huge rock, four feet close together with an ungainly
daintiness, given his rangy, quarter-ton bulk, while surveying a route
through the jumble of piled stone. He picks his way over and between
rocks as big as automobiles until he reaches the trees, where he shoulders through that thick stand of young spruce. Crunching the corn
snow of spring underfoot, he comes at last to a meltwater stream
where he drinks deeply. He follows this defile down the mountain to
where the snow gradually dissipates and the first green plants come

into view. There he may feed on any succulent greens sprouting at the snow edge, to purge his guts for the feast of rotten moose flesh to come. To his brain comes an image of the others feeding on *his* moose; coyotes with their allies and *penates*, the ravens and whisky-jacks. He reads the wind intently, and his stomach growls in response to the message it contains. Led by his nose and spurred by his stomach, he hurries toward the promise of the feast, moaning with impatience, armed and ready for the combat with any competitor he encounters.

But as he stalks off down the mountain a strange cloud comes between the earth and the sun. The daylight fades back into a near night and it begins to snow. But the snow does not melt when it falls on his nose as it should. When he licks it, it tastes not like snow, but like rock flour, like dust. He stops for a moment and peers up at the sky, then sits on his haunches and looks at his shaggy arm, which has turned a ghostly grey.

When he runs in among the feeding white coyotes and the white-shouldered ravens perched on the white pines, it's as if a spectral bestiary has convened to feed upon the ghost of a moose. The great bear rips open the moose's belly from gullet to gut loops, and the red and purple tangle of its insides flow out over the remnant snow and the ashes of that uncanny spring. He falls to among that raucous caucus of carnivores, scattering them from time to time amid howls and croaks of complaint. Eating on and on, he washes down the liver with a mouthful of snow, and swallows the stomach well-salted with another sprinkling of pumice from the bowels of Mount St. Helens.

SIX

THE HIDDEN ROAD

In September 1980, Warden Halle Flygare found an old bear trail, hereto-
fore unidentified, that led down from Mount Norquay to the edge of the
Trans-Canada Highway across from the Whiskey Creek "swamp" as it was
then known . . .

THERE ARE TRAILS NEAR the timberline, connecting between
the ranges, whose purpose is known to very few, because they are not
part of the trail system used by humans. Known as bear roads, they
tunnel through the krummholz and slide alder where most people
stop, baffled, unwilling to get down on all fours and crawl, unsure of
their welcome in that hedged darkness. They are roads of ancestral
knowledge, passed on from the mother bear to the cubs, imprinted in
the brain to be recalled later, perhaps some years after the cubs have
dispersed, maybe long after the siblings have gone their separate
ways. Mothers and cubs might meet again on those roads, and recognize each other, and pass each other by without doing harm.

One road, of many such, crosses rock slides where the shale is
packed into the interstices between great fallen blocks of limestone
by the coming and going of padded feet. Here a hole in the path marks
where a boulder the size of a small car was grappled and shoved out
of the way, and sent rolling down the mountain like local thunder.
This road winds across avalanche chutes, over the flayed trunks of

old-growth trees that can be three feet or more in diameter, trees that lived for a century or longer before a winter avalanche finally called them to account, leaving their bones like giant pick-up sticks between the boulders, the trunks now scarred by claw marks. Here and there will be a drift of snow, insulated by a layer of broken shale that fell, piece by piece, from the precipice high above earlier that spring, as meltwater loosened the rocks, so in the heat of summer there are still places where the traveller beast can stretch out and rub its back and cool off in the icy slush for a moment below a boiling of frustrated deer flies. The bear road curls through a mossy gulch now and then, where a brook purls down the mountain to form a pool of icy water in which a bear may stop to bathe its hot, cracked footpads in the mud while slaking its thirst. And if, later, you came upon the spot by chance, you might think that a huge man had stood barefoot in the mud; you might wonder if the stories about Sasquatch are true, and then you might note how the mud is punctured at the end of each toe pad. And this fact will make you stand up quickly; it will make you turn around, and listen, and listen.

In the old-growth forest, where the deep layers of duff and moss sometimes serve as the flimsy roof over a rock crevice, a place to be sniffed at and passed by carefully, or else out on the flatter lie of a bog, the road is marked by tracks a foot deep and a foot or more long. These tracks were made over the centuries by the padded humanoid feet of bears that journey between mountain ranges; each has put its front foot and then the corresponding rear foot down in the same print the first of its tribe made here centuries before. It may seem as if this were a trail made by human footsteps, but you will look in vain for any other sign of their habitation or resort. There are no axe blazes, no fire circles or rusty tin cans. The road may be grown in with fresh green moss as if it had been unused for years, but it has not been forgotten, and won't be as long as bears are allowed to live.

As Sticky Mouth walks the high, hidden road in the dark of night, the quietude gives way to a constant rumbling from the valley floor below. He sees the glow of strange lights so unlike the scattered prickle of stars in the night sky. These lights make him blink; they are far too bright. He smells the tantalizing odour of food, and this smell draws him on.

Every day he is growing fatter and more powerful and every day he feels the need to be bigger still. But now when there should be clusters of red berries to assuage his hunger, there are only sparse offerings of former excess. His weight and his strength are his glory; they secure his mating rights and the passing on of genetic material. (Considering that he would eat his offspring if he got the chance, perhaps our conclusions about breeding success among grizzly bears are somewhat anthropocentric.) But a thick layer of fat under his hide is what promises his survival in the winter den; that was the fuel his body burned all winter while he slept. But now that fat is diminished and so finding food is his first concern.

No creature he meets on that trail is his peer; none can look him in the face without turning away to show their deference, and every living thing he encounters gives up the trail and hurries out of his way. Surely the same will happen in the bright, rich-smelling valley below?

It must have been very early in the morning when there are long intervals between vehicles on the highway that he came suddenly out of the trees as if he had walked there for his whole life.

He crosses the ditch with a crunching of gravel underfoot and stops at the asphalt margin of the highway. He remembers this Meatmaker; that is, his stomach reminds him that it had fed him once before, long ago. He bends his great head down to examine it with his nose; he smells the foreign odour of gasoline, of spilled oil, the sweet poison of antifreeze, and he sniffs loudly, for he detects the tentative nose-candy richness of pooled cruor. The odour tells him that a male bighorn sheep was killed here a few days earlier. He can almost taste the musty tang of its scent glands that lingers in the roadside grasses and on the pavement. It rouses a picture in his head of a meat-beast with massive horns. He prowls back and forth in the ditch for a few moments, looking for the carcass, but there is nothing there but scent.

The smell of blood makes him salivate, and he tests the asphalt with his pink tongue. He is not prepared for the heat it still contains from the previous day of sun, and he recoils from the warmth. He rears up on his hind legs and stares, front feet in the air, feeling the heat waves radiating still in the darkness. He inhales sharply, as a breath of cool air from the river floats to his nostrils. On all fours now, he steps onto the warm pavement, then breaks into a rough gallop for the other side. But the tacky warmth of the road on his padded feet puzzles him, and so he hates it: the earth should be cool and firm at night and give some relief from summer's heat. Reaching the graveled verge he rounds on it, slams a forepaw down on the pavement with a rattle of great yellow claws, lifts and strikes again, then pauses, paw raised as if in admonition, and emits a low, querulous moan. (The thin grey scars he leaves in the pavement might have been understood by a good tracker, the kind that has been dead a hundred years now, but only from sun-up to noon, after which the heat of full day anneals the scar to black again.)

He turns slowly away from the warm body of this Meatmaker road as if to show that he is not intimidated, but a shaft of brilliant light makes the rock cut above the highway jump out of the darkness, full of brooding stone faces. The grizzly gallops in among the trees before the oncoming headlights illuminate his retreating form. The old trail has been abraded by machines and lost. Hidden in the forest and enclosed in the night, he follows the ancestral memory with a deliberate, pigeon-toed shuffle until he comes to a stream, where he slakes his thirst for the last time that night. Within earshot of the water, there is a thick stand of willows. There he bows down on his forearms and knees, where the fur is worn down to the hide underneath, shrugs his way through a low opening a coyote would have hesitated at, and finds a hidden open space, layered with a nest of branches worn smooth by restless bodies over the decades.

To the west the peaks show themselves with a rosy flush of alpenglow announcing the coming of the new sun. Where the Twolegs were not, he felt free to go abroad at any hour, but here their scent is strong in the air, and their scent prompts him to be crepuscular and secretive, except when the tendency is modulated by the overpowering urges of his stomach. Here he will lie up a while. He settles with his nose into the night breeze where he had last lain within the circling protection of his mother's great limbs, some seven or eight years earlier. He sleeps, snoring slightly like an old man wrapped in a fur robe and hidden in a hobo jungle, dreaming his way back to the Motherdark, to the safety of the winter den . . .

What he remembers first is darkness and in it the warm breath of the Motherdark, and the rich smell and pleasant taste of the Motherdark, the taste of warm fat that flavours the milky proteins that course through the blood, to expand into growing muscle and bone. The Motherdark covers him with a pelt of warm comfort.

Another is there, a small thing whimpering like himself, suckling with a loud chirring noise also to the Motherdark. Often they rolled together and slept in a ball, lulled to sleep listening to the beating of each other's hearts, and the slower muffled tympanum of the Motherdark. The Motherdark is vast and soft everywhere and seemed to be of no end or beginning, unlike that other smaller one. But in a dream or a sudden moment of lucidity, he hears the Motherdark itself suckling at something, a wet warm tongue licking, and when he sticks his head in to the wet centre of that great paw to share the wet pleasure, long spines that feel as hard and cold as the stuff under the nursing bed clench gently on the side of his small skull. He whimpers and burrows deeper into the Motherdark, away from the weapons, the weapons that imply a boundary, a finite edge to the bounty. He finds the teat again and suckles greedily.

When satiated, he nuzzles those weapons once more and feels the same things at his body ends and feels them scraping over a hard surface when he moves. This hard thing feels cold, unlike the Motherdark and he recoils from its touch. But there is food, and the end of food is sleep. There is no fear because there is no hunger, only appetite which is constantly satisfied. There is no day and night and so there is no time. Time begins at the end of pleasure with the light, claws of light raking at his eyes, and fear will come with it. It will come without warning, when the Motherdark is transformed into a silhouette, suddenly bounded and limited, rising as if to confront the flood of light. But now this mutation is moving upward, its edges silvered with brilliant shards of painful fire, moving away, leaving only cold shadows behind. Now there comes the feeling, for the first time, that he is separate from the Motherdark, that their oneness has been shed by this new medium that burns his eyes with the miracle of sight. He bawls out in terror, and hears his sibling whimpering in the back of the den. Heart pounding, he does not wait, but finds his feet and staggers, then scrambles up after the sound of weaponed feet scrabbling on stone, almost snared by protruding loops of tree root that seem alive. And when his eyes clear at last, this terrifying thing no longer a shadow towers up starkly, darkly in the stunning brilliance and terrific white cold, a shaggy quadruped taking sharp outline from the brilliant blue vault overhead. And what was felt at the edge of her body are now these long sharp talons tipping raised paws. The Motherdark has vanished, leaving this huge stranger: the Mother.

Things unlike the Mother grow up through the white cold under his feet and all around. Space, a gaping endless vista, tips away from the black hole in the snow edged with melted earth that had opened onto this sheer brilliance. The breath of something not seen riffles through his fur with a cold breath unlike the Motherdark breath. There is Up and Down, and there is vertigo, which is felt in the throat with a dizzying rush. He looks up in fear again and the Mother's eyes burn into his eyes, like nothing else in this no-darkness. There is nothing else with eyes in that towering world of stone above and snowy cliffs below. The Mother bends her huge head to him and suddenly he smells again the welcoming odour of the Motherdark and senses the presence of Her again. A maw of teeth opens; she fastens on the scruff of his neck and he is carried back, squalling a protest into the embracing shadows that soothe his hurt eyes, to the bed where the other not-Mother thing cowers timidly, now no longer invisible, now a shadow in the shadows.

There will never again be darkness so profoundly comforting as that first darkness before the birth of light. So, shivering at the first taste of a frightening outer world of light and cold, he cowers again under the cloud of the Mother. But light trickles in, writhes in serpentine patterns over the nursing bed and glints back from the rocky vault above, from facets of quartzite that line the mountain's insides. Light has revealed at last the Mother and the not-Mother. Time has begun, marked by fear: a great hunger soon will follow.

— SEVEN —

THE LANGSHAW EFFECT

"Never pass an infraction without taking action."
BANFF PARK SUPERINTENDENT PAUL LANGE, 1978

CHIEF PARK WARDEN Andy Anderson began the 1980 bear season
with the odds stacked against him. He planned to move as many bears
out of town as he could manage; meanwhile his wardens would be
knocking on restaurant kitchen doors in an effort to get the managers
to cooperate in cleaning up their bins and making them bear proof.
He was hampered by Parks Canada's institutional reluctance to lay
charges against local businesses, especially big businesses, especially
CP Hotels – call it the "chicken shit effect." By which I mean that if
wardens caught Joe Citizen throwing away an itty-bitty pop can, they
would pull him over, lecture him righteously about littering, relate a
horror story about a coyote that got its nose stuck in a pop can, and
issue him a summons to court. But if you were CP Hotels, and every
day setting out bins of garbage that bears could get at, thereby endan-
gering the public as well as the bears – you got a free pass. Laws, like
taxes, were for the little people, to paraphrase the late Leona Helmsley.
 Another handicap for Anderson was the fact that Parks Canada
campgrounds attracted even more bears than commercial operations
and people's homes, a situation that undermined the credibility of
his wardens; call it the "laughed-us-out-of-court effect." Finally,

Anderson and his superiors, Superintendent Paul Lange and Operations Manager Tom Ross, were further hoist by their own petard as the result of their decision the previous September to charge warden Eric Langshaw with insubordination after Langshaw used his police powers without their explicit approval.

Langshaw had done the unthinkable: he had laid charges against CP Hotels for improper storage of garbage and illegally setting out food for bears. The decision to charge the warden for insubordination, when he was only doing what he was hired to do, had a demoralizing effect on other wardens; call it the Langshaw effect.

In the spring of 1979, with the bear season following on the heels of melting snow, Park Superintendent Paul Lange had sent a letter to all businesses, including CP Hotel's Château Lake Louise, taking a tough stand on the garbage storage problem. "Bins must be bear-proofed," the letter said. "Grease containers must be placed in the bin to prevent spilling . . . garbage must not be left out at night to attract animals." And Lange put some teeth in the letter by promising to prosecute offenders and suspend their business licences.

"I thought, at last we're going to get some management backing and clear up this mess," says Langshaw. "I couldn't have been more wrong."

Warden Langshaw had been the bear control coordinator at Lake Louise for the two previous summers. He had seen some bizarre sights in the mix of tourists and grizzly bears at the Château, but the hot-buns-bear episode was most memorable. The hot-buns bear was an incorrigible food-habituated grizzly with a taste for fresh-baked buns and prime rib. This big fellow had been trapped and tranquilized three times. Each time the wardens had him flown out in a helicopter cargo net over 100 miles into the backcountry, where he was released. Each time he'd returned within a matter of days, crossing passes and glaciers, heading back to where the golden hot buns were blooming, on the banks of Lake Louise. He was a ticking time bomb, bound to blow up at some point and injure a tourist.

On July 1 the grizzly returned to the Château and soon had a gallery of spectators, who followed him as he stalked his prey: the garbage bin behind the Fairview Dining Room. The bear didn't like folks infringing on his space, and he ran at the people on either side of the bin to try and move them away. It was a chilling sight to anyone who knew the violence an aroused grizzly could unleash. "They were all around the bear, snapping pictures," recalled Langshaw. "They scared the hell out of me."

Langshaw grabbed his .308 rifle and quickly got between the bear and the crowd. He was about 80 feet away when the bear made a bluff charge. Facing a charging grizzly is like playing chicken with a runaway truck. The interesting thing about a bluff charge is that not even the grizzly knows for sure, in my experience, whether it is bluffing or not until the last minute. In this case, the bear hove to in a spray of gravel without making contact, almost giving Langshaw an underwear moment. The bear backed Langshaw up, ignoring the garbage bin. His quarry was a trolley of hot food behind Langshaw that had been left outside the dining room door temporarily by staff (not for the first time), because there was no room for it indoors. Langshaw did the wise thing – he stepped aside.

"After nosing aside the silver plate covers, and vacuuming up the grub," I later wrote in an article on the Langshaw debacle, "the beast chopped its fangs together appreciatively, half turned as if to leave, then stopped, sniffing the wind. Turning back, it snapped up a box of hot rolls in its massive jaws and carried it off into the woods for future reference."

The Château's manager, Michael Broadhurst, had already been told by his own security staff on June 7 (as later testimony revealed) that garbage and spilled grease were attracting bears to the hotel, a problem the security staff considered dangerous to the safety of guests and hotel staff. Despite more warnings and evidence gathering by Langshaw and his colleagues, the problems continued. By July 10, the wardens had responded to 14 bear problems at the Château. Sometimes four wardens were busy day and night trapping and tranquilizing bears there. By season's end, three aggressive grizzlies and three black bears had to be destroyed in the Lake Louise area – two of them close to the Château. Langshaw made repeated recommendations that charges be laid against CPR Hotels. All he got was a memo from his bosses saying that they wanted to "wait and see." It's true that if they waited long enough, winter would come and the bears would go into hibernation – until next year.

Langshaw didn't want to wait and see. He'd already witnessed what a grizzly bear could do to a human being, how it could tear through flesh and bone. It had been his lot to stand guard over Wilf Etherington's body, at the head of Totem Creek, while the helicopter pursued the grizzly that had killed him. He would not wait for more needless deaths. On July 1, the hot-buns bear tore the plywood doors off the Château's garbage bin once again. The next night he cornered two workers trying to repair the damage, and a CP policeman fired warning shots to drive him away. The bear, previously a good-natured old fellow, suffered from worn-out teeth, and he was becoming increasingly desperate to get food. "There was no place left for him," Langshaw explained. "I had to find him and shoot him."

Langshaw and an RCMP officer destroyed the old grizzly a few nights later.

On September 12, 1979, Eric Langshaw had had enough. He swore out three charges against CP Hotels, astonishing the chief park warden and the superintendent. CP Hotels was dragged into the provincial courthouse, where it was treated like a common litterbug, to the delight of the media from coast to coast. On November 1, Provincial Judge Albert Aunger fined Canadian Pacific Hotels a total of $600 for improper handling and storage of garbage. "Park wardens have a difficult job to do," the judge noted sternly, "and they should be supported in their efforts to do it." The maximum fine for each offence was $500, and the judge expressed surprise that no jail term could be imposed for default of payment. CP's lawyer asked for time to pay. Perhaps CP Hotels was strapped for ready cash: the company had recently budgeted $12 million to renovate their western hotels in the next two years.

"Two weeks to pay," said the judge, with a smile.

Langshaw's moment of triumph did not last long. On November 5 he was ordered to answer to a charge of insubordination. He was ushered into a meeting room at the Kremlin, as locals styled the Park administration building, with Superintendent Lange, Andy Anderson, and Tom Ross. At one point Lange slid a document across the table to Langshaw and said, "Sign it." The document called for Langshaw to acknowledge that he was guilty as charged.

Langshaw slid the paper back across the desk. "I can't sign that," he said.

"Why not?" demanded Lange.

"It's not an official bilingual document," said Langshaw. "It's not legal."

Langshaw says that Anderson turned red and choked on a laugh. "I thought he was going to explode," he recalls. Lange stared at Langshaw. "Very funny," he said.

"If there's nothing else, I'll be getting back to work," said the warden. There was no response, so he picked up his hat and left.

Anderson told me that he had assigned Jack Woledge, a senior warden at Lake Louise, to talk to the hotel manager, and Woledge had received a promise that the hotel would cooperate. "Langshaw decided he wasn't moving fast enough and we should be charging them," Anderson alleges. "So he went to Canmore and laid his charges. I gave him a couple of days off and chewed his ass out, pulled him out for a couple of days or something like that. But at any rate there was no going back and changing what he had done. It was just the way he went about it."

Langshaw now had a reprimand on his record, which would stay there for three years. Tangling with the federal bureaucracy, as I have learned, is like prodding a sleeping elephant: if it rolls over and starts to smother you, you can pull its trunk and rouse it. But the elephant doesn't like having its sleep disturbed, and an elephant never forgets. Langshaw was not only hurt and offended by his employer's treatment, he also developed bleeding ulcers from worrying about the effect of the episode on his career. He eventually hired a lawyer and launched an appeal to have the reprimand lifted. On December 4, William Turnbull, director of Parks Canada's western region, ordered the reprimand to be withdrawn and, on behalf of Parks Canada, apologized in writing to Langshaw. Turnbull regretted, he wrote, "the breakdown in communication."

In 1980, I had interviewed Superintendent Lange for my story on the Langshaw episode. Lange, as I remember him, was a product of the old school, in which wardens spoke when spoken to. He had a long and successful career with Parks Canada and was well known throughout the hierarchy, having worked as an administrator in a number of parks and in Ottawa, before coming to Banff.

"There are two ways of doing things," he'd explained to me in measured, professorial tones. "If you don't like the decisions that are handed down, you can appeal, right up to this office, and get the final word. Or you can act the way this warden did and accept the consequences. The end result might have been identical; we might very well have decided to lay charges anyway.

"As a matter of fact," he went on, "I plan on commending the warden for the good presentation he made in court."

As Lange talked on about the need for discipline in a paramilitary outfit like the warden service, my mind drifted back to a previous meeting with him, in the spring of 1978. I, too, was a warden then. We'd petitioned the superintendent with a list of complaints about the way in which the warden service was being managed. Angered by our statements, Lange retorted that we had much room to improve in our law enforcement function. He said we weren't issuing nearly enough parking tickets for the loading zone at a nearby picnic spot. "Never pass an infraction without taking action," he'd ordered us. "That could be a good motto for you people."

Not long before the first mauling in Whiskey Creek (which occurred just three months after my article was published), I asked my old mentor and partner John Wackerle for his views on the Langshaw effect. He summed it up succinctly as only he could do: "It just goes to show," he drawled, his English flavoured with an Austrian accent, "that if you vould only 'vait and see,' you vould never get in trouble vith the administration."

It was Langshaw's peers, who had witnessed firsthand what happened when one of their own tried to enforce the law, that Parks Canada was now counting on to enforce the same regulations in the back alleys of Banff in 1980, the year of the volcano. It is to their credit that they just gave their heads a shake, as if ridding themselves of a bad taste in their mouths, and got on with that thankless but necessary task.

EIGHT

COUNTING COUP
THE FIRST VICTIMS

To kill an enemy is praiseworthy, and the act of scalping him may be so under certain circumstances, but neither of these approaches in bravery the hitting or touching him with something held in the hand. This is counting *coup*.

GEORGE BIRD GRINNELL
Blackfoot Lodge Tales (1962)

STICKY MOUTH IS A shadow and he moves from shade to shade leaving no tracks, leaving not even a pile of dung to be discovered. No one sees the black grizzly enter the Whiskey Creek wetland; no warden knows the date of his arrival there that summer. In this part of the grizzly bear's range, the black colour phase is rare, accounting for perhaps only 1 percent of the cohort. Few wardens had ever seen a black grizzly in the park: some even denied they existed. Based on later events, it is clear that he was there long enough to explore every hideout and corner of the swamp before August 24, without being detected by humans. The black bear tribe sensed his arrival, however. It was like a stone falling into a pool and they were mere water striders, pushed away by the ripples.

Irritated by the noise and lights of the town that lay nearby, Sticky Mouth likely kept to the outer cover for a few days. His kind had evolved to live on the great plains, but it was the mountains and the mountain forest that harboured and protected him now, as they harboured and protected the black bears that could not survive without them. The tree cover and openings he finds are familiar aggregations that prompt him to seek out berries, but they are in poor supply and not worth the effort. There are no heavy boughs laden with crimson fruit to grasp in his claws and bend down to his lips and tongue.

This lack of fruit makes him uneasy; he has experienced this loss before and he recalls it as a relentless hunger followed by a long, restless sleep. So on the drier ground now he feeds on horsetail plants growing close to the protective boughs of the big white spruce trees, distracted at times by the noise of traffic on the Meatmaker, made by a torrent of vehicles beyond the friendly churl and rumble of the creek's modest waters. Along the creek in the shadowlands under the trees, he grazes like a huge black steer on sedges and hair grass, but he leaves no tracks on the beds of grass and moss. Most plants are past their peak; they fill his belly but do nothing to increase his stores of wintering fat.

Occasionally, a human voice intrudes on his solitude as he lies in one of several day beds hidden in the forest, but he lets them pass and listens as they wade in the creek; listens until they pass by again, making their loud noises and *ha ha* sounds and fading into the trees, moving back to their dens. The absence of their puzzling stinks (tobacco, cosmetics, and insect repellents) and their noise is a balm to his nerves, but the smell of their food is an exquisite torment. The sweet aroma of seared blood from fatty barbecued meats, the exotic pungency of grilled fish and chicken fanned and vented out from scores of local restaurant and residential kitchens, combined with the fermented deliquescence of sun-warmed garbage from dozens of bins, wafts out from the town and creates a smorgasbord of enticing odour, drifting through the thickets of Whiskey Creek.

The carrion odour of garbage is the most enticing of all. He pictures writhing legions of sweet, nut-flavoured maggots; recalls the zesty crunch of carrion beetles on his palate: all these treats to him both esculent and excellent are massed in tender, ripened flesh. His stomach rumbles in anticipation, but he hears the human blare and babble of the town and the Meatmaker rumbling back in some kind of constant greeting of allies, things allied against him, and it chastens and confuses him.

As he traverses the swamp, shaggy and dark as the boughs of the swamp spruce, exploring its limits, probing its depths, he finds where the black bears have dragged human food into the bush; there are too many such trails to miss. We might imagine him chasing a family of coyotes clear of such a prize. See them (as I have), circling around him in the timber, jesters around a king, watching, grinning as he claims the crumbs they have left him. Imagine him growling when he gets wind of the canine funk of these arch manipulators. There is no feud like an ancient family blood feud: bears and dogs share a common ancestor, and though coyotes pose no real threat – bear cubs have been seen at times playing with coyotes – their cousin the grey wolf is one of the few predators capable of separating a grizzly bear sow from her cubs, perhaps a luckless one that can't find room to hide under her belly when the pack closes in, circling and slashing with teeth that can eviscerate a little bear in one bite.

Sticky Mouth broods over this canine picnic. There is little left to eat; the remains are netted in a shiny black skin, shredded by teeth and claws, inedible. The little false wolves have pissed on it and their stench infuriates him. He swats at it with a front foot, then holds it down, biting and ripping it apart in frustration.

That summer the Whiskey Creek Swamp was lifting with black bears like ticks on a deer's back. If the grizzly could have jumped a black bear on its day bed, he would have prospered in fat. But no cached carcasses of black bears were later found, stewing away under a pile of dirt and branches, no remains were found strewn in a frenzy of feasting. The black bears eluded Sticky Mouth and eventually fled the swamp to escape him.

There was one black bear in particular that left his mark on the rubbing trees and his scat, reeking of fatty meat, on the trails between his day beds. This one had a scarred face and he moved with a rotund swagger. This was the black bear tattooed as B054, last seen by the warden service on July 9, when he was captured by the Banff bear management team and flown out to the Clearwater area some 50 miles north of town and released. Based on the records, and my experience with black bears, I doubt that B054 spent much time in the rugged Clearwater country, a land of winding rivers, lakes and high peaks. There was a homing beacon of neurons in his head and it was connected directly to his stomach. In a certain direction, indicated by the setting sun, there were tottering piles of fat scraps; in the Clearwater country there were few berries and there were too many grizzly bears, meaning for a black bear, more than zero.

B054 was big for a black bear in the east slope Rockies, where they seldom reach more than 300 pounds, and he had put on more weight since the warden service handled him in July.

When B054 came in to feed at the Caboose Restaurant garbage bins, the lesser black bears moved out of his way, and if they did not, he moved them, like a minor grizzly bear himself, huffing and swatting at the gravel if they dared not to give him his space and priority at the best morsels, or chopping his teeth together in a blatantly suggestive manner they clearly understood. He was the dominant bear in the Whiskey Creek Swamp, as far as he and the other beasts knew. The resident moose learned to avoid his routes; the coyotes were attuned to his speed and power. Among his own kind, he was soon used to having his way with the pick of human leavings to be found close to the forest edge.

There was another element in the swamp that summer. Several dogs frequented the bush, though the law said they must be penned or leashed in the park. There had always been locals who felt their beloved pets were born to run free, or at least free enough to avoid the nuisance of walking them on a leash, and that this need trumped the needs of the park wildlife to live without being harassed by uncontrolled dogs. In particular, there were two husky-like mutts that had the run of the area, clever and furtive and hard to catch up to. We know from past experience what grizzly bears think of dogs, and we know that dogs, like bears, can cover big stretches of terrain, and that they have a tendency to suss out any big game whose path they cross. So I wonder whether that or some other variation of canine harassment insulted Sticky Mouth's dignity, on top of his having to dodge people every day to find the food he needed to assuage his raging hunger – a hunger fuelled by the absence of native fruits or other rich victuals, such as a road-killed elk. Perhaps Sticky Mouth felt a great resentment that he was ready to visit upon the next hapless bird-watcher, or lapdog, or fisherman that blundered into the area.

When I interviewed former chief park warden Andy Anderson in Banff in 2003, he had a different theory altogether. He believed that the first trespasser on the big bear's turf that Sunday morning, August 24, was not a human being; it was the scarface blusterer, B054. He believed that B054 left the encounter nursing a grudge; he believed then, and still believes, that B054 was primed and ready to unleash his frustration on the first vulnerable creature to cross his path.

On August 19, a young man from eastern Canada, who was trying to climb Cascade Mountain wearing street shoes, attempted a steep rock pitch and fell 20 feet into a waterfall pool, suffering serious injury. His companion rushed down the mountain to notify the authorities. The warden service rescue team decided to extract the victim by helicopter sling. The flight path was right over the Whiskey Creek wetlands, and since the accident was only a few miles away, the flight rescuer was lifted up on his sling rope right from the warden office pad and flown under the machine into the scene. Once extracted, the victim would be flown to nearby Mineral Springs Hospital.

Sticky Mouth has already learned that the quiet of the forest could be shattered by an overwhelming sound dominating the sky overhead. The noise was made by a monstrous, long-tailed insect; a roaring, *whop-whop* noise instead of a buzz. That day Sticky Mouth hears the roaring fly working itself up into a rage again as it always does before springing into the sky. Sure enough, here it comes, just above the tree tops, rushing toward him. He slips under a spruce tree's thick lower branches and stares up as it approaches, turning to watch it pass overhead. He has seen hawks fly close overhead with small, four-legged meat clutched in their feet. Now he sees that the roaring fly has captured some meat; it has a Twolegs hanging under its belly. He watches carefully until the huge fly goes out of sight, before emerging from cover.

The intoxicating scent of restaurant scraps tickles Sticky Mouth's nose. It smells as though a great dead beast, half beef cow and half fish, is fermenting in a vat of spoiled fruit, rancid butter and deep-fry fat, perfuming the atmosphere with its captivating putrescence. He lies quietly, his nose made drunk with excess aroma, and he listens to the ominous clatter and metallic hum of the railroad and the constant engine roar of the town.

Still distrusting the tumult, though under cover of darkness, Sticky Mouth steals in to feed behind the Caboose, gorging himself on the meat mounds there. His nostrils flare at the rancid joys; his stomach sings hosannahs. In the early hours of August 23, the frigid mists give way to a killing frost, harbinger of the long cold season to come.

As dawn approaches the bear prowls restlessly, nosing the moose tracks in the long grasses, ears perked up for the sound of approaching game, ready for the ambush, but to no avail. He has already fed once that night, but the frost pricks him with the urgent need to gorge again. Now he will risk feeding at the Caboose in daylight. As if prodded from cover at spear point, he steps forward from the depths of the forest, fearing the light but determined. He comes out onto the railroad right-of-way, a long narrow clearing paved with river gravel and surmounted by alien structures. These objects are neither stone nor tree yet they give off the smell of trees mixed with toxic odours like those of the Meatmaker, along with the earthier fragrances of urine and human waste. (These are the buildings of the CPR station, sheds and small warehouses of local businesses, and the offices and fuel tanks of bulk fuel dealers.) The glistening steel rails, the smell of Twolegs and their poison make him hesitate. If not for these odours and the constant noise from the Twoleg dens nearby, he would make his bed right in the garbage enclosure itself. The smell of grease and meat and rotting fish draws him on again; he moans with hyperphagic anticipation, aching to gorge and gorge again on flesh. He is stalking slowly into the open, following his nose directly to where the seductive cowfish kill oozes its welcome with the stirring of the mountain breezes.

August 24, 1980, 7:30 a.m.
The garbage enclosure across from the CPR depot was equipped with chain-link fencing topped with a few strands of barbed wire. The black bears enjoyed scratching their bellies on the barbed wire when they climbed over the fence, which was about 12 feet high. I do not know if the grizzly bear broke the enclosure's gate open earlier that night or if B054 had done the B and E at some point. I suppose the question is academic: Warden David Cardinal, when inspecting the site, found the gate would open with a "gentle tug."[26] Warden Perry Jacobsen, who walked by those bins on the evening of August 24, reported that the gate was open, the bins were upset "and garbage was spread both inside and outside of the enclosure." At that point, however, the Caboose management may have been ordered to stay clear of the bins until the emergency was over.

Sticky Mouth is instantly on the fight that morning; the grub-pile is already occupied by the underling bears, long-eared, sharp-nosed nuisances that heretofore frustrated him with their arboreal elusiveness, their sky-high escapes. Here they are, stealing his food when they should be up in the trees, eating clouds. He lowers his head and flattens his ears as he stalks deliberately over the gravel, feet toed in and heart provoked to violence, his great humpback finned up, the muscles rippling beneath erect guard hairs. Drool drips from his open jaws. One of the larger females, more nervous than the rest, chances to turn away from the feasting for a moment and gets a glimpse of the black grizzly coming in: she lets out a wail of distress. Sticky Mouth swings his head from side to side and huffs a warning, shakes his head in anger.

Tin cans and bottles fly from under paws. Claws scrape on rusty metal; there is the jangling squeal of stretched barbed wire then the snapping of dry branches as the frantic sloth of bears takes to the trees. Up they go, mothers pushing their cubs ahead of them, followed by dry sows and some juvenile males kicked out by their dams that spring. They go up so high there is hardly an inch of treetop left; they bend the leaders into bows and fearfully back down, but not an inch farther than they have to.

Sticky Mouth does not deign to pursue these imposters. His nose is fixed on an easier prize; this great grub pile smelling of fish and meat. He pries the gate open with one paw and swings it wide. It swings back with a protesting metallic squeal and bangs into his rump as he goes by. He wheels and answers this insult with a swat from his front paw that sends the steel gate, to him as light as balsa wood, crashing against its hinges. But when he goes to the bins where the treasure is found, and stands up to peer, in turn, into their depths, he smells the musky reek of underlings over the reek of wet garbage, and it makes him roar out a protest. The bin has been plundered, the choicest tidbits scoffed down by these thieves. Angered, he takes out his frustration on the dumpster bins, grappling them and knocking them over with a bang and a crash so that they spill their contents on the ground. He deals one a few heavy swats to finish it off – with a force that would easily tear an underling's head from its moorings, or knock a deer's brain back into its rectum; he is a fur-coated terror, furious to find his cache already ransacked.

Meanwhile, back in the swamp, B054 had long since explored every foot of the Whiskey Creek wetland, and found it a pleasant place of good odour and comforting escape trails leading into the deep cover of sturdy climbing trees. The most alluring place was one he could not get access to, though he had explored its perimeter fence and probed its buried foundations; this was the garbage transfer station next to the government compound at the southeast end of the wetland. Here the daily deposits from the entire area were centralized in massive containers before being loaded on trucks for the trip to landfills near Calgary for disposal. This time the fences really were bear proof, and there were humans and motorized vehicles coming and going frequently there and in the adjacent Parks Canada compound, so bears soon dispersed to forage elsewhere. The Caboose garbage enclosure was one of several prime targets advertised on the west wind. After his first visit there that summer, B054 established his claim to the best tidbits among the eight black bears that had been counted feeding there.

On the morning of August 24, B054 came in to feed as usual, probably hungrier than ever; lately there was not as much grub on hand as there had been earlier that season. He stopped near the edge of the trees, hearing a commotion from the garbage enclosure. Previously, he would just give a loud *woof* at this point to announce his importance, which would have scared the smaller black bears away from the banquet, temporarily at least. Perhaps he stands up and peers through the fringe of trees, trying to improve his view, looking for the source of the brouhaha. A noise above catches his attention: one of his rival cohort is 40 feet off the ground, hugging a spruce tree trunk. If a black bear could grin, this one might grin now at B054. For the bully bear is on the cusp of enlightenment. It is a shame that park bears don't have a sense of irony; it might help them to appreciate their lot in life. But this treed bear does know what fear is: he turns and stares down at its epitome, which remains hidden from B054's view, then turns and stares back down at B054, opening his mouth, panting.

The big black bear peers toward the bins and emits an imperious *huff* of warning to any interloper lingering there. In response, there comes the sound of flying gravel, then a big, dark blur bursts through the fringe of trees. Bear 054 glimpses a nightmare doppelganger of himself, right down to the scarred face but twice as big: it rushes at him with ears back and jaws open. He hesitates a second, but no more. He swarms up a tree with a heartbeat to spare, shreds of bark rain down from his passage upward: a 350-pound dominant boar black bear, shitting himself with fear in those desperate seconds of sheer survival. His moment of glory in the swamp is finished in an instant; his small victories are overturned.

Experts assure us that adult grizzlies don't climb trees, but I have seen where they have wrestled their way up a tree 12 feet off the ground, when the branches were low enough to offer them a start. But the grizzly's long, somewhat straightened talons cannot grip the tree effectively as they could during cubhood; they are no match for the shorter, curved claws of his arboreal quarry. B054 rolls his eyes and chops his teeth together, a half-hearted admonishment, an embarrassed attempt to threaten that sounds more like a plea for mercy. This only makes the grizzly roar back at him then grapple the tree, which is too thick to uproot by far, yet he will make it sway and creak nonetheless. The black bear bawls like a frightened calf; his bowels empty themselves.

The green and black ordure filters through the branches, and some splatters down on Sticky Mouth's face as the underling wails in distress. Wiping it off on his furry arm, he smells the rich fat molecules and he moans in frustration as he drops to all fours, aching with the need to sink his teeth into that soft underbelly, those steaming intestines, those layers of wintering lard, the delicious liver and lights. Fat! He does not have a name for it, but he knows it when he smells it. He craves and aches and swoons for the taste of it.

The grizzly returns to the bin, to fret over and rummage through the contents once more. There are still some good remnants there after all. He is intent on protecting them, as if he were defending a carcass.

But now a railroad maintenance truck enters the siding and the big bear, who would not otherwise yield to anything on two legs or four, is intimidated by the sheer size and the clattering roar of this behemoth. He retreats into the woods as slowly as dignity allows. He resents the interruption right to the root of every erect hair on his back. (Apparently, his presence went unnoticed by the CP crew.)

After allowing some time to make sure his enemy had left the scene, the big black bear hooked his claws into the tree trunk, clambered down, and disappeared into the forest. At that moment, it would have been dangerous to encounter either bear, each dominant among their own kind; each forced to retreat from a valuable food source by the sudden arrival of a larger rival. A grizzly can kill a grown steer with one bite, it's true. But a big adult black bear is no slouch: it will jump on the bovine like a cowboy steer wrestler, grapple it by the nose with one forepaw while holding the withers with the other, and break the animal's neck.

In August 1980, Albertans were looking forward to the Labour Day holiday (September 1). Not only was it the last long weekend of summer, but it was Alberta's seventy-fifth anniversary, and special events were planned, at a cost to the provincial government of $1.3 million. There would be fireworks and parades and a CFL football game between arch-rivals: the Edmonton Eskimos versus the Calgary Stampeders. Calgary was giving away 10,000 of its trademark white cowboy hats. In Edmonton, Jim Comfort, a mountaineer, had pledged he would climb 75 mountains before the end of the year. In Banff, veteran warden Monte Rose, known for his quirky sense of humour, heard of Comfort's pledge and said he, too, would celebrate the event. He vowed he would capture 75 bears before they went into hibernation. Some wardens were not amused by Rose's promise. One remembers counting 11 bears in the holding pen one morning waiting for a flight out into the backcountry. He thought that was about eight bears too many, that Rose was out of control and needed to be reined in.

Rose remembers that occasion also. It was a hot day, and he misted the trap with cold water to keep the black bears from overheating. "I remember this one," he says. "He just lay on his back by the door, by the bars. I remember we had a package of wieners, I broke them up in little pieces. I poked them through the bars, and he would just gently take them with his claws, just as gentle as could be and eat. There was no paw swats, he was just like a friendly dog." But the bear was a three-time loser, and Area Manager Paul Kutzer ordered Rose to destroy it. He disobeyed, and flew the bear out into the bush instead, which resulted in an angry confrontation with his boss. "I was getting tired of killing," was how Rose explained it to me.

Despite their efforts, the park wardens had for long been compromised by their own employer in trying to clean up the bear problems in the mountain parks. They were unable to solve the real problem – garbage management – but were forced to respond to the crisis it caused every night. Alan Westhaver was a young warden getting an eyeful of the situation that summer on the bear control team. He had studied under bear expert Chuck Jonkel at the University of Missoula. Westhaver admired Monte Rose and felt the summer spent trapping bears with him was an invaluable experience. As for Rose, he would give it his best shot, but he was destined to miss the mark by 15 bears when the quarry went to earth that November.

In 1980, the chance of being injured by a bear in Banff National Park was about one in two million.[27] Calgary salesman and fisherman Ernest Cohoe, age 38, beat the odds; like the reverse of winning a lottery, he hit the bad luck jackpot during a fishing trip only 500 yards from the back door of his fishing partner's home in the town of Banff.

On August 24, the wardens on duty in Area 1 were busy with several issues. There were bear sightings at two local motels, and a warden was also dispatched to Fish Lakes on the Clearwater River to post a warning sign about grizzly bear activity there. Warden Ian Pengelly, who had just transferred to Banff and was waiting arrival of both wife and furniture, began his shift assisting Assistant Chief Park Warden Paul Kutzer arresting a dope peddler in the public washroom behind the museum, the RCMP being too busy to respond just then. Wardens were patrolling the campgrounds, checking for carelessly stored food and garbage, which continually brought bears into the area. The public safety team, led by Tim Auger, was dispatched to patrol the river below Bow Falls by jet boat, looking for a missing canoeist. Hauling the boat and trailer behind his rig, Auger scooped up Warden Pengelly to assist him in the search, thereby interrupting the pot bust. Roaring down the river that day, Pengelly was worried about Mr. Brown, his chocolate Labrador retriever, locked in the empty house and upset about the change in surroundings. In the town, people's thoughts were on the last holiday of summer, on beers and barbecues, not bears and bugaboos. For the merchants in Banff the holiday was crucial: it was a chance to make some big tourist bucks, before the slow "shoulder season" began. People would start pouring into the park as early as Thursday evening, if only the weatherman co-operated. One thing that threatened to mar the celebrations aside from rain clouds or, god forbid, an early snowstorm (which had been known to happen) was the ongoing brewery workers' strike; many taverns had to ration out their supply of beer. Albertans were forced to swallow their national pride and either purchase beer flavoured American imports or go without the staple drink of summertime.

Ernest Cohoe, a medical equipment sales rep, was the kind of man who enjoyed sharing a beer with a fishing buddy on a summer weekend. The Cohoes, Ernest, wife Geraldine and 14-year-old son Steven, were spending the weekend of August 23 in Banff, staying with their friends Bob and Julie Muskett and their eight-year-old son, Kelly. The two families had been friends and neighbours in Calgary for many years, and the connection continued after Bob Muskett accepted a position as manager of the Canadian Imperial Bank of Commerce and moved his family to the Marmot Marsh subdivision on the edge of Whiskey Creek. The two young fathers were avid skiers, fishermen and bird hunters; their families were included in the many camping trips they made along the east slope of the Rockies. Muskett and Cohoe had planned to take their sons fishing the next morning, but they were slow to get moving on the Sunday. The youngsters, eager to get going as usual, were dispatched to fish at a nearby pond just beside the railway tracks, with the two dads to follow after a leisurely breakfast.

Steven Cohoe had fished the area before and already knew it well. "There was a massive amount of fish in those little creeks back there," he told me during an interview. "We went fishing there after supper with no adults with us. It was like 'What's back there that could hurt you?'"

Sunday, August 24 was a cool day, which is not unusual for August in the mountains. The weatherman called for rain showers and a high of only 12° Celsius, so Cohoe donned his blue windbreaker to ward off the chill. The tall, solidly built Cohoe and his affable friend Muskett, the shorter of the two, left their wives chatting in the kitchen around noon, followed a footpath through the forest fringe to walk down the railway tracks and soon joined the boys, who were fishing by an old wooden bridge on the railroad "Y," a length of track used for switching cars that branched off from the main line. Steven Cohoe and Kelly Muskett had been joined by a neighbour's boy who was tagging along for the day. It was decided the boys would remain there while the two adults hiked north on the main stem of the Y, which dead-ended within easy distance of Forty Mile Creek. There they would see if the trout were in a mood to strike at a spinner, although the noon hour can be a slack time for fishing. The two men had much to discuss. Muskett was Cohoe's banker as well as his friend, and Cohoe's financial picture had been changing for the better.

In 2005, I interviewed Steven Cohoe to get some insights into his father. Steven is a leaner version of his father, but inherited his dad's height, five foot ten inches. He remembers Ernest as a strong man, with powerful wrists and forearms. He was handsome and proud of his good looks. According to Steven, Ernest was "the most fun guy you ever met," a guy who made friends wherever he went. Steven remembers that his family had little money when he was small, but that was rapidly changing for the better. Along with two partners, Cohoe had developed a line of testing equipment that hospitals were eager to purchase. So crucial was Cohoe to the enterprise that his partners had recently purchased a $300,000 insurance policy on their salesman.

Neither Cohoe nor Muskett was particularly concerned about bears that August afternoon as they left the Y and headed across a stretch of wetlands to the forest edge, picking their way over the tussocks of grass, "frost cushions" as they are known. Both had seen black bears on numerous occasions while camping and fishing in the Kananaskis forest reserve south of Banff. When bears ventured too close to their camp, they had simply run them off, yelling and banging pots together. In the town of Banff, dumpster-diving black bears were so numerous in the subdivision in that summer of 1980 that Muskett saw them coming and going like so many stray dogs. He used a sling-shot to drive them out of his yard, which is, incidentally, against the law in a national park. But now the two friends left the shop talk and the noise of town and all thoughts of nuisance bears behind them and shouldered their way through the willows overhanging a well-worn game trail. After a hundred yards or so they came to some crystalline trout pools on a branch of Forty Mile Creek. The water looked prom-ising. The two tied on small spinning lures, suitable for short casts in confined, brushed-over pools where the trout like to hide under over-hanging banks. Giving each other room to cast, they sent the bright spinners whirling into the dark green water.

Within the boundaries of Banff National Park, Forty Mile Creek takes its rising north of Mystic Lake and comes down brawling and clear from between the arms of the Vermilion and Sawback Ranges, north of the Banff townsite. The torrent, foaming white over boulders and pellucid in its backwaters, plunges into the town's water reservoir, which is contained by a dam bridging the canyon between Stony Squaw Mountain and Cascade Mountain. The overflowing waters pour down the canyon; the stream rounds the bluff east face of Stony Squaw then rolls under the Trans-Canada Highway bridge and rattles into a stretch of willows, marshy meadows and old-growth forests, the northern edge of the Whiskey Creek Area. Here, in the space of a mile and a half, the stream meanders in confusion, splitting into two channels, gnawing restlessly at its banks to form deep pools and eddies that are a trout fisherman's dream. Then it draws together again but still winds in U-shaped turns through moose meadows and willow groves, a stream floored with rounded stones, yellow, brown and green, rolled down from the heights and cobbled in to form the stream bed in a temporary arrangement waiting for the transforming hydraulic power of the next flood. It is a stream overhung with big spruce trees trailing yellow wolf lichen on the breezes; it is a treasure known mainly to the locals and not to the general public. It goes winding out at last under the Norquay Road, its rock-rumbling threats calmed in a placid horseshoe turn to the north around the Fenlands. Its far bank, fringed with forest, serves to divide the fens from the Vermilion Lakes. A small stream flows into it from the lakes and now its name changes to Echo Creek, a sandy-bottomed stream and a romantic stretch of canoe water. It flows out under the railroad and debouches into the Bow River on the west side of Banff, not far from the railroad station.

Cohoe and Muskett had not been fishing long when they were joined by Steven, who had found the pond unproductive that day. The other boys had agreed to stay behind and keep trying for trout.

Fishing a forested stream is an absorbing task. On that stretch of the creek there were fallen trees here and there bridging across the pools. Muskett and Steven clambered back and forth on these now and again while Cohoe, who had borrowed Muskett's waders, worked his way along the stream bed. For a fisherman, the play of sunlight on running water has its own mesmerizing charm. The sound of running water overtakes your brain; it is all you hear after a while. But in bear country, even where no bear tracks have been observed, you must remain vigilant. The noise of the stream and the tree cover can mask the approach of a predatory bear. Though such attacks are not frequent, bear expert Steve Herrero has documented a case where three young boys were killed by a black bear while fishing in Ontario. I have read of other cases, including two attacks in Alberta, one involving a black bear and one a grizzly. In both, the fisherman was jumped from behind and killed. There have been some close calls, and cases of anglers being robbed of their catch by an aggressive black or grizzly bear.

The party of three fished their way downstream for about 150 yards. On that cool, cloudy day the fly hatch was small and the trout were not inclined to rise. Then the silence was broken by Kelly Muskett's voice shouting from the bush upstream. He and his pal had followed the game trail down from the railroad Y. Muskett scrambled back up the bank, concerned. The terrain was too rugged for a small boy; the water was swift and the pools dangerously deep. Cohoe dispatched Steven back upstream to return the two youngsters to the wooden bridge on the railroad Y. "The last time I saw him alive," Steven told me, "he was standing watching me fish wearing his hip waders and with his own fishing rod in his hand." Steven Cohoe owned a big dog at that time, a wolf–husky cross that would fight anything that approached. "It started to follow us into the bush," he'd recalled, "but my dad made it go home." To this day, Steven wonders if the presence of the dog would have changed the course of events that day. It is possible of course, depending on the dog and how well it obeys its master. Things might have gone better, if the dog had distracted the bear while the humans escaped, but they might have gone even worse, if the dog had antagonized the bear and then fled back to its owners, bringing the vengeful bear down upon the youngsters.

Bob Muskett and Ernest Cohoe, having no luck on Forty Mile, decided they would shortcut southward through the bush, try the fishing on Whiskey Creek en route, then meet the boys at the bridge. The boys followed the train tracks south on the Y. As the two parties went along, parallel but about 200 yards apart, they called back and forth from time to time the way people do in a thick forest, reassuring each other with their presence that all was well, filling the wilderness with the echoes of their passage.

On a day bed in the heart of the willows, the black grizzly, Sticky Mouth, sleeps, hungry and alone and not caring that he is alone. All morning he has tracked the big underling through the wetland with his nose to the ground, his blood still up from being pushed off the richest cache of flesh he has found by a noisy rolling thing that was too big to bluff or to rub out; he was forced to hunt other grub when he should have been spread-eagled on the cowfish kill, gorging and sleeping.

There is a scar on his muzzle and it aches when he comes too close to the haunts of man. It is aching now. (Alberta bear expert Dennis Weisser believes the scar was made by a bullet. Steve Herrero thought it was made by the bars of a culvert trap.)

The underling had followed the creek bank, then wormed his way through a willow thicket and crossed into the open. Sticky Mouth might have pursued him except for the long, broken-backed serpent that came rolling and roaring through from the east, and then returned again from the opposite direction, making the boggy ground quake as if it might open and swallow him up. This huge entity, segmented in a rainbow of colours, squeals and chatters its teeth together with the sounds of rocks colliding on a slide, then cries out a high, wolfish note that echoes from peak to peak across the valley. Its appearance is random, always surprising. So he turns back, but the smell of the fat underling bear is everywhere, coming and going, and the smell of other wandering bears is mixed with his among the long grasses, though the sulphur stink of bog mud that oozes out to fill the tracks shows them disappearing into the bush.

So here in the willows he sets his ambush, lying up in a half-sleep, his eyes and broad, rust-coloured nose twitching at the deer flies and mosquitoes that have followed him into cover. When night falls, safe under the cloak of darkness he will be drawn inevitably back to the grub pile reeking of beef and fish. In the meantime, he waits behind a log in the thicket, where only his ears poke up in the shadows, hoping for a chance at other meat, where underlings and the occasional cow moose with calf at heel cross back and forth over the bog.

Blood and darkness fill his dream; a pelt of Motherdark covers his head and, dreaming, he drinks from a pool of fat and warm moose blood and hears a soft drum pulsing like his own heart. But then the shrill Twolegs voices wake him suddenly from the dream and he gasps like a drowning man. He hears them snapping branches, far too close – little ones. Then nearer still, the deeper, dangerous voices of the big ones rouse him to instant alert. Sticky Mouth's small eyes narrow and focus on the direction of the threat; his strength coils and ripples within him, quivering, compressed, and ready for instant triggering.

The black bear B054 had several beds in that stretch of willows on either side of the meadow. He had crossed the bog undeterred by the chance of being seen by the naked bears, these beasts without fur that went on two legs and left prints in the river mud so much like his own. He had come to know them so that the smell of them made him think always of their meat-hoards and sweet-hoards, but he preferred to avoid them, whenever possible. The naked bears had entrapped him, so he remembered their iron cave that smelled of rich fish. It had swallowed him up once, so he avoided it. They had trapped him again but he could not see the how of that. That time was by night, in the middle of their dens near one of their hoards. He remembered feeding, straddling the hoard and ripping into the sweet pleasures there, then came a blinding sun in the middle of night. There was pain, a big splinter in his rump. He turned, tried to escape, but his legs soon buckled, and they were all over him, the naked bears, hurting: the smell of them was like a cloud covering him. He could not move; could not drive them off. He saw that picture now, he felt the fear again. That picture led to a worse one: a big flying insect that shone like a sun and filled the sky with its voice. He had often heard its stuttering roar. Its den was close by, and whenever it came near he crawled under the trees and hid. He remembered it carrying him off; remembered feeling weightless over a void, followed by the silences of a strange country where he wandered in confusion.

He'd turned south finally, following the stars and the sun back to the valley as before. There were several memories, a confusion of images. But the fear and hatred of the other bear, the big claws that had treed him that morning, dominated his thoughts. He had winded it; what he had seen in front of him at the meat-fish hoard was now behind him. There was a dread in his brain, dread and simmering fury. He moaned in rage. His swamp had been taken over by a usurper. Yet hunger must draw him back to the hoard eventually.

That night, fear of meeting the grizzly would prod B054 to go eastward, to forage among the houses in the Marmot Marsh or Whiskey Creek subdivisions. He had crossed the bog then circled back toward his line of travel. He had a bed where the grass and bush had been scraped away down to the earth. It looked outward to whatever

COUNTING COUP: THE FIRST VICTIMS   93

might come from the forest at the edge of the open ground. But then the breeze calmed, the air lost its warnings. He forgot about his enemy for a few moments, and fell into a troubled sleep. In his sleep his body trembled; his nerves remembered something was coming, something dangerous. The shouts of children roused him suddenly; then he heard the sounds of men approaching, coming closer.

Too close. He was on his feet, his hair was up, his ears were perked up and he was ready to fight, if he had to or flee, if he could.

When I interviewed Bob Muskett in 2005, I asked him if a weapon would have been of any avail to him or Cohoe that day in 1980. "I can assure you," he responded, "that there's absolutely no way that a pistol or any kind of a gun would have been any use to us at all. It happened that fast. Didn't even have time to bring it up."

"We have pepper spray nowadays," I said.

Muskett nodded. "I carry it; it would not have worked."

"You would not have been able to get it out in time?"

"No," he said emphatically.

There were no official trails in the Whiskey Creek Swamp in 1980, only game trails (paths worn in the ground by elk, moose, and bears). Ernest Cohoe and Bob Muskett, walking south back to town, pushed their way through the bush single-file, and emerged into a small clearing where knee-high shrubs of willow covered the ground, and larger willows formed the backdrop. They spread out, walking shoulder to shoulder, as Muskett described it, to pick their way through the area, with Cohoe to Muskett's right. The long grass swished on their legs; dead branches were tangled beneath it, thick tripwires. Walking was awkward for Cohoe, wearing the borrowed hip waders. It was around 2:15 p.m. when Muskett, an experienced deer hunter, as was Cohoe, heard a loud noise behind him and to his left that sounded like an elk getting up from its bed. The source of the sound was about 30 yards to the east and between the two adults, close to where Muskett figured the boys were walking. In the bush, when one surprises a bedded elk or a moose at close range, the noise it makes in its panic to escape, charging off through the dead branches that protrude over the game trails, is startling. But it took only a second or two for the men to realize that this animal was not running away, it was coming straight at them. Muskett had time to see a big, dark blur approaching at full speed, bending the thick willow stems to either side like an approaching wave, crashing forward. The animal made no other sound as it came in.

Cohoe, still looking over his shoulder, shouted: "Bear!"

In the official statement for the authorities that he wrote on September 11, 1980, Muskett stated: "We both took off running in a similar direction towards Whiskey Creek. I did not proceed far, and might have taken two or three steps looking back, tripped and fell. When I turned around and looked up, a large bear was standing on his two hind legs looking down at me. From that laying-down position, the bear looked very large and did not at all look like the usual black bear that is often seen in the townsite of Banff. The bear was very dark brown in colour and had no distinguishing marks on him. It looked much larger than the normal bear, but from laying down anything would likely look large. The time seemed like an eternity, but it was likely only a matter of seconds that the bear looked at me. As I froze in panic staring back, I heard noises to my left and [assumed] that Cohoe was running through the bush. The bear turned its head then turned its shoulders and I got up and ran." Muskett had the impression that the bear continued to watch him as he made his escape. "I kept running as much as I could, collapsed in exhaustion, continued to run until I came to a creek which I jumped into, discovering it was waist-high, and waded through. I proceeded, I believe, along the creek until I came out at the wooden bridge. Sometime before I jumped into the creek or soon after, I heard three loud screams from Cohoe, then silence for a short period, then three loud cries from the bear. At the time I could, in my mind see the bear over the top of Cohoe, having finished his kill."[28]

Muskett doesn't recall beating his way eastward through the bush to arrive finally at the bridge, shouting warnings to the boys as he moved forward. He remembers telling himself that if he could make it to the creek, he would be all right. This idea was, of course, completely without basis. A mere creek would do nothing to deter an angry bear. The bear could have easily caught up to him at any point had it chosen to do so. The creek seemed to be an impossibly long distance away. What drove him on was fear for the boys "and what might be transpiring in the bush," because "the bear would have been in my opinion directly in the middle of where I was and where the kids, I thought, would be."

In fact, the boys were still in the bush, having dawdled along on their way back north. Strangely enough, they had heard nothing of the warning shouts, the attack, or the noises made by the bear. Being young boys, they might have been making too much noise themselves to have heard anything else. Bob Muskett made it back to the wooden bridge at the railroad Y, and stared back down the tracks. He was chilled to realize the boys were not in sight; they were still in dangerous proximity to the bear, which might well be lying in wait again, just to the west of them. He ran down the track, shouting for them. Steven Cohoe heard his shouts and called back.

"Get out of there!" yelled Muskett. "There's a bear in the bush!" The boys came out of the willow bush on the run.

Steven Cohoe recalled that moment: "I remember just coming out of the bush, and there was Bob Muskett standing on the railroad tracks with his back toward us. He had his hunting knife in one hand. He turned around and saw us there, and his hand went to his chest. He was stressed out and trying to catch his breath. I'll never forget the look on his face; he was in great distress."

"Steven asked where his Dad was," Muskett recalled. "I told him he had been hurt by the bear and to run as fast as he could home and phone the police and the wardens and meet me behind Whiskey Creek." The boys dropped their fishing gear and ran.

At our meeting, Muskett told me that the bear turned, "and looked at Ernie, looked back at me, turned and jumped on Ernie. Ernie had a bright blue jacket on, and I was dressed in earth tones, for no particular reason; that's just what I had on that day, so he saw the colour, and jumped on him. Ernie screamed and I ran. When I went back in there [later] with the wardens, I was absolutely amazed at how close Ernie was to me. We were walking shoulder to shoulder. But my fly rod was laying there, my hat was there. And where he attacked Ernie was just really close."

Muskett said Cohoe had tried to scramble up and get on his feet. That's when the bear went after him.

This was one of those classic situations where, in the absence of a weapon (bear spray was not an option in 1980), the experts recommend that you lie still, on your stomach, feet spread to try and keep the bear from flipping you over and with your hands over the back of your neck, because you'll never outrun the bear. Muskett had a hunting knife, but there was barely time to draw it, and it would take a strong and determined person indeed to ward off a large bear with a hunting knife, although such feats have happened.[*] So all you can do is play dead and possibly endure some serious wounds before the bear is satisfied that you offer no threat and leaves. In fact, many people have survived such assaults using this method over the years since, some escaping with only minor injuries. (Such was Muskett's case, although his lying down was inadvertent.) Others have been killed or terribly damaged for life.[**]

"Never stare directly at a bear," was one item of advice commonly heard 30 years ago. Steve Herrero has a provocative passage in his book *Bear Attacks* where he advises you not to do this unless

---

[*] For example, Chris McLellan, 32, was attacked by a mother grizzly he surprised at close range on August 15, 2007, near Grovedale, Alberta. McLellan had a large knife (12-inch blade). As the bear grabbed his left arm, McLellan stabbed the bear between the neck and shoulder, mortally injuring it. Fortunately, he survived the attack with a broken arm and severe bites; the sow's three six-month-old cubs were orphaned by the event. (Derek Logan, EdmontonSun.com, Friday, August 24, 2007)

[**] The advice has also been complicated by what we know about predatory behaviour in some black bears these days; in this case, we must stand and fight with whatever we have on hand. But Steve Herrero's *Bear Attacks* had not yet been published, and these above recommendations were not nearly as well known to the public in 1980.

you deliberately mean to try and intimidate the bear. Staring is a dominance behaviour that is a threat to an animal that is dominant over all other beasts. Bears that confront each other for mating rights or feeding position will ritualistically turn their heads to one side to avoid provoking an attack. If conflict ensues, they will sometimes rear up and grapple each other jaw to jaw to see who is king for the day. And so that is perhaps why bears may elect to attack the human face in bear–human conflicts, if the victim is unable to keep it hidden.

I wonder if it goes beyond that, though; we readily recognize intelligence in the eyes of other people, and in many animals also. Perhaps there is some intensity in our eyes that is threatening to a bear. It seems likely that Ernest Cohoe looked into the eyes of his attacker that afternoon: Muskett told me that, for his part, all he saw was teeth, that and the hair standing erect on the bear's neck. But the bear pinned Cohoe to the ground, and he could not move. Then the dread jaws closed on his face; its teeth tore through flesh and mandible bones in one horrific bite.

After sending the boys home to call the police, Muskett hurried across the railroad tracks and climbed up on the berm that separated them from the nearest homes. He stood trembling, with his friend's screams still echoing in his head. From there he could watch the swamp until the police and ambulance arrived. Help was literally minutes away. The warden dispatcher would receive the first call at 2:37 p.m., via the Banff RCMP detachment, and immediately dispatch the ambulance and park wardens to the scene. Meanwhile, Muskett stared wildly out over the forest and beaver ponds in disbelief, that moment of waiting feeling like a lifetime.

This was a place he had wandered peacefully with fishing rod in hand, a place where he had allowed his small son to fish unsupervised; such had been his faith in the benevolent calm of the beaver ponds and spruce groves. That would never happen again. What lay before him now was a place whose shadows were not the cool refuge of summer but the heart of uncompromising ambush. The forest had betrayed him, his family and friends; it had assaulted them and cast them out.

Turning from scanning the neighbourhood for any help he might find, he looked back at the swamp and froze, amazed. His friend was "wandering out" toward him along the railroad Y. "I first saw that he was walking and both arms were moving, and I could not believe my eyes. I would guess him to be 400–500 yards away." Muskett shouted a greeting and waved his arms. Cohoe managed to shout a response: "Get help, as quick as you can."

Fearful that the ambulance might not have received the call from Steven, Muskett ran down the street looking for assistance. There he saw local residents Helen Kennedy and her fiancé, Paul Vawdrey, busy cleaning a car. The couple were to be married the next weekend and their thoughts were of the happy days ahead, when suddenly they were confronted by a wild-eyed Bob Muskett, soaking wet and splattered with mud. Kennedy, who, as it happened, was a part-time dispatcher at the Banff park warden office, remembers that Muskett was in a state of panic, hyperventilating and having a tough time getting any words out that made sense. She finally heard the words "my buddy" and "bear" and concluded that somebody had been attacked. Kennedy rushed in to phone the warden dispatcher, then she grabbed some blankets and towels to do instant first aid if needed and hurried back out. Meanwhile, Vawdrey followed Muskett out to the tracks. When he saw Cohoe approaching, he ran out to assist him. Muskett gaped at his friend as he drew near. He saw that there was "something wrong with Cohoe's head." He realized that his friend had not been fortunate after all. Most of his face was gone. Muskett recalls that the sight brought him to extreme panic: he ordered Cohoe, who had reached the street leaning on Vawdrey for support, to sit down on the curb. Cohoe was bleeding heavily and Kennedy, shocked at the extent of the wound, tried to staunch the blood loss and comfort the injured man. Cohoe was still wearing the waders; the right was badly torn and the left had several punctures above the heel, but there were no wounds there or on the rest of his body.

Muskett remembers that he rushed out to direct the ambulance in. The paramedics arrived as Vawdrey and Kennedy were tending to Cohoe.

The first warden to arrive was Larry Gilmar, an officer who had seen his share of mangled human flesh in car crashes on the Banff–Jasper Highway. He had just gone home for a late lunch break when he'd received the radio call. But when he got out of his truck to check on Cohoe's condition, he was momentarily immobilized by what he beheld. Cohoe, who had been sitting on the curb, collapsed, falling backwards, and the bloody towel fell off, exposing the wound. Helen Kennedy was traumatized by what she saw that day, and her description sums up the injury: "He was hurt about as bad as you can get hurt and still be alive. He was trying to talk to us, but he was aspirating blood and unable to get the words out. I just kept trying to reassure him that help was on the way."

Cohoe's eyes, which were uninjured, stared up dazed at the sky with the look of a man who knows himself to be hurt but who has not yet realized how bad the damage is. From the concave shape of the wound, seen from the side, it looked as if the bear had delivered one massive bite. Cohoe, alone in the bush with the bear still near at hand, must have been full of dread, wondering if the bear would attack him again or attack the boys next. He must have felt it was up to him to get out and get help. That he managed to walk out through the thick bush in his condition is a tribute to his enormous courage.

The paramedics took charge. Working quickly, they bundled Cohoe onto a stretcher in a recovery position so he could breathe, and lifted him into the ambulance. Eight minutes after the initial callout, he was in the Mineral Springs Hospital.

Muskett was left behind, reeling, trying to answer questions from the police and park wardens. He thought of his wife, and of Geraldine Cohoe and their children, of their questions he would soon have to answer.

There is something particularly distressing in the destruction of a human face: it is after all the first aspect of ourselves by which the world knows us, and by which we know ourselves. We look at it every-day in the mirror, sometimes pleased, other times discouraged by a blemish or the clear signs of aging. There we are, for better or for worse but recognizable always to ourselves and others. Cohoe's injury was so shocking to those involved that the dispatcher's log describes the damage as a "partial decapitation," based on the information she received from the field. Yet the plastic surgeon who would later work on Cohoe pointed out that he had seen the same kind of damage inflicted on people by dog bites. Indeed in 2005, a French citizen lost her entire face when she was attacked by her pet dog while she was unconscious, one of thousands of people who are seriously injured by domestic dogs every year. In her case, a deceased donor and advances in surgical technology resulted in an amazing surgical feat – a facial transplant, something not available in 1980 to Ernest Cohoe.

Cohoe's injury was assessed quickly. It was decided to transfer him immediately, by helicopter, for specialized care in Calgary. Pilot Geoff Palmer of Okanagan Helicopters would fly the injured man to Foothills Hospital. Twenty minutes after the ambulance was first dis-patched, Ernest Cohoe was airborne on a 30-minute flight to the city, headed for six hours in the operating room. His condition there would be listed as critical.

NINE

THE HUNT BEGINS

In following one of these trails one will find, every little while, where the bear has made a circuit to the side and rear, so as to get to windward of his own back trail, and so assure himself that no danger follows on his track.

WILLIAM H. WRIGHT
The Grizzly Bear (1909)

THE FIRST OFFICIAL RESPONSES to the mauling of Ernest Cohoe were prompt and efficient. "When the mauling took place," recalls Chief Park Warden Andy Anderson, "I was in my vehicle and was on the scene within minutes. I realized that if we did not get the bear quickly we would be in a situation where we could have to destroy several bears; or if the bear fled the area we would be in for a long hunt." Anderson ordered a general callout of all park wardens. Most mustered at the office within minutes. It was as if the service had been waiting on tenterhooks for just such an ursine disaster, which is not far from the truth. (Speaking personally, I had been waiting for the other shoe to drop ever since Wilf Etherington's death – he was the first person to be killed by a bear in Banff National Park – though it was a tossup where disaster would strike first, between hungry garbage-habituated bears at Lake Louise or their famished cohort nearer to Banff.)

Anderson ordered an emergency meeting at the warden head-quarters on the east side of the Whiskey Creek Area. His assistant chiefs, Peter V. Whyte and Paul Kutzer, would coordinate the hunt for the bear. Whyte was head of resource management and public safety, which included backcountry patrols, while Kutzer headed the "front-country" or high visitor use management function, that being Area 1 of the park, where law enforcement was a major mandate. Senior wardens, or "lead hands" as they were sometimes called, such as Monte Rose, Keith Everts, Perry Jacobsen, Bill Vroom, John Wackerle, and others would supervise in the field. They were all well-rounded generalists, skilled at all aspects of the job. Responsibility for overall operations rested with Anderson, reporting to Superintendent Paul Lange. On Anderson's recommendation, Lange would order a closure of the entire area including the Fenlands and the Vermilion Lakes. (Anderson sent teams of armed wardens in to make sure any park visitors found there would be escorted safely out.) Decisions to close park areas were not popular back then, but these days they are more widely supported by the public. A slogan heard in 1980 was "Parks are for people," and any closure of park areas tended to draw criticism, first from local business or recreation groups, then from Ottawa.

Anderson's priority was to mount a cordon of officers around the entire Whiskey Creek Area (an area that, ironically, included the warden office itself) in the hope that the attacker was still in the forest. There would be time to set culvert traps for the bear after that was accomplished. Answering Anderson's call for assistance, Sergeant F. Gardiner, commander of the Banff RCMP detachment, sent all available officers to augment the warden staff. By 3:45 p.m., there was a cordon of patrol trucks and squad cars on three sides of the area, emergency lights flashing, while armed sentries stood at intervals by the roadside, or stood guard along the CPR right-of-way. The area looked like a mega-crime scene investigation. The sentries were to keep each other in direct sight at all times, but a hundred yards or more separated them in places: it was a thin line of defence against an elusive predator. It would prove to be porous in the days ahead.

During the first hour of the operation, the sentries knew little about the details of the attack, other than that a "large dark-coloured bear" was the perpetrator. It was a description that could apply to either species of bear. Considering that some of the police had no real experience dealing with wildlife, any bruin that ventured out into the open risked being shot. Nowadays, more effort might be directed at capturing the bear alive, using leg snares if possible, to collect DNA evidence based on tissue and hair samples to tie it to the mauling before deciding whether or not it should be destroyed. In 1980, knowledge of DNA testing in regard to animal attacks was not well advanced, and the Banff wardens had little to no experience using leg snares. Human blood or hair found on the bear's claws might tie it to the attack, but the most certain method was to kill the suspect animal, then do a necropsy to check for human tissue or pieces of clothing in the digestive tract. This "terminate with extreme prejudice" approach is preferred in some North American jurisdictions to the present day.

The swamp was eerily quiet, diminished by the surrounding tumult of road and rail traffic but implacable and offering no clues as to the whereabouts of the attacker. Staring into its forests, the wardens wondered which of them would be selected to enter there and take their chances with the Whiskey Creek mauler. Wardens were trained to conserve and protect bears; some of them had tracked and killed bears in the past, but mostly those were bears seriously injured by collisions on the highway or railroad. Few Banff wardens had experience hunting down an adult bear that had previously attacked a human, and attacked without provocation, according to the survivor, Bob Muskett.

Chief Warden Anderson had experience with bear–human conflict involving both black and grizzly bears as a park warden in Banff and a former chief park warden in nearby Yoho National Park, but it was the first time he had dealt with such a large-scale operation to locate a marauding bear. Anderson had risen from the ranks to become a top-down-style administrator. He assumed leadership during a time of radical transition, known as centralization, where wardens were moved into park towns to assume a more technical and science-based role as "resource officers," who would conduct studies on park inventory and habitat. However, if a bear bit Little Johnny or if a forest fire threatened a local motel, the people expected a warden to show up carrying not a field guide and a sampling kit, but a gun or a fire hose.

In my opinion, Anderson seemed frustrated at times in his attempts to push an operations-oriented outfit into a role that worked only in theory, not in practice, Anderson perhaps compensated on occasion by slipping into obsessive periods of micromanagement, such as reorganizing the placement of desks in the main warden office, to give one example. The chief warden tended to rely for advice on a small clique of trusted colleagues (friends, in other words), which is, of course, not uncommon in bureaucracies, whether public or privately owned. Bill Vroom was Anderson's trusted confidant among his subordinates. Vroom was the park's in-house authority on grizzly bears: he would be detailed to make the first probe into Whiskey Creek, looking for the mauling site.

The late Bill Vroom was well regarded by many, including Steve Herrero. The tall and rangy biologist with an ever-present smile is a skilled bush man himself, but he paid Vroom the ultimate compliment during my interview with him in 2006: "I worked with him a lot," he said and added, with disarming candour: "I got to admit, I loved him." Herrero and his associates had worked with Vroom on a grizzly bear den study. "Yeah," he continued, pensively, "I always regarded him as very quiet and competent in the out-of-doors. We always learned something from him. His knowledge of horses was second to none. For a while, we had horses involved in our operation and he was a great advisor and steerer for us."

Bill Vroom was a quietly courageous man, at his best when the chips were down. On a couple of occasions, while guarding contractors working for Parks Canada, Bill faced down a charging female grizzly with cubs at heel. Knowing that grizzlies sometimes initiate bluff charges that end without contact, he had allowed the bears to come very close and held his fire. They had veered away at the last moment so both men and bears had escaped without a shot being fired, a measure of his coolness under pressure.

No one questioned his skills, but Bill could be maddeningly slow when relatively mundane decisions were needed quickly. Bill was a top hand, nevertheless. As for the rest of the wardens, despite previous criticisms that had not been resolved, and notwithstanding some misgivings in the days ahead, they closed ranks under Anderson's leadership and attended strictly to business.

At the outset, Anderson suspected the attacker was a grizzly bear. He had Bob Muskett brought in for an interview after the mauling. "Bob Muskett was able to give a good description of the bear," he reported, "although he stated he only had a good look after he fell and the bear stood up and then turned and chased after Cohoe. He described the bear as a large brown-coloured black bear. He stated by the head it could be a grizzly. However, when questioned he could not remember seeing claws when the bear stood up. He felt that he would have noted the claws. He did note the broad head, and was quite sure the bear was a dark brown, dirty brown, in colour with no light patches on the chest or front and no 'grizzly colouring' on the back." (In other words, the bear had no grizzled or silver-tipped guard hairs characteristic of the species.) "In size he stated he could not be sure as he was seeing the bear from his position lying on the ground. He could only say that it looked large."

Muskett in his written description of the bear said, "The bear was very dark brown in colour and had no distinguishing marks on him." Later, however, the bear would be described by others, including Anderson, as having a white chest patch. The presence, or absence, of a well-defined white chest patch was important; this feature often occurs in the American black bear species but does not occur in the grizzly bear.[29] However, grizzly bears, which can vary in colour from a creamy white to jet black with ranges of brown in between, can have lighter-colour markings, such as a light brown stripe, for example, across the chest and over the shoulders, which confuses the issue. The Stoney Indians believe that this light brown stripe signifies the most powerful grizzly bear, the one they call *Wahtonga*.[30] In the grizzly bear, the front claws, which can be three to four inches long if not too badly worn, are often streaked yellowish-white in an older bear and are very evident. They are even more prominent when the bear is a dark colour, is standing on its hind feet some seven to eight feet above the ground and facing you at very close range, with its paws hanging below its chest.

Muskett's description did little to allay Anderson's suspicion that the attacker was a grizzly bear, but the lack of prominent claws raised a red flag nonetheless.

Shortly after Muskett's interview, it was decided that a two-man team led by Bill Vroom would probe the general area where the mauling took place and try to find the actual site. A Mountie (whose name has not been recorded) was sent in with him to investigate the site and recover flesh that was missing from the victim, Ernest Cohoe, as required by law. Wardens Perry Jacobsen, Lance Cooper and Earle Skjonsberg, all experienced hands, would back them up in the vicinity of the railroad Y. Other wardens spread out along the Norquay Road or watched the Calgary Power electrical line right-of-way to the west of the road. It offered them a narrow clearing in the forest and a safe shot at the bear, should it cross at that point. Apparently, Muskett was too badly shaken to guide them at that juncture.

Vroom would definitely shoot the bear if it obliged by showing itself, but failing that he hoped to collect more evidence to try and identify the species and also to understand why the bear had attacked; was it guarding an animal carcass, for example? If so, the bear might well be shot right off the carcass, since grizzlies often bury the meat and make a bed on top of it to protect it from competitors. There was some uneasy speculation about what such a carcass might be, however, the happiest thought being that it might be merely a dead elk; the darkest worry that it might be a dead "hippy," as transient campers were labelled in that era.

The voices of approaching humans had roused the bear from its bed and, already vexed from its losses that day, it would not tolerate the threat they posed. When it seemed like they were about to discover its hiding place, it had attacked. One intruder had dropped to all fours and crawled off. The other one had opened his mouth and shown his teeth; the bear had seen this one as a threat. His eyes had glinted like the shine on a metal weapon, like the gleam of light inside the iron cave where his kind cached their kills of ripe fish. His eyes jumped and burned into the bear's eyes, so it had set upon him to make him stop. It had met the challenge jaw to jaw, as it had done with rival bears many times before, but this creature's bone and flesh parted with surprising ease.

After the noises stopped, it had dropped the strange-tasting flesh from its mouth and watched the foe writhe for a few seconds. Confused, it held the challenger down with a front foot and worried at his leg with its teeth, biting through the strange greenish skin there: the taste was bad. It had pawed and snuffled at the fallen one, which now lay still, moaning, no longer a threat. The bear, gurgling a warning, did not press the attack on Cohoe further, but turned its lowered head and stalked back into cover. Once hidden safely again, it stopped and stood listening for more threats. It heard the voices of the younger ones; more distant, not threatening.

In Whiskey Creek the smell of human blood fogs the air and stirs a restless disquietude along Sticky Mouth's nerves. Then he hears the bush crackle not far to the north, and pictures the long-eared underling on the move. He rears up on his hinders, whiffles air into his nares, trying to scent it, to see it. An enticing tang of musky underling stink rewards his inquiring nose.

Human screams of distress had barely stopped echoing in the woods when the male black bear, B054, hears something big breaking through the willows, heading his way. The smell of blood is printed on the wind; it is in his nose like strange fruit in the back of his mouth, he could taste it, like no other taste in the forest. He bursts into a frantic gallop and in seconds reaches the safety of the nearest stout tree and swarms up the trunk as fast as he can climb. The grizzly comes into sight, at the lope. He stops, his small eyes burning fiercely and stares up at B054. Gurgling with frustration, he wraps his arms around the evergreen as he had done on the first encounter, and shakes it like an apple thief trying to dislodge a bushel of Granny Smiths. Shards of old bark fly from beneath his long, thick talons. Bear 054 squeals in protest at the narrow escape and clings to the trunk like death, crying out twice more. He peers down at the big claws and rolls his eyes in consternation, panting with distress.

Sticky Mouth leaves off and stalks slowly back into cover to wait and watch for the prize to come down. But B054 is too wise to fall for that trick. After a while he climbs down the spruce to reach some limbs big enough to make his wait more comfortable, but still far beyond the reach of his enemy. He drapes himself over them, paws dangling, listening and waiting, still panting lightly from the fright. The woods are quiet now, and soon the black bear's eyes begin to droop, but a high-pitched whining noise shatters the afternoon and thrills him to alertness. He's heard this sound before, but now it comes from all around the wetland; there are many creatures wailing or honking in a myriad of voices and notes, monstrous geese and coyote cries. In the foreground below, he hears his enemy moving restlessly in the bush. After a long interval, the wailing stops. Then he hears naked bears approaching once more. They are downwind, he cannot get their smell. A branch snaps and the bush trembles. The big-claws bear is on the move again, but moving away.

Sticky Mouth, sensing a new threat, stalks forward, forgetting about the underling for now. Catlike, he drops to his stomach and wriggles between the thick willow trunks for a few more feet, then stops. He gathers his limbs, ready to attack or to retreat depending on the threat. Hidden behind a screen of boughs and leaves, he watches the Twolegs moving slowly past him in single file, hunting. The first, smaller one holds his attention: it carries the oiled metal smell of extreme danger. This one stops suddenly; its eyes dance back and forth, then it moves on again. As the second one comes by, the grizzly smells the same weapon. He eases back down; he slides under the lid of a shadow, lets them pass.

He rises, stalks silently after them through the bush. Coming to a muddy patch, he steers around it and leaves no track discernible in the tall grass underfoot. He lets the green boughs and dry twigs slip over his fur like water. The wind favours him; he stays well back, tracking the Twolegs by their scent, avoiding their actual path.

Now he catches wind again of the great cowfish kill; he knows that the Twolegs are upwind and between him and that feast and now he is aimed at them like a projectile. The western breeze is like the page of a book that his nose reads. Though veiled by the odour of ripe flesh, by the perfumed tang of spruce trees, and the sulphur muck of the bog, the oil and graphite smell of the weapons nevertheless comes faintly to his nose. This scent triggers a memory of pain, it makes him hesitate, trembling with emotion.

They turn now and move back toward their dens, passing him by. Sticky Mouth blends into the shadows, only his glimmering eyes show among the willow stems.

The moment of losing all restraint passes. He follows them back; he watches between the tree trunks as they come out of the forest and stop. There is a pack of Twolegs there. They stand around jawing at each other, making that yak-yak noise; he shrinks back deep into the woods.

Meanwhile the black bear waits, ears pricked up and listening, trying the air for a scent of danger. Finally, hunger overcomes fear. He grips the trunk, sinks his curved black claws into the bark and begins to ease his way downward like a fur-coated telephone lineman.

Back at headquarters that Sunday afternoon, Anderson and Whyte monitored the radio conversation between the hunter teams. The hunters were surprised and sobered by the thickness of the brush they had encountered, and the long marsh grass which masked all tracks. Rain showers that wet the grass showed dark in spots where animals had moved through, but everything faded into the impenetrable tangle of the bush eventually. Anderson believed that the bear was still contained within his cordon; that it would feel safe in such thick cover. But could he hold it there? His own trained manpower was limited to 22 wardens at that point, including the hunting teams as well as men new to the area and untried seasonal wardens. He knew that he could not count on deploying the half-dozen RCMP officers indefinitely; responding to human-caused mayhem was their first priority. All he could do in the meantime was to keep up the pressure to locate the bear. The hunters had not seen any other people in the bush – that was a bonus. Finding the mauling site would have to wait until the morning. Anderson decided to call Vroom out and send him up in the helicopter with another shooter to try and spot the bear, while other hunting teams pushed into the wetlands on foot.

Pilot Geoff Palmer was notified while returning from his flight to Calgary, where he had delivered Ernest Cohoe to Foothills Hospital, in the company of a physician. The surgeons were evaluating the damage to his face. He remained in critical condition. Once on the ground at the helipad behind the warden HQ, Palmer removed the rear doors from his Jet Ranger, so Vroom and his partner could shoot from either side of the machine unimpeded. The Outfit had used this method to take out the grizzly bear that had killed Wilf Etherington. Warden Monte Rose had been the shooter during that crisis. At the very least, the low-flying machine might flush the bear out to the guns of the waiting sentries.

At 4:30 p.m. the helicopter lifted off and the aerial search began. In 1980, pilot Geoff Palmer (I interviewed him in 2007), was 30 years old and had been flying helicopters for some seven years. He is a compact five-foot-seven, with a trim and efficient build suited for the cockpit, and his fine-boned features often arrange themselves into an engaging smile. In the Jet Ranger that afternoon, Palmer was focused on flying a methodical grid search, 50 feet above the highest treetops, while his passengers in the back seat leaned as far out the doors as their seat belts allowed to get a better view, rifles at the ready. He was angling across the northeast quadrant of the wetlands when he caught sight of some movement at the edge of the trees. There was a dark-coloured animal below, digging at the ground. He kicked in some pedal and eased the collective over to turn the machine as he descended, trying to give Bill Vroom a look at the animal from the right rear door. Palmer realized that the animal was indeed a bear. "The bear looked up," he recalled, "kinda like we're just a mosquito up there. It turned as if to go back to what it was doing. Then it suddenly changed its mind and ran off into the woods."

After the first Twoleg hunters leave the swamp, Sticky Mouth roams in a desultory fashion through the bush, having temporarily forgotten about hunting down the fat imposter bear but aware only that he is very hungry. He is uneasy, wandering in the broad daylight this close to the dens of the Twolegs, but, roused from his day bed by them, he is temporarily out of sync with his habits. What holds his attention still is the odour of ripe fish and beef drifting in the wind.

His belly is doing any thinking he is capable of just then, and it pushes him toward the cowfish kill. He can smell it in the distance, and he drools at the rich stink. He pauses in a small clearing, detained by an ancient red ant nest that humps above the frost tussocks. Ever the ready opportunist, he tears into it with one paw and begins licking up hundreds of tasty ants and fat white larvae with great relish. The tart and ticklish pleasures of that feast are suddenly interrupted by a roaring noise to the east. He turns and sits back on his rump, his face swarming with ants, which he licks with absent-minded insouciance off his chin with a long, pink tongue. He cocks his stubby, rounded ears, listening. (Now he is a Winnie the Pooh–like bear, not the thing of nightmares that those who have felt the power of a grizzly bear will remember for the rest of their lives.)

The sound is familiar: what does that familiarity trigger in that great whisky barrel of a head? Perhaps an image of a cyclopean dragonfly, the very one that now roars into sight. This flying thing often frightened the sky above the swamp. He had learned to avoid its huge glass eye and watch it carefully from deep cover. The speed of its approach this time catches him in the open. He rises from his haunches and turns, showing as much dignity as he can under the circumstances, about to stalk back into the bush, away from the bellicose insect. This time the flying thing comes closer then it ever has before, making his hackles rise in protest. Its hot breath blasts down at him, rattling the willow branches together and riffling through his fur. Thrilled to fury at something with the nerve to reach out and actually touch him, he turns his great head, his ears flattened against his skull, to glare at it, and he smells its oily breath that is neither meat nor insect, but more like the smell of the sticky Meatmaker in hot sunlight, the smell of those shiny beasts on black feet that roar and whistle as they roll down that hot trail.

This thing tore through the sky, insisting on dominance, yet if at that moment it had come close enough, he would have seized one of its long shiny feet and tried to wrestle it to earth.

Sticky Mouth is emboldened by having cover to retreat into. Let the dragonfly follow him, he will ambush it. In the clearing there is nothing to hear, see or smell but the machine. His acute senses are overwhelmed by this dervish of noise and engine exhaust. He turns now, slips away under the spruce tree canopy to evade it, then breaks into a gallop, the hind feet springing forward well outside of the front paws. He hears the deafening chatter and chop of the great bug's teeth as it whirls and follows; he stops under the boughs of a friendly spruce tree to ambush it and fight it if he must. After a while the thing moves away, looking for other prey.

While the helicopter was on the east end of the area, a two-man hunting team cautiously advanced in the general direction of the machine, which could be seen in the distance, and the other wardens moved in behind them for back up. The idea was to drop the bear if the helicopter sent it in their direction, otherwise they hoped the shooters to the west would take it out. The whole exercise was a bush-beating operation aimed at encircling the bear and pushing it into a safe clearing where a shot could be obtained. The overriding concern was that if the bear was allowed to escape on this occasion, it would inevitably return to this populated area to obtain food, and more human casualties would be the likely outcome. In the meantime, Warden Monte Rose and Seasonal Warden Alan Westhaver had been ordered in to meet with Assistant Chief Warden Peter Whyte. Later, they would prepare live traps for setting after dark.

At an interview in Jasper, Alberta, Whyte recounted the subsequent events. "We started looking through the bear control records to try and find any matches. The worst fear was that we had a habituated bear that we had handled and whatnot, and that had been responsible, hence the liability of the Crown. Of course, our first response was the public safety aspect. Second was to get in and find out what had happened. Our access to Cohoe was pretty limited. The doctors, of course, didn't want us getting anywhere near. We abided by that, we didn't press it. We were getting info trickling out from his surgeon and the nurses who would be talking with him, even though he couldn't talk and was putting [writing] stuff down. We got a number of notes back from him.[*] The major witness we used was Muskett. And he was very calm, cool, and collected about the things he'd seen. But later, it wasn't a case of him changing his testimony but he became less sure as time went on. The bear had charged him and he had fallen down; the bear reared up over top of him and then had gone out chasing Cohoe. Bob [Muskett] had got a really good look at the animal and had, again, described it as a large back bear. Of course, we kept saying, 'Are you sure it wasn't a grizzly?' and he was quite definite that he didn't think it was."

The records search was inconclusive: there was not enough information to separate out one "very dark brown" black bear from several hundred similar bears handled in recent years.

Warden Perry Jacobsen began the first of many all-night vigils as part of the team of hunters pushing their way through the bush along the

---

[*] I was unable to find any such notes in the official records.

railroad Y. The men were distracted by the helicopter's noisy patterns overhead. When I interviewed Jacobsen at his home in Cochrane, Alberta, he recalled, "We started to hunt him on foot. We didn't know what we were after, and I'm telling you that was dangerous. You've walked through there, you know what it was like. The willows, you couldn't see from here to that TV. I remember I went through on the first sweep and I thought, My god, if this bear does charge, our chances of even stopping him are almost nil."

Perry Jacobsen remembered one comment from the air-to-ground radio conversation during the late afternoon hunt, which he monitored on his handheld radio set. Someone, in all that radio traffic, asked Bill Vroom "What is it?" and Vroom replied, "All I can tell is — just a bear." In 1990, Bill Vroom described this moment: "We made this flight looking for the bear, and we saw a bear briefly from the helicopter, and what I recall from that brief observation was that I saw the back end of a dark-coloured bear go under the limbs of a spruce tree. It went out of sight under the tree."[31]

So at this point in the hunt, the information Anderson had from his expert, Vroom, was that the species was still unknown. Although the colour might indicate a black bear, Anderson could not rule out the possibility that the attacker was a grizzly.

Lance Cooper, who has long since left the service, was hunting with Warden Earle Skjonsberg. Cooper was sure the attacker was a grizzly bear right from the start. I interviewed him at Alpine Helicopters in 2006, where he is base operations manager and one of three pilots certified to fly helicopter sling rescue operations. I worked with Cooper in the olden days, when he used to sling underneath the type of helicopter he now prefers to ride inside. A shrewd move on his part. He is a fit, economically built man with a grey beard, an understated man of few words, and no stranger to danger, so when he says of that hunt "I was not comfortable," that indicates to me a situation where many people would not only be uncomfortable, but paralyzed with fear.

"I used to hunt bears, both black and grizzly with my dad before I joined the warden service," he told me. Cooper felt that if you were going to send a team to hunt a grizzly bear, it should be a team that had at least hunted bears together before. He and Skjonsberg had worked together before, but not as bear hunters. In Whiskey Creek, he recalled, "The willows were so thick we had to part them by hand to move forward. We were on hands and knees at times. I remember thinking, 'This is not good.'" He laughed at the memory. "I asked myself what my father would do," said Cooper wryly, and he chuckled. "I already knew the answer – he wouldn't be in that bush to begin with." I asked Cooper what he thought of the whole operation. He considered the question carefully before answering: "I thought it was a bit – disjointed," he said.

Wardens Perry Jacobsen and Rick Kunelius were probing the bush west of the railroad spur while the helicopter flew its grid search ahead of them to the north. As he listened to Vroom's voice on the radio that day, Jacobsen stopped and stood still, staring hard into the shadows ahead of him and to either side, deafened by the tumult overhead. I asked him what went through his mind at that moment. "We were scared shitless," he said vehemently, "due to the prop noise." Scared, because they could not hear the bear coming over that racket. The range for visual contact with the bear was only about 15 feet, so their ability to hear the bear charging toward them was critical. If it came out of the bush, they would have a split second to shoot before the bear struck into them.

He had to wonder if he could stop the bear at all with the .308-calibre government carbine, which he felt was too light for a head-on attack. Maybe he could shove it down the bear's throat as it bowled him over, and pull the trigger. A short-barrelled 12-gauge Defender-style shotgun loaded with heavy slugs would have been preferable at close range, but there were only two such weapons on inventory at that point (which were already in use), not nearly enough to cover a situation like this. It occurred to him that if the helicopter had rousted the bear, it could be headed straight toward his team at that moment, could be a few heartbeats away. The other hunters, working nearby, shared the same thought. As they stared intently into the bush, they braced themselves to receive the bear's charge. But that long moment passed. The bear had bolted into the woods. It was headed away from Jacobsen's and Cooper's positions and moving west. Palmer turned the helicopter to follow it. He caught a glimpse or two of the bear before it blinked out of sight in the thick cover.

Sticky Mouth shrinks away from the light, darkening into the shade of the spruce. The cowfish kill will have to wait. The sky is fading now; night is his only ally in this noisy place. The eclipse of day in that season floods him with undifferentiated emotion; he will plunge into that soft pelt of Motherdark and be safe and welcome. He crawls into the heart of a thicket and sprawls out in the shadows, dark as the entrance of a pit where life and light are swallowed in sudden equanimity. He hears other Twolegs moving westward through the bush, and perks his ears to track their movements. Now he is a shadow; later on, he will move through the woods like a vapour float-ing between the stars.

The hunting teams, monitoring the air-to-ground radio traffic, spread out and moved west, hoping to get a shot at the animal if it turned back toward them. Right then, they had not found so much as one clear track that would have warned them of the presence of a grizzly bear. All tracks were indistinct in the wetlands, blurred by the coming and going of people and their pets, or chopped up by the sharp cloven hooves of the deer family. As they worked their way through the creepers and shintangle of willows to where the heli-copter was flying its grid, they tried to keep each other in sight, or in earshot when that was not possible. At the same time, they had to watch their step to avoid tripping and to manage their weapons to avoid accidents. Doing these things, while at the same time trying to move quietly and in concert with each other, and watching for a sudden glimpse of an attacking bear, had them wired to the max. But the helicopter was a constant distraction, due to the terrific engine and rotor noise in the foreground. When they lost sight of each other occasionally, the hunters were isolated and jumpy, unable to hear each other moving, unable to hear a bear should it come charging out of the shadows. In retrospect, the addition of the helicopter may have been more of a hazard than an aid.

This was not at all like sport hunting; this was strictly armed combat where there might be only enough time to shoot by instinct, not over the sights. This requires a long acquaintance with the chosen firearm; some form of combat arms training should be a job requirement. To my knowledge, there was nobody in the warden service, or any other conservation agency in Canada, that was trained by the employer to shoot under those conditions in 1980. In my day, a few of us did take the time to practise instinctive shooting with the two Defender shotguns available to us out on the rifle range, out of concern for our own safety. (Nowadays, wardens must pass professional shooting courses before being issued weapons.)

The team advanced slowly until their superiors, apprised of their difficulty by radio, ordered them to stay put for the time being. They waited, rifles and shotguns at the ready.

Black bear 054 stops several times as he makes his way westward through the forest, to watch his back trail for signs of oncoming danger. He comes at last to a rubbing tree where he has left his sign before. This time he vents some of his frustrations on it, rearing up on his hind feet to smell at the tree where other bears left their mark. Then he bites into the trunk as high as he can reach, savaging the bark with his teeth. It's a warning to other bears that he is not to be trifled with, to be pushed up a tree like a squirrel. He turns and leans his back against it, rubbing up and down against the rough bark and stubbed-off branches, grunting with pleasure, giving himself a good scratch while coating the tree with his musky stink. He is thus engaged when the roar of the oncoming helicopter rushes into his ears. Startled, he drops to all fours, scuttles under the spruce boughs, and turns to peer up.

The sound brings back the memory of being carried off, trapped and helpless. His old sky-enemy is hunting him again: popping its

jaws in hungry anticipation. He must stay out of sight. This time
the thing lingers overhead, dancing a bit from cloud to cloud. He
turns to retreat through the bush, keeping ahead of it, not picturing the great flesh-hoard anymore, intent now only on escape. He
remembers the big-claws bear moving in the shadows; he glances up
again and sees this bug-eyed thing hunting from the sky. Terrorized,
he flees westward through the forest.

On the Norquay Road to the west of Jacobsen's position, wardens
Keith Everts and Will Devlin were putting up "Area Closed" signs and
also keeping a look out for the bear. They monitored their handheld
radio sets, which were equipped with either chest or belt holsters at
the time. They knew the bear was headed their way and that they
must try and stop it from crossing the road and escaping into the
Fenlands. As yet, there had not been time to even sweep the area and
make sure all people had left.

The Fenlands and Vermilion Lakes are replete with wildlife, and
have for long been popular with the public. It is a place where you
might see a moose with calf wading through the shallows, where
ospreys plunge after surfacing trout while flotillas of waterfowl grace
the still waters of the lakes. With the Labour Day weekend only five
days ahead, people were planning to visit the area, hoping to find the
leaves changing colour for the fall, a glorious time for photographers
and artists. Now they would be denied those pleasures until the bear
was either captured or destroyed. Should it reach the Fenlands, the
bear had many escape routes. It might cross the Bow River and flee up
Brewster Creek toward Mount Assiniboine, in British Columbia, or
work its way upstream, cross the Trans-Canada after dark and escape
the valley to the north. Should it escape, they knew that the memory
of the food it had obtained in Whiskey Creek would inevitably bring
it back to the area, likely before the November den-up time.

Keith Everts, a burly, dark-haired man with a memory for detail
and a quick intellect, was a well-trained warden and an old hand at
backcountry work. He was a natural leader who would be a steadying

influence throughout the hunt. He had studied engineering technology before joining the Outfit, and spent some winters on avalanche control in Glacier National Park, British Columbia, before transferring to Banff. Although a competent marksman, his real expertise resided in a larger and more dangerous weapon. He had helped design the park's automated avalanche control program. The system employed radio telemetry to detonate explosives previously placed on slide paths that threatened the access road to Sunshine Ski Resort each winter. Now, out of the corner of his eye, he caught a glimpse of movement and turned, raising his Browning .308 carbine, thumbing the hammer of the lever-action piece to full cock. A large, dark brown-coloured American black bear, darker on the front quarters, was halfway across the road, moving quickly and intent on gaining the cover of the forest. Everts realized this might be the chance to end the entire hunt with one bullet – but he held his fire.

The report states that Everts (who has since passed away) did not have a safe shot at the bear. (Will Devlin did not wish to discuss the events of that summer.) Perhaps there was oncoming traffic on the Norquay Road. A misplaced copper-jacketed slug might skip off the pavement and ricochet through a motorist's windshield. Any such mental transactions would have happened in a few heartbeats – leaving Everts, no doubt, cussing under his breath at the missed opportunity – then the bear crashed into the woods and disappeared into the bush of the Fenlands on the west side of the Norquay Road close to Forty Mile Creek. Everts called in the sighting to the warden dispatcher. Despite the efforts of hunters, sentries, and aerospace technology, the predator had eluded the predators.

In the emergency operations centre at the office, Peter Whyte kept one ear on the ongoing radio traffic as he followed events with Andy Anderson. The two men listened intently as Everts described the bear. His description seemed to tally well with Bob Muskett's information and Vroom's partial sighting. This appeared to be the same bear, spooked by the helicopter and headed west. Now Everts, a very experienced hand, had identified it as a black bear. Was this then the attacker?

Andy Anderson told me he did not believe the black bear was the attacker at that moment in the operation. But the black bear was the only bear they had spotted in the area. The only way to eliminate it as a suspect was to kill or capture it for examination. Still, the nature of the attack seemed more like that of a grizzly than a black bear.

Puzzled by the discrepancy, Anderson phoned Steve Herrero to see if he could drive out to Banff for a consultation, but he was unavailable. He had just returned from a board of enquiry in Montana on the Ammerman and Eberlee deaths and was on his way to Alaska to testify in court on a bear mauling matter there.

With the helicopter working westward, Jacobsen and his crew continued their sweep, looking for tracks, making sure there was no other bear answering that description in the swamp. Meanwhile Whyte and Anderson pondered the map of the Bow Valley; the area that now must be contained, which included the Vermilion Lakes, had instantly doubled or even tripled in size, and also in complexity, due to the various water bodies and bogs involved. The helicopter seemed like the best tool to cover a lot of terrain quickly. They would gamble on getting it out in front of the bear, hoping for one clear shot at the quarry. Given the bear's propensity for constantly seeking cover, the chances were not good.

On the road, a half-dozen wardens, having overheard Everts' description on the radio, converged in a green-jacketed huddle on the scene to plan their next move. Warden Dale Loewen, a senior hand called in from Lake Louise for the hunt, did not believe the attacker was a black bear, and said so. He told young Tim Laboucane, his partner that day, that the attack was too ferocious and direct for a black bear. Laboucane, who had some experience with bears in other parks before transferring to Banff, concurred. Loewen predicted they would find grizzly bear tracks leaving the area. While they conferred, the helicopter appeared overhead and began a grid search over the Fenlands as Palmer and his crew attempted to locate the bear.

The hunters split into several parties, some to cover both sides of the Fenlands loop trail, others to track the bear as it moved west. The trackers found plenty of tracks in the Fenlands where the deer and the hiker roam, along with moose, coyotes and domestic dogs, but no definite sign of the bear.

Forty Mile Creek, as described previously, makes a classic horse-shoe bend north near the foot of Mount Norquay and then south around the forested Fenlands before joining with Echo Creek. This lower reach of the stream was once very popular as a short canoe route from the Bow River into Whiskey Creek wetlands. Having paddled that stretch back in the day, I wonder how many couples fell in love during an evening of paddling on this ribbon of flat water while listening to the flute-like trill of the hermit thrush.

In the few minutes it took for the wardens to regroup and organize the new search, B054, noted only by the eye of the red squirrel, moved quickly westward through the old-growth forest of the Fenlands. He hid as the helicopter angled past, then plunged into Echo Creek and splashed across to reach the tall grass on the opposite side. Soon he made his way into the forest between the first Vermilion Lake and the CPR line. Later, when well out of sight, he would furtively cross the tracks to the south and fade into the bush between the Bow River and the railroad. The hunters spent a tense hour and a half traversing the Fenlands, following the trails or cutting through the forest, checking every mud flat for bear sign, stopping every few minutes to listen intently for the attacker. Meanwhile the helicopter made a futile search over the lakes which are girded by willow-covered peninsulas of marsh and bog. Finally, at about 7:30 p.m., one of the sweat-stained crew cut the bear's trail where it had forded the creek. The track was that of an adult black bear, not a grizzly. What Loewen had to say about that discovery was not recorded.

Soon they were moving west along the railroad line, tracking the bear south and west toward the Bow River. Knowing they were now tracking a black bear, not a grizzly, would have eased the tension a little. It might be a man-killer, but it was still only a black bear and they had enough guns to take it out the moment it showed itself.

The black bear was well concealed and moving quickly through the forest, heading west, stopping frequently, no doubt, to check his back trail, which is the habit of an intelligent predator. The hunters followed him across beaver dams, slipping and sliding in the special kind of mud found there – known to westerners as "goose shit" – and swatting occasional mosquitoes and flesh-eating bulldog flies. Known to hikers as horseflies, and cursed by equestrians as hiker flies, this specimen is equipped to carve a minuscule steak out of your hide, which it carries off to a handy perch to consume at its leisure.

The bear had crossed the tracks and kept on angling toward the river but he stayed clear of its edge, not trusting such a clear expanse that might reveal him to his pursuers. Meanwhile Lance Cooper and Rick Kunelius had been assigned to hunt westward along the riverbank. In the forest, the bear moved between the two teams of hunters. He may have heard, or caught scent of them from time to time, but it is more likely that he simply outpaced them. He was completely at home in the forest, a maestro of the shintangle who shambled through willow hells with Olympian detachment, where men could only curse and crawl. It is quite likely that he knew the terrain more intimately than his hunters, and even if he had last moved through it years earlier, he would have remembered it better than the humans, such was the map of the mountains imprinted in his neurons. The wardens followed slowly, losing ground, circling to find his track as the light was fading, then losing the trail completely as darkness fell.

Assistant Chief Whyte called them in for the night. Those along the railroad right of way straggled back down the tracks in soggy boots, thirsty and defeated. Cooper and Kunelius returned along the river. In the gloaming, they came to a stretch of muddy riverbank north of the Banff boat rental landings. There in the mud they found the tracks of a large grizzly bear. Under the circumstances, the sight made their scalps prickle and they stared hard into the forest in front of their noses. Cooper was confident in his rifle, a .270 loaded with 180-grain bullets. He had killed Lord Grizzly with it before, but he was leery of taking on a grizzly bear after dark.

Finding grizzly tracks on the riverbank might have been a heads-up to Anderson and his team, but instead this sighting was treated as just one of many leads under consideration. The warden office was getting phone calls and tips everyday from anxious residents. Some callers were convinced there were no grizzly bears in the area, others claimed to have seen tracks and actual bears of various colours and types on several different occasions. Wardens were sent out to check each lead that came in. "It all went in to the mill," Peter Whyte recalled. The fact was that no grizzly track had yet been found directly associated with the mauling site, and no dark-coloured grizzly bear had been seen in the area by wardens or reported by the public. Like the tracks that Monte Rose discovered, the Bow River tracks were seen as one more thread in the weave of events, a thread that so far led nowhere in particular. Everts had seen a black bear, and they had found a black bear track crossing at Echo Creek. Cooper did not believe the attacker was a black bear, but neither could he prove that this particular grizzly was suspect. It might be one of a dozen bears making a circuit around the town to feed at outlying garbage bins, such as those at the Rimrock Hotel on Sulphur Mountain whose lights glimmered down from the forested heights overlooking the town.

Cooper and Kunelius worked their way back slowly along the darkening shore to the edge of town, then hurried back to headquarters to file bear occurrence reports on their findings. Meanwhile the summer help poured into the local pubs for a cold beer after a day in the tourist trade. Cohoe's tragedy was the talk of the town, with many wild embellishments concerning the injuries he had suffered. As the American import beer flowed, the locals regaled the "Gorbies," as tourists and newcomers were called, with ripping yarns about their own escapes from the jaws of death while braving the wilderness on their days off, or traded old saws like the one about the young trapper who asks his partner "What do we do if we meet a bear?"

"Start running," says the oldtimer.

"But we can't outrun a bear," says the greenhorn.

"Don't have to outrun the bear," comes the reply. "Just have to outrun you."

The late Jon Whyte, celebrated Banff poet and author, disparaged the instant mountain men found among Banff's transient seasonal workers, many of whom hailed from eastern Canada. He once defined a true Gorbie for me as "someone from Toronto who has been here for two months, describing someone from Toronto who has been here for one month."

That evening the cordon around the swamp would be reduced in strength as the police returned to hunting down speeders and collaring drunks. But Cohoe's attacker was not the only bear wardens hunted that night. While revellers roamed the brightly lit main street looking for a pub that was still open, wardens stalked bears in the dim back alleys a few yards away. Warden Rose was the lead hand on one of the two bear management teams working in the Banff high visitor use area that summer, Alan Westhaver was his assisstant. The teams had been working overtime even before the attack on Ernest Cohoe to keep up with bears raiding the townsite and campgrounds. Westhaver recalled, as we have seen, that it was as if something was pushing the black bears into town, there were so many sightings.

On August 23, wardens had live-trapped two black bears at the town recreation centre near the banks of Forty Mile Creek. On the day of the Cohoe mauling (August 24), the crews were as busy as ever. Rose and his assistant darted an 85-pound black bear at the garbage bins behind the Rimrock. They hauled him down to the helicopter hangar where they caged him up in the "bear jail," a large holding pen, for future reference then went out after another furry diner down at the Voyageur Restaurant on Banff Avenue. That night the garbage bins behind the Voyager were overflowing, and later, while still shaken from the day's gruesome events, they live-trapped a repeat offender, black bear 067, at that location. This bear had been trapped in the wetlands on August 9 and flown to the Dormer River Area. Here he was again, bolder than ever, willing to forsake the forest to make his way among the houses and patios to forage on the edge of

main street. His huffy attitude in the dark alley that night made
Monte Rose nervous, although his size did not tally with Muskett's
description of the Whiskey Creek attacker. Yet the bear was definitely a resident of the swamp, so guilty by association. Rose decided
to dart the 175-pound male and place him in stir temporarily while he
consulted with his supervisor on the animal's fate. He needed to move
traps into the Whiskey Creek wetlands and get them into operation.
Westhaver, who would be detailed that winter to get the bear-proof
garbage container issue resolved, recalled that at that phase of the
hunt, bear control teams "were not inclined to be forgiving to a bear
that looked like a threat." Rose would later be ordered, on August 27,
to destroy these "repeat offenders" as a potential hazard to the
public. He didn't realize that the decision would be bruited about in
local saloons and coffee shops as an example of trigger-happy wardens
blasting every bear that moved. The same tongue-flappers had
wardens blasting away at shadows in the swamp, killing elk, moose,
and deer with panicked disregard – the usual mix of BS, lies and
slander dumped on government workers by a cynical and poorly
informed public.

Assistant Chief Kutzer, never touted as a wild-eyed park idealist
but given to a utilitarian frame of mind, decided he would stake out
the Caboose Restaurant area every night, in the belief that the bear
was bound to return sooner or later and probably sooner. If anything
could draw the attacker back that Sunday night, it would be the rich
supply of calories behind the Caboose. The bulk stations and lumber
yard had to suspend their operations while the hunt was on, but the
Caboose would keep churning out restaurant scraps in the days ahead
with nary an objection from park management.

Owner Louis Kovacik told me that it was tour bus traffic that kept
the business going during the crisis; the locals were staying away. In
the station yard behind the Caboose, Kutzer and warden Tim
Laboucane set up their ambush, relying on headlights and six-volt
lanterns that could light up the entire area. Government shotguns
were few, but buckshot ammo was in good supply, so Kutzer had

brought his personal shotgun along. Twice that night, the telltale rattle of empty tin cans had the two stepping out of their truck, Kutzer easing his goose gun past the door frame on his side, both men chambering rounds into their weapons. With one well-placed bullet the entire operation might come to an end. Kutzer flipped on the lights and shouldered his shotgun, ready to squeeze off a shot, but grinned sheepishly at what was in his sights: a lactating female black bear. She weighed less than 175 pounds, by the look of her. She stared into the lights, then turned tail and went crashing off through the forest to rejoin her cubs. Later on that night, when the lack of action on the stakeout was making the men's eyes glaze over, there came another rattle of cans and bottles. An immature black bear stood in the floodlights, blinking at them, a confused actor in a bad play. He dropped his head submissively, like a big dog caught raiding a chicken coop, and padded off across the gravel to fade into the night. It was the last bear they saw on their late-night shift.

On September 21, Warden Earle Skjonsberg and his Alsatian search dog, Faro, would discover the remains of five transient camps in the wetlands. He would report that the food left behind in those camps had been fed on by bears.

Sticky Mouth pads quietly through the trees, light on his feet despite his great weight, until he nears the station yard, where he pauses. There is a pool of shadow on the gravel where the arcs from the lights on either side fail to illuminate the yard. He creeps out from under the trees and steps almost daintily out as if the darkness were a bridge over a deep canyon. The smell of the cowfish kill is like a cable through a ring on his nose, pulling him steadily forward. But he freezes in his tracks like a outsized bird dog on point, smelling an odour that had not been here before among the funkier acridity of men. He recognizes it at once; the smell of their weapons. He perks up his round ears and listens until he hears the faint mutter of something else he recognizes, stirring inside his ears as if spiders were crawling there. It is an itch he cannot scratch, this sound of Twoleg voices.

There is the slight squeal of a metal door opening; he has heard the sound before and hearing it again is a warning note. Across the yard, in the darkness, the truck door opens; he has no understanding of what that is, but he makes out the vague shape of a Twolegs moving, he hears a splash of liquid falling and the night breeze wafts over the smell of urine. The odour is mixed with the graphite and grease smell he fears. Eyes narrowing, ears laid back, he turns slowly and retraces his steps, not disturbing the gravel under his huge padded feet, and vanishes, a black ghost in black shadows.

That night Sticky Mouth prowls along the trails that radiate out from the station, stepping clear of any patch of ground where he might leave a clear track. To his eyes the paths are as if painted with phosphorescence. If you travel enough in the woods at night, you will begin to see them that way as well, though never in as much detail as a bear does. On these trails he will find some scraps from local garbage bins scattered by the other bears through the bush; he scoffs down anything that has a shred of flesh clinging to it. The downslope breezes from the west speak of a hidden cache of grub he has not detected before. He turns into the wind, the scent drawing him forward, until he enters a small clearing and finds an abandoned man bed protected by a roof of branches and deadfall arranged in a cone shape. The human food is piled inside. Here there is meat in a swollen, transparent skin that has burst open, releasing a glorious stench of old pork. He butts it gently with his muzzle, and a whiff of outrageous potency bursts like a scent orgasm in his nose. He bites eagerly into it, savouring the blue cheese texture of advanced decay, and his whole body has become a giant tongue. Next he turns, licking his delighted chops, to find potatoes, a package of melted butter, an open can of jam graced by a murmuring of trapped flies. He laps down the butter, crunches down the potatoes, savouring the starch and grease. But the jam puts his tongue in a state of ecstasy once more.

Entranced, he laps his way to the bottom of it, cleans up every drop. When it's gone, he groans like a man in despair, then takes out his frustration on the other cans, pouncing on them, biting and punching holes with tooth and claw. He takes them up and chews them open in his jaws. His mangling oozes canned fish and canned fruit out on the forest floor, a carpet of odours and flavours that soon mollifies his temper. It would all be a delicious smorgasbord, over far too soon. Mere snacks like these will have to sustain him until he can gain access to the main banquet. Though he cannot claim the prize, he never forgets it is there, never forgets that it belongs to him, and to no other.

Warden Monte Rose and his helpers would get no sleep this night. They were busy moving traps from outlying campgrounds and setting them just inside the forest, in case Cohoe's attacker returned. Along the edge of town where the houses lay close to Whiskey Creek, the locals stared into the dark of their backyards and recoiled mentally from the very notion of entering the old "station bush" or allowing their children to roam freely in its shadows, where Banff's children had roamed, uninjured and unafraid, for generations. The wilderness had reclaimed Whiskey Creek, and it was the old primeval version, "nature red in tooth and claw," not the Disneyfied fantasies served up by the tourism industry they relied on for their daily bread.

In the wetlands, Sticky Mouth listens to the sounds of the people moving in a clanging and rattling of metal. It makes him uneasy. Denied access to the Caboose bins, he roams the night away, nose to the grass, alert to the sound of anything moving there that he might run down, but any moose and elk foraging with calves at heel have fled the area, alarmed by all the human invaders. As for the black bears, they are off hunting trouble in the back alleys of town; they leave plenty of stink behind, but he cannot eat stink.

The black grizzly's eclectic picnic has left his stomach churning. (Compacted plastic will turn a bear's intestines gangrenous if it lodges in the digestive tract, leading to a slow and painful death.) His response is to doctor himself by grazing along the creek on whatever coarse grass comes to hand. This will give his guts a healthy purging and help rid him of contamination. He steals around the perimeter of the wetlands, where a fence made of brilliant light glows between the trees, and the voices of the hunters are heard when the rumble of traffic stills.

All night he roams, haunted like a vampire by the scent of human blood in his nostrils, confused by the noise of humanity boring into his ears, burdened by his carnivore genes with an insatiable hunger for fat and protein. Memories strum the web of neurons in his head; he is compelled by appetite to make his home in a place where he cannot rest and compelled by the sounds and smell of mankind to retreat further into the mountains. Always he hunts the darkest shadow he can find, returning later that night to the forest edge near the Caboose once again, frustrated again by the presence of men there, his stomach growling a complaint. He wends his way westward at last, following the banks of Forty Mile Creek, any sound he makes muffled by the flowing water, his tracks washed out of the gravel. He has remembered a dark cave where the water flows under the Meat-maker trail. It leads to a forested retreat to the west. He comes to the place at last, and above the sound of water rushing through the cave he hears the sound of the hunters moving along the road. He stands in the water, close by the bank, screened by an overhanging spruce and watches with narrowed eyes as two brilliant talking lights approach slowly and float along the edge of the Meatmaker. He stares into the cave, feeling himself drawn to its promise of safety. He pic-tures the treasure of meat he is leaving behind, and he stands there in the cold water waiting for the impulse that will move him westward to safety, or eastward back into hazard. It was probably just some chance occurrence, such as a man-shape lingering on the bridge as some sentry stared down at the hypnotizing sheen of running water, that caused him to turn and retrace his steps, back into the Whiskey Creek wetlands.

TEN

THE RANGES OF A BEAR
HUNTING WITH GUNS AND TYPEWRITERS

"The answer lies in the bear itself."

CHIEF PARK WARDEN ANDY ANDERSON
Edmonton Journal, August 27, 1980

THE WHISKEY CREEK INCIDENT was the fourth bear attack in Alberta in a two-week period. Albertans were still reading accounts of the oil rig workers killed at Zama, Alberta, on August 15 when news of the Whiskey Creek attack reached city newsrooms. The response to the Cohoe mauling was staggering. Radio, television, and newspaper reporters from Calgary, Edmonton, and Lethbridge were dispatched immediately to Banff when the story broke. Before the full debacle ended, the coverage would stretch to the national and international levels, and the actions of the park wardens would be under intense media scrutiny. The experience would give Parks Canada cause to re-evaluate all aspects of its relationship to the press; ultimately it would result in the muzzling of some park officials and the imposition of official spokespersons between the warden service and the public.

As writer Ian Frazier once pointed out, an important part of a bear's range these days is within the pages of the local newspaper, with predictable results. To paraphrase Frazier: once the bear becomes a major character in the press, news of its exploits are eventually followed by news of its demise. On the morning of August 25, Andy Anderson found his adversary, which had escaped the net of hunters around Whiskey Creek, ranging for hundreds of miles through the morning papers. That was not surprising, since he himself had given interviews regarding the bear to some of the country's dailies the day before. His phone had begun ringing with calls from reporters even as Cohoe was being flown to the hospital; media pressure would only increase in the days ahead. For Anderson, as he lit up his first bowl of pipe tobacco that day, the news included an update on the American hostage crisis in Iran, and a blow-by-blow of the aborted military rescue attempt of April 25. Human violence continued unabated in Canada also, making a face-mauling bear appear almost reasonable by comparison. In Mississauga, Ontario, a 37-year-old man was charged with murder for throwing his neighbour's baby off a bridge into a 75-foot-deep ravine. And there was the first headline, in the *Calgary Sun*: "Fisherman mauled by bear." But the chief warden, used to being the spokesman for conservation issues in the park, could not have been amused to find the *Sun* portraying the RCMP (an agency as adept at garnering credit in the press as it was at retreating behind a veil of secrecy) as the lead agency in the hunt. "'We're following it by helicopter and we've spotted it a few times,' but we keep losing it in the heavy bush,' said an RCMP spokesman," the paper reported.

"If we do catch it, we'll shoot it – that's for sure," said the spokesman, who also offered the learned opinion that the bear "could be sick or something" and advised that the police would "autopsy" the bear when they finally caught it. In fact the RCMP had no mandate to "autopsy" (the correct word is necropsy) bears, nor were they leading the hunt for the bear. The RCMP had no bear traps. Perhaps they planned to handcuff the bruin and lock it up in the drunk tank. There was also still a chance that the bear might be live-trapped, not just shot on sight, though no doubt it would wind up dead one way or another. To cloud the issue even more, the spokesman had identified the bear as a grizzly, while Anderson was still undecided as to the species he was looking for. The tracks that Cooper and Kunelius had found on the riverbank were inconclusive as far as Anderson and his team were concerned, since no grizzly tracks had been found in the Whiskey Creek or Fenland areas. He suspected a grizzly was responsible, nevertheless, but what Keith Everts saw was a black bear, and what Bill Vroom had caught a glimpse of also sounded like a black bear; that was the only likely candidate so far. Anderson was keeping his options open just then, and didn't need other agencies steering for him. In fact, the *Sun* also reported that "Banff park officials suspect the bear to be a male black bear approximately 375 pounds, last spotted 5 km west of Banff. 'We're following it by helicopter and we've spotted it five or six times but it keeps running into heavier timber,' said Andy Anderson, chief warden of Banff."

Anderson, both as a warden and as a resident of the town, knew that accounts of gory bear maulings frightened off tourists and alarmed local residents. He didn't want to label the attacker a grizzly unless he had conclusive proof, as this would inspire even more panic in the press. Instead, he sought to be reassuring: "Ninety-nine percent of the time people are safe in Banff woods," he had told the *Sun*, adding: "This was just a fluke. It shouldn't have happened." Anderson had "stressed how unusual the attack really was since there was no apparent provocation or reason."

But the *Sun*, and most other papers were not to be spun easily off the scent of blood and the ancient feud between men and bears. The *Sun* pointed out the frequency of attacks that summer and reminded its readers about the recent Zama incident. To the public, there appeared to be an epidemic of bear attacks, particularly of black bear attacks (for those who knew the difference between the species), and the fact there was an attack in Banff, involving a black bear once again, and that the head bear wrangler in Banff did not know why the bear had attacked, was not reassuring.

The most even-handed accounts of the Whiskey Creek debacle would be filed by Brian Patterson of the *Calgary Herald*, a reporter with contacts in the warden service. In the Monday evening *Herald*, he noted that "Reports conflict on whether a black bear or a grizzly bear is responsible for Sunday's attack." Anderson had told Patterson, "As far as we know yet, there is no reason why the bear would attack. It doesn't appear that it was for food." Anderson would repeat this theme on August 27, telling the *Edmonton Journal*, "This bear attack more than any other I've seen is completely unexplainable . . . The bear had ample opportunity to move off. It wasn't provoked. It wasn't surprised. There wasn't a cub. We've combed the area and there's no carcass or food cache . . . The answer lies in the bear itself." So the mysterious, violent nature of the bear's character and motive were left up to the layman to ponder and any role man may have had in causing the problem in the first place was not mentioned. Hardly reassuring, contrary to the jovial head warden's intention.

Anderson's statements raise several questions. True, the wardens had not found a carcass in the area, which would have led them to suspect that the attack was made by a grizzly bear defending a meat supply. But there was ample food in the form of garbage, which Anderson was well aware of. His own experience seems not to have led him to equate a rich supply of garbage with a carcass or "food cache" that must be defended, as far as a grizzly bear is concerned. Anderson had been in close proximity to grizzly bears foraging for food in the Lake Louise dump. He had seen people moving in close to the bears to get photographs. Though he had intervened in the situation, he had not witnessed any real threatening behaviour from the bears, which were busily gorging on high-calorie human food. But I would compare this to the situation today in Katmai National Park, Alaska, or the Khutzeymateen Grizzly Bear Sanctuary in British Columbia, where people are able to move around grizzly bears without much threat when the bears are stuffed with salmon. The bears allow each other a certain amount of room to feed, and they seem willing to grant humans some room as well. But if you follow an apparently docile grizzly bear into the woods, as I have done, you will note an immediate change in its behaviour. The animal will likely stop and stare over its shoulder at its back trail. It may stand up and gaze intently in your direction; it may suddenly take to its heels as if intending to leave you far behind, or it may fade into dense cover to wait in ambush. And if you press it too close, it may finally perceive you as a threat and come charging back down the trail. The food-habituated bear that seemed so docile, that even allowed you to approach, has suddenly disappeared, and in its place stands the foremost predator of the wild, wild woods.

There were at least three factors in Whiskey Creek that differ from landfills and salmon streams. First, the east slope of the Canadian Rockies is a relatively arid and unproductive habitat for bears to begin with, not at all like the lush habitat of the Pacific coast rainforest, with its spawning salmon, its beds of eel grass and clams, and its varieties of berries. On the east slope, any rich source of calories, including dumps, will be soon exploited by bears. Second, the resource at the Caboose Restaurant, though rich, was not like a big landfill or salmon stream: it was limited in volume, more like a carcass. Third, the actual feeding area also was limited in size, forcing bears into close proximity with limited escape routes. This can cause stress and lead to conflict, including conflict between bears and people who wander into the area under dispute. True, there were other garbage bins on the edge of town. But the Caboose bins, which were close to retreat cover for both species, were the prime food source available at that time, hence they were coveted by all bears moving in that area. In a case like this, the dominant bears will come into conflict until one bear prevails. Other bears will feed at the pleasure of the king, when present. The whole dynamic of food competition among these bears, all of which were anxious to put on fat for the winter hibernation, was fraught with danger for any human wandering into the area. But as we have seen before, bears feeding around people was the norm in Banff park: we had been letting them get away with it for decades.

Another reason for the attack – a bear surprised at close quarters and reacting defensively – was not advanced by Parks Canada spokesmen. In other words, Muskett and Cohoe had been making lots of noise, so the bear should have moved away. But in recent years, although no one has yet tallied up the incidents, we have learned that the most counterintuitive human-caused noise, namely gunshots, may act like a dinner gong for some bears: it brings them to the hunter on the run. Over the decades, there are many incidents of bears robbing hunters of their kills, so watching for incoming bears is absolutely crucial when hunting in grizzly country. For example, in October 1995, two hunters, Bill Caspell and Shane Fumerton, were killed by a grizzly after they shot a bull elk outside the south boundary of Banff park. According to bear expert James Gary Shelton, four other hunters in British Columbia were mauled by grizzlies that year.[32]

The brouhaha in the press, with conflicting statements being made by the RCMP and Anderson, came to the attention of Ken Preston, head of public relations at Parks Canada's regional headquarters in Calgary. Preston, now retired, knew a bit about the garbage management problem and the delay in installing bear-proof containers. "I think they had hoped they could buck it off back to Ottawa," Preston explained during an interview in his Calgary apartment in 2006. Anderson, of course, had pointed out to his bosses that closing the dump without first installing bear-proof garbage containers in the park could bring bears into conflict with people. But that was not something Parks Canada wanted in the newspapers.

News of the attack must have been received like a sun-fermented tuna sandwich by the honchos in Calgary, particularly by the director, the late W.C. Turnbull. According to Preston, Turnbull was a former department store executive before coming to Parks Canada, and more concerned with financial management than wildlife management. Biologist Bruce Leeson, who worked for him, said Turnbull didn't know much about national parks or "what you actually did on the ground out there" but he was a good manager. Leeson recalled arguing for wilderness values over development at a meeting with his boss and other staff. "Bill looked at me and he said, 'I know you know lots about wilderness, but do you know what wilderness is for me?'"

"What is it, Bill?" asked Leeson.

"Wilderness is Saturday afternoon with a case of beer and the barbecue, out on the balcony of my apartment."

Although Turnbull was briefed on events every day, he left it to Superintendent Paul Lange and his officials to handle the disaster out in the wilderness of Banff. As for Ottawa: "We never heard anything from them," Preston told me. "Their attitude was we have a regional office, so let them handle it." In 1979, Parks Canada came under the jurisdiction of Environment Canada. After the election of 1980, John Roberts (Liberal) was appointed minister. The minister would soon be in nearby Lake Louise for the cabinet conference, and he would not want to see his name on the front page connected to a story about bears eating tourists in one of his national parks. To date, I have not found any record of communication from Minister Roberts to his regional office during this period – which doesn't mean there was no communication, of course.

Preston, who had come to Canada from the United Kingdom originally, was assigned to handle all press relations from his Calgary office. This should have taken some pressure off Anderson, who was under siege by the media at the outset, but it was difficult to convince reporters, who were hanging around the administration building and tracking him down to the warden office that morning, as he went to meet with Vroom and Whyte, that they should get their quotes about what was going on in Banff by phoning up a spin doctor back in the city. Besides, Anderson was not one to avoid the media. He felt it was up to him to set the record straight and try to reassure the tourists. He continued to comment for the record from time to time in the days to come. "Andy was a nice guy," said a grey-headed Ken Preston, gazing out his window overlooking the Stampede City, "but he didn't understand reporters, in my opinion, and I was one of them for a long time. I don't think he realized the basic thing about newspapers. The bad news goes on page one; the good news goes in the back pages. If your name goes in the paper, you definitely don't want it on one."

Preston was wise to the ways of editors, having worked for city dailies from Vancouver to Ottawa. He still had a nose for a good story, however. He confided that he saw a good story in Banff and was chomping at the bit to get up there. It was as if he wanted to cover the story himself. Instead, he had to manage the sleuth of journalists that was sounding the air for the sweaty whiff of failure or the cheesy tang of duplicity. Bruce Patterson remembers some park officials (he declined to name them) comparing the situation in Banff to the movie *Jaws*, where a dangerous predator threatens not only people's lives, but also the tourism industry in a coastal town. In New England, they had "Jaws" and a city father who wanted to keep the beaches open for the fourth of July holiday. In Banff, we had "Paws," and a business-as-usual attitude with the last long weekend of the summer a few days away. Judging from some of the quotes Preston gave the media that summer, the sensational story sometimes eluded the efforts of the spinmeister to rein it in.

In Ottawa, when Parks Canada executives saw the name of one of their chief wardens on page one, I imagine they winced. The name would have called up vague memories of memos prophesying mayhem of the ursine kind. Something to do with bear-proof garbage containers being needed, which seemed a laughably low-priority item among all the issues confronting Environment Canada. Then there was that incident the previous year where some junior park warden had pressed charges against CP Hotels – and got on the national news. Who knew where this business was going to end? One park visitor maimed for life, and the bear still out there looking for more victims, no doubt. The situation was turning into a horror flick.

I am guessing they preferred to avoid any public comment. Let the staff at regional office stickhandle this one; keep the press clear of the minister, otherwise they would ruin his time at Château Lake Louise with possibly unpleasant blow-back upon his return to Ottawa. This – what was the name? – Anderson, he might wind up a hero yet: in which case good for him. He might also finish up in a lawsuit, tongue-tied, under a ton of toppling torts. So I picture Ottawa executives smiling thinly at the thought of this possible outcome before slipping out into the muggy streets of the capital, headed for another taxpayer-subsidized lunch.

Bill Vroom started as a park warden in the 1950s, when Banff was divided into districts, each one being assigned to the care of a senior warden, sometimes assisted by a junior, sometimes not. The headquarters might be located on a park highway, or far in the backcountry, depending on how the boundaries were drawn. In the mountain national parks, wardens patrolled the backcountry on foot and horseback, monitoring wildlife activity, watching for outbreaks of wildfire, enforcing regulations, and assisting hikers and equestrians. They supervised trail crews, and also did a fair bit of trail maintenance themselves, clearing trees from the route with chainsaws packed on horseback and repairing bridges and washouts as needed. In my era (1960s and 1970s), we also maintained many miles of the single-strand forestry telephone system in our districts, which was strung from tree to tree on glass insulators in the forests and from pole to pole (or from cairn to cairn) over alpine passes. One of my packhorses was often loaded with the pole-climbing harness, rolls of number 9 wire and boxes of insulators, while another might carry a chainsaw, fuel and hand tools. A series of log patrol cabins augmented by tent camps provided accommodation and storage of trail maintenance gear and provisions, as well as emergency caches for first aid, fire fighting, and mountain rescue. Up until the early 1970s, we were required to live in the park year round and we paid only a modest rent for the use of the cabins, which we also had to maintain. Those chosen for this role were of necessity self-reliant and not averse to their own company, since it was often the only company they had, aside from their horses and the wild critters.

With the advent of centralization in the early 1970s, most wardens were moved into town to work under more direct supervision. Theoretically, we would have an upgraded role as "park resource officers," conducting wildlife studies and working on a biophysical inventory of the parks among other things. For such technocratic pursuits, the term *park warden*, used since 1909, lacked suitable scientific cachet. In reality, the backcountry, where fewer park visitors roamed, came to be neglected in favour of dealing with human-caused problems in the high visitor use management areas near town, despite the fact that the backcountry is far more important in preserving ecological integrity than the settled areas where it has been compromised by man. (We didn't hear too much talk about ecological integrity back then.) In Banff park in the 1970s, centralization, despite some very worthwhile scientific goals, tended to be a squeaky-wheel-gets-the-grease system. Banff then averaged 2,750,000 visitors per year, and their activities and needs dictated what wardens did each day, from putting out illegal fires to tranquilizing bears or searching for lost children and mountain climbers.[33] This was still the situation in 1980.

When Parks Canada elected to hike rents upward in accordance with real estate values in Banff's superheated market, it lost the right to enforce park residency for wardens. Many wardens moved out of the national park to buy property where it was less expensive. This meant that it sometimes took longer to round up wardens to respond to emergencies than it had in the past.

Bill Vroom was raised in the bush by a rancher who was reputed to ride barefoot at times to save on boot leather. Vroom was a natural candidate for backcountry life in Banff park, where housing was a log cabin with only cold running water – running by the door, that is. But by 1980, he and wife Maureen had gone way uptown, in a sense. They were living in one of the new condominiums on the edge of Whiskey Creek. Glancing out his living room window on Monday morning, August 25, Vroom saw that it was going to be a cool day, a good day for hiking in the bush. And maybe, just maybe somebody would get a clean shot at the bear, and the whole sorry business would be over. Who knew, maybe he would be that guy. Vroom had just the weapon for the job; a customized .30-06 with a reduced barrel length: a gun with lots of power and range of motion, suited for the forest.

When it got down to shooting, Vroom hoped the bear did not try to bust out past one of the new recruits. Vroom, like other veteran wardens, had some concerns about their lack of experience with weapons. In 1980, the service had no formal firearms training program. The oldtimers had all come into the service complete with shooting skills learned on the ranch or, as in my own case, in the military. Many had been trained by their fathers to hunt as a matter of survival. In the late 1970s, park panjandrums had not yet caught up with the fact that the new generation of better-educated recruits, whom they now favoured as hires, were increasingly coming from an urban background. They were being hired for their formal education in resource conservation or natural science. Game warden skills, such as shooting, animal tracking, horsemanship, and wilderness survival were secondary; they could learn those on the job, presumably from the older wardens, who would gladly impart those skills, according to theory, so that the new guys could get the promotions that the old guys could not get (due to their lack of formal education in resource conservation and natural science!).

As for shooting, it was already a serious mistake in 1980 to assume that such recruits knew how to handle a gun, as it is now a mistake to assume graduates in resource conservation or biology have any interest in the blood sports. As he drove over to the warden office that morning, Vroom had some definite preferences on who should back him up in the swamp. One of the older hands, like Earle Skjonsberg, a Second World War veteran with a long career full of many dangerous twists and turns already behind him, could be counted on, as could Lance Cooper, a younger man, but a serious hunter from boyhood, known as a crack shot and a steady hand. Monte Rose was another good guy in a tight corner. Rose had direct experience with man-killing grizzlies, as we have seen. But the two men were sometimes at odds in those days; Vroom was a serious-minded guy, though not without a sense of humour. Rose was a bit too flippant and cynical to suit the more even-tempered Vroom, and was notorious for his black sense of humour, having seen too many gory human fatalities doing mountain rescue work. I believe Rose was fed up with the parks garbage management policy, or rather lack of policy. Perhaps in self-defence, he had begun to make a game out of trapping bears, refusing to get emotionally involved with animals he might be ordered to destroy. Although he may not have known it at the time, his days on the federal roster were drawing to a close.

Lance Cooper, who was also destined to leave the federal employ later that year, was a regular member on the mountain search and rescue team led by mountain guide and park warden Tim Auger. Cooper, a .44 magnum guy built on a .32 calibre frame, had an enquiring brain and great physical endurance in the bush. He was intense, focused and taciturn, except when partying and loosened up with a rum and coke. I had worked with him on avalanche control at Sunshine Ski Village one winter. We would depart the office every day before dawn, headed for Sunshine, me yakking away about lord knows what, and Cooper saying nothing. After a few days of this silent treatment, I had demanded an explanation. Cooper had fixed me with his grey eyes behind steel-framed glasses, slightly steamed as I recall (the truck heater was failing) and said tersely:

"Mar – tee!

I do not speak.

Until noon."

The compressed eccentricity of his riposte left me speechless.

If Anderson was going to insist on using the helicopter again, then Cooper would be a good man to have overhead. If he got a shot, he would not miss – as long as no one distracted him with small talk.

At the warden office that Monday morning, those on duty and those who had worked all night and were too overtired to go home just yet were convened in the conference/ops room to drink dispatcher's revenge coffee and listen to Whyte brief the troops for the day's operations. Rose's traps had not tempted the Whiskey Creek mauler to enter. He was still very much out there. The wardens were joined by Constable Dennis Krill of the RCMP, who would accompany Vroom into the site.

The briefing was short: the day would be a repeat of the previous one, with hunting parties in the bush on both sides of the Norquay Road and the helicopter spotting for them overhead, and sentries posted at vantage points all around the area. Warden Halle Flygare would be paying a visit to the Caboose this day. He would not be issuing a summons requiring manager Louis Kovacik to appear in provincial court and explain the condition of his garbage storage. Instead, that gentleman would be given yet another warning and ordered to "install approved garbage containers" by September 3, 1980. Though privately owned, the restaurant after all was in a CPR train station, its garbage bins were on CPR property and Parks Canada, in the Langshaw debacle the previous year, had made it clear that there was a different law for the venerable railroad. In my experience, Canadian Pacific letterhead was enough to make park managers nervous. When discussions centred on the need to enforce park laws, CP Hotels was still the elephant in the room that everyone pretended not to see – or smell.

As I have pointed out, the Caboose was by no means the worst offender when it came to human garbage management and food storage; the worst offenders were Parks Canada-run facilities. The most serious problem for enforcement officers was the fact that their employer, Parks Canada, had compromised their credibility with the local judge by its own lax practices.* As for the Caboose, Kovacik decided after Flygare's visit he would no longer use the enclosure; he would henceforth haul the restaurant leavings to the transfer station in his own truck. The back door of the restaurant opened onto CP's paved passenger landing. The Caboose's pickup truck was parked there, its box loaded with kitchen scraps by the restaurant staff. However, it seems the enclosure continued to be used by the other businesses that operated at the depot, the three bulk-fuel stations and the coal and lumber merchants.

---

* Wardens spent 12 trap days at the Caboose in 1980 and captured two bears. The trap days and bear captures for three other selected eateries, at the Timberline Hotel, Rimrock Hotel, and Canadian Pacific Banff Springs Hotel, were respectively 20(3), 18(10) and 15(0). The data for Parks Canada-run facilities was as follows: Tunnel Mountain Village 1 campground 90(4), sanitary landfill 70(7) and Two Jack Campground 30(1).

Vroom and his party left the office, dodging journalists' questions, and headed for the Whiskey Creek subdivision. There they loaded their firearms, shouldered their packs and began working their way into the bush and bog on the west side of the railroad Y. The Y itself was patrolled by Warden Larry Gilmar, a heavyset but active man, a serious amateur hockey player, and a good guy to have onside if things went south. He would watch for movement in the bush and come to their aid if needed. They had Bob Muskett's account of the mauling as a guide; Muskett had agreed to be brought into the site to describe again what had happened on the ground once they determined it was safe.

Vroom led the way, flanked by Skjonsberg and Krill. The tall marsh grass was wet from an overnight rain, making tracking extremely difficult. No clear bear tracks could be discerned, though here and there grass that had been trodden down into the bog by the passage of heavy feet was slowly straightening up toward the light again. They worked their way slowly through the area west of the railroad Y. The family corvidae provided the only birdsong, magpies and whisky-jacks making occasional raucous interjections, punctuated by the *conk-conk* notes of ravens overflying the wetlands. The scavengers were all on the lookout for road-killed deer, elk, or bighorn sheep on the margins of the highway. As he moved quietly through the bush, Vroom had the eerie feeling of being watched. The uneasy quiet was soon disturbed by the sound of the Jet Ranger's engine warming up on the helipad to the east.

Today's version of Dennis Krill is a brown-eyed, sandy-haired stocky gentlemen with a kindly face I cannot easily associate with a former Mountie who finished up his career as a homicide detective. Krill and I met at the Sylvan Lake golf course, west of Red Deer, Alberta on a May morning in 2006. I'm not comfortable in such places; golf courses make me feel like I have strayed down a wormhole into a parallel reality.

Krill's assignment that morning in 1980 was much more exciting than the usual duties. "Banff was not particularly interesting from a police perspective," he confided over lunch. "Obtaining food and lodging by fraud was one of the common offences. For the police, the here-for-a-good-time mentality resulted in dealing with a lot of domineering drunks. There were many callouts to deal with drunks in campgrounds, and we got frustrated with wardens refusing to throw them out."

Listening to his comments, I recalled how the police referred to the warden service as "F Troop," after the comic Warner Brothers television series (1965–67). We had some choice epithets for the horsemen in return, best forgotten now. The police were supposed to deal with people versus people problems in the park while our law enforcement mandate, like our public safety mandate, was under the heading of "protect the park from the people and the people from the park." Most campers, including the rowdy element, arrived by private car. We had the same police powers as the RCMP to deal with drunk drivers and other criminals when no RCMP were available to lead the action, but unlike the RCMP we had no breathalyzer equipment to prove drunkenness conclusively for the court and no holding cells to detain belligerents. In 1980, we also had no self-defence training, no pistols issued (many of us purchased and carried our own, which peace officers were entitled to do), no nightsticks, no Mace and no handcuffs, and the lack of these last three weapons was a good thing, because we had but limited police training in how to use them. I for one declined to evict drunk drivers out onto the public highway unless the police were waiting to check them out. I feared for the safety of the public, which included my friends and family, not to mention being sued for negligence in case of accidents. The cops were sometimes slow responding to campground complaints; on the other hand, when the chips were down, they saddled up and moved fast. They saved me, and others from a serious shit-kicking on several occasions. We returned the favour by helping them clean up at highway crash sites as needed.

On that morning in 1980, Krill, schlepping through the pond slime, found himself a part of the warden's world of ursine violence and Catch-22 bureaucratic ineptitude. He took some kidding from Paul Kutzer on his choice of firearm that day. Krill had decided to take a pistol to a bear fight. In addition to their service revolvers, Mounties also had .308 bolt-action rifles with scopes, excellent for picking off snipers at political rallies I suppose, but a liability in the bush. By the time you found the Whiskey Creek mauler in the scope he would be all over you like a bad haircut. Open sights are your man in the bush. But the police did have 12-gauge shotguns with the plugs out, loaded with five slugs, good for taking out armed criminals and engine blocks and also the weapon of choice at the time for shooting attacking bears at close range. Krill, however, carried nothing but a snub-nosed .38 revolver of the kind detectives prefer and told Kutzer that was all he would be needing, since the wardens with him were all armed with rifles. Kutzer, a fan of the shotgun, chortles at that memory to this day.

Calibre isn't everything of course. In the spring of 1953, in Alberta's Swan Hills, a 63-year-old First Nations woman named Bella Twin, who was out picking berries, was threatened for right of possession by a large grizzly bear. She killed the bear by shooting it through the eye to the brain with a single-shot .22 long-rifle round. Mr. Grizzly weighed around half a ton and is still the largest grizzly bear ever taken in Alberta. Bella Twin was obviously a very good shot, and the luckiest person in Alberta on that day.

As if quoting from an old manual of procedures by heart, Krill told me his job was to "possess and retain body parts for the medical examiner's office."

"Were you fearful?" I asked him, cutting to the chase.

He considered the question seriously before answering: "It was like going in to a murder scene when the suspect is still at large," he answered. "I was certainly looking over my shoulder, but confident that the wardens would deal with the bear." He sipped his coffee, remembering that day. "When we first got the call, I heard something like 'A guy just walked out of the bush with the whole lower face knocked off.'"

The team moved very slowly through the willows and bog, looking for tracks and bear scat and for objects left behind by the victims. Dennis Krill parted the bushes in front of him at one point, and there was a fishing rod lying in the long grass. The team stopped dead, staring hard into the shadows of the trees. Bill Vroom called in the find to dispatch at 10:40 a.m. The helicopter approached; Palmer was at the controls and watching for them, scanning the trees for signs of movement. Cooper leaned out the side door opening, rifle in hand, and headset in place, to see the small figures below flashing dimly between the trees where the sun caught their uniform shirts. He knew what they were up against and he didn't like the setup but, he told me, "We had an obligation to go in there. I just thought we should wait and try and get the situation on our side, to greater advantage anyway. It's kind of like how far do you push a rescue? There's no point in hurting somebody else, especially after the fact, in this case."

Cooper saw Vroom, some 150 feet below, raise the two-way radio to his lips and suddenly heard his voice over the static in his headset, calling Palmer. The ground thrummed with the roar and rotor wash and Vroom, deafened by the tumult, waved them off, wanted them to back up out of there. The helicopter turned away to hover in the distance, and Vroom paused for a moment, adjusting to the quiet again, listening hard for movement in the bush, then continued on for another six minutes into a little bit of a clearing, watching the ground, watching the shadows. Suddenly he stopped, shocked into temporary immobility. He tore his eyes away from the sight and turning both ways stared hard at all the shadows, rifle up and ready, then looked down again.

Judging by the torn-up bushes and broken boughs it looked like some horror show maniac had gone quaquaversal with a powered brush cutter. As he called Krill over he could see blood fanned out on the branches of the willows from a stain in the grasses: the dried, wasted blood of a strong man in his prime. At the centre of the scene lay part of the victim's face, including the nose and nine upper teeth, which had been removed with a part of the underlying bone. This mask of tragedy lay there like a forgotten Halloween disguise, bitten off then abandoned by the bear, who if it saw even its own visage reflected in a pool might slash the offending water with a heavy, indignant paw. There was a message for any man to read in the grass: there was a tenant in this bush, obdurate and ancient in his purview, and there lay his statement of claim.

Dennis Krill smiled up at the waitress as she refilled his coffee cup and turned back to answer my question. It had made me wince merely asking it. "My thoughts seeing the mandible lying there? Well, I was used to that, from dealing with car crashes where body parts would be strewn around. But I was thinking about the poor guy having gone in there with his kids to go fishing. And then for him to walk out later. Walking out of the bush in that condition." He shook his head at the pitiful, amazing courage of Cohoe's action.

"In essence," Krill continued, "I was looking for a crime scene. A mauling scene, in this case. You find the scene, and you get some evidence." So it was as simple as that, though of course nothing is simple that involves human suffering. Krill was able to add some closing reference to the file and account for the missing flesh of the victim which he would turn over to the medical authority. There was no technology at that time to reattach the torn flesh and bone. The flesh, the blood-spattered and trampled mauling site confirmed Bob Muskett's statement of the facts for the official record.

At some point on August 25, Muskett was brought into the mauling site to relate again the details of the event. Vroom listened carefully to his account of the attack. "The bear came from that direction," concluded Muskett, pointing to the northeast. According to Bill Vroom's diary for the 25th, Muskett gave an imitation of the sound the bear had made. Vroom would note, "After bear mauled person it made noise 3 times about like a black bear does when it's in a trap, sort of wailing sound." Anderson, who later interviewed Muskett personally, described the bear's cry as "three short squeals."

Rifle in hand, Vroom eased his way through the thick cover, following a line where he could see dry branches had been snapped off by the bear's progress through the bush. "Approximately 50 ft. east-erly from where the mauling took place," he reported, "there is one place where a bear may have bedded down and 20 ft. farther on is another place where it looks like a bear bedded down. Where these beds are is the direction Mr. Muskett said the bear came from when it attacked."

That same day, Vroom guided Andy Anderson in to view the mauling site and to examine the bear beds. A bear bed can be a mere shallow depression scraped in the duff down to mineral soil, the kind where a bear can lie down on some cool, shaded earth on a hot day or it may contain bedding material such as spruce boughs and moss dragged in by the bear. Anderson told me that the size of the beds indicated they were made by a black bear. Vroom and his team had scoured the area looking for grizzly bear sign, to no avail. The soggy, marshy ground and the high grass made tracking inconclusive, and no grizzly sign was found at the mauling site. The area was criss-crossed with the comings and goings of big game animals, but the trails were like wet streaks on a rain-covered window, beginning nowhere, merging, intertwining in an endless maze.

Anderson now had more corroborating evidence of a black bear attack, albeit circumstantial. He listened to Vroom relate what Muskett had heard. They both agreed that they had heard black bears make a squealing noise before, when caught in a culvert trap, but they had never heard a grizzly bear make such a sound. The burly chief warden glared into the thick bush as if willing the bear to come into range and settle the issue right then and there. "I need to talk to this guy," he growled at last and he called the dispatcher on his VHF radio to make the arrangements with Muskett.

"I was skeptical at the start," admitted Anderson during our con-versation. "I thought it's too ferocious. The black bear thing didn't quite agree with me."

In an e-mail he sent to me in 2006, Anderson recalled the August 25 interview with Bob Muskett:

He was aware the bear had attacked Cohoe and stated it was squealing like a pig. He maintained it was a black bear. I suggested it may have been a dark-colored grizzly, but he was sure it was a black [an American black bear, that is]. I remember asking him if he could picture it in his mind and he replied, "Yes, vividly." He went on to describe it as a large black with a white spot on its chest. [In his statement Muskett had not mentioned a white spot.] I asked him if he noticed the claws, he replied, "No." The questioning was conducted informally as a conversation to put him at ease and no notes were taken at the time. It was obvious that he believed what he was saying. I was still skeptical; however, I had to consider that most local persons with some knowledge of bears would be more likely to expect it to be a grizzly. He had to be given some credence.

Back in 1980, Anderson would go on to place a much greater emphasis on the three short squeals described by Muskett, and Muskett's description in general, which pointed to a black bear attacker. Muskett, on the other hand, has forgotten over time the bear making any noises at all, even though he described them in his written report on the attack the day it happened. He still maintains that he did not see the white spot, but he also recalls that he saw little else but the bear's teeth during the incident. At the time, he was the only witness Anderson had. Cohoe was undergoing intensive care and was under sedation; the hospital was under siege by the local media, eager to learn the gruesome details of the attack, and the medical staff was not permitting anyone other than immediate family to visit. According to Anderson and other informants, the hospital told the press that Cohoe had been transferred to a plastic surgery facility in the United States, just to get rid of the reporters. Unfortunately, through some apparent confusion, they gave Anderson's office the same story, so Cohoe was never questioned by the warden service or the RCMP.

Anderson had told the press that the bear he was looking for was a black bear, and it is true that the evidence so far pointed to that, but his default position, which was not for public consumption, was far more conservative. The wardens would set traps throughout the area and try to take the bear alive that way, but otherwise they were to shoot on sight any large bear they saw of either species that was frequenting the Whiskey Creek wetlands, because no one was absolutely sure which species was responsible for the mauling.

It was at this point, when Anderson was seriously questioning his own gut instincts that this was not a grizzly bear attack, but a black bear attack, that Warden Rose called in to report he had found the tracks of a large grizzly bear on the eastern edge of the Whiskey Creek wetlands.

— ELEVEN —

THE BAD NEWS BEAR

The grizzly is the only animal I know who appears to be fully aware
that he is leaving telltale tracks. He will make unthought of turns
and doublings to walk where his tracks will not show, and also
tramples about to leave a confusion of tracks where they do show.

ENOS A. MILLS

The Grizzly Bear (1909)

THE BLACK BEAR TATTOOED in blue ink with the number B054
had not forgotten the perquisites of the Whiskey Creek forest any
more than the wardens had forgotten him. The memory of delicious
greasy tidbits acted like another force of gravity on his orbit through
the Bow Valley. He had reached the limit of his trajectory away from
the Caboose. Now he began a spiralling loop back to Whiskey Creek.
Neither two-legged bears or ghostly big-claw bears mattered to him
just then: he was a grease junkie and he had to get his fix.

On August 25 the wardens hunted the Whiskey Creek and
Fenlands forests from dawn to dark, looking for a crafty, dark brown
coloured bear who wasn't there. As far as they knew, he was out in
the skunk cabbage somewhere west of the Fenlands. There was no
clear track to be found, so it was hard to believe there was a bear anywhere in the area. So why was it that all the time they were going
through the motions of looking for him, they felt hairs lifting on the

backs of their necks as if an uncanny hot breath was wafting there? Occasionally, a hunter heard a slight crackling of bush on his back trail, or off to one side that he could not explain. If there was no bear there, why did they have the distinct feeling of being stalked, or sometimes of being circled? Who was the hunter, who was the prey? The Whiskey Creek bear seemed to have his own ideas. These intuitions had them looking over their shoulders at one moment and staring intently into the bush ahead of them the next.

The lean and taciturn Monte Rose was one of many wardens who, from the start, believed a grizzly bear was the mauler of Ernest Cohoe, not a black bear. Rose hunted through the wetlands partnered with warden Rick Kunelius by day, then worked late at night with young Alan Westhaver monitoring the live traps. Kunelius, who cut a romantic figure in Stetson and black handlebar moustache, was inclined to agree with Rose. "It was just too violent an attack to be a black bear" – that was his opinion, in retrospect at least. Lance Cooper was another who believed the real target must be a grizzly bear.

Given such suspicions, those on duty on August 25 were not unduly surprised when news spread that Rose had found signs of a grizzly bear in the Whiskey Creek Area. It was sobering news for Peter Whyte and Paul Kutzer. Neither one was happy sending their people into the dense bush looking for the mauler. Andy Anderson took Bill Vroom and warden John Wackerle, another experienced hand in grizzly country, in to the site on the east edge of the wetlands where Rose had come across the tracks while setting up a bear trap for the attacker. The funky fish aroma of Rose's bait wafted from the trap and came to the nose with a stomach-turning piquancy, as they huddled over the tracks and felt their ridged patterns with bare fingers. There were the distinctive front pads with the holes punched in the mud from the big claws at the tip of each toe pad. There was the rear foot, complete and like a man's, but weirdly different, conjuring up images of sasquatch or windigo. For Anderson, this could have been the moment that confirmed his fears that a grizzly bear had mutilated Ernest Cohoe. Such news would spread fear through the town, especially among those with young children. But in fact the bear that left those tracks had been prowling around the back-yards off and on since May. Anderson listened with mixed emotions while his wardens discussed the tracks, which showed a maximum length of about nine inches. They felt these prints were older than Monte Rose's estimation by several days, and that they were proba-bly made by the blonde grizzly bear that warden Perry Jacobsen had spotted earlier that summer. The bear had been seen several times close to the path that led from the subdivision to the warden office. Maureen Vroom, the head dispatcher, who had travelled in grizzly country with her husband, Bill, had described tiptoeing past it on two occasions on her way to work. The consensus was that the blonde grizzly was not particularly aggressive, and was highly unlikely to have been the attacker. Young bears, particularly females, are more likely to hang out near human food sources, in the absence of adult bears. So was this the animal that had been follow-ing wardens around in the bush, out of mere curiosity perhaps? It seemed unlikely.

Anderson stared down at this mud autograph and pondered the situation. The attack still felt like a grizzly bear attack to him, but what Muskett had seen appeared to be a black bear. True, Muskett had not seen grizzly bear-type claws, yet the bear he had seen was broad in the head – more like a grizzly. Then there were those day beds, from which the attack appeared to have originated: they were too small to have been made by a grizzly. If only they had found some tracks near the mauling site! Anderson still had reservations (there were those grizzly bear tracks discovered outside the area by Cooper and Kunelius), but it was necessary to make sure all his wardens took the possibility of a black bear attacker seriously. Meanwhile, Anderson would not tolerate a garbage-habituated grizzly bear, good-natured or not, in such close proximity to the town. Rose was to con-tinue his efforts to trap it for removal, but failing that the chief's order to the rest of his hunters was succinct: "If it comes back into the area, take it out."

Perhaps the blonde grizzly was loitering nearby, and maybe it could hear, as the Stoney Indians believe, when people were talking about it. More likely, it may have got a good noseful of Sticky Mouth and left the area *tout de suite*, since it was not seen again.

The black grizzly meanwhile had made his presence known only by a play of shadows at the edge of small clearings, by glimmerings, rustlings, vanishings. The hunter teams reported that they heard a large animal moving stealthily in the thick bush on several occasions, but could not close upon it. Once or twice they had come near to his hidden day bed, and he was poised to charge out among them, but always the smell of their guns, and the deliberate way they walked through the forest, made him hesitate, and the moment passed. Sometimes the hunters made a lot of noise, as if trying to drive him out of cover. Compelled by an angry curiosity perhaps, he picked up their spoor and followed after, hearkening to their hoots and hollers and stalking close enough to hear their whispers.

The hunters had at first travelled through the bush in a grid. When that was unsuccessful, they tried being more geometrically creative, moving in a series of spirals back across the grid. It happened that sometimes they spiralled back past the grizzly, and he found himself in an outer gyre around their route of travel. It was hard to know who was hunting whom, but there was a difference between the bear and his human pursuers: they did not know where he was but he knew exactly where they were.

At night they left him alone at last, and only the false sun hunted the black grizzly in fitful moments when the clouds parted, and he was suddenly revealed for a moonlit instant before withdrawing again behind the curtain of the spruce. This was the second night the grizzly had spent grazing horsetails and wild sweet peas for sustenance, or mouthing the few scraps left behind by other scavengers as he moved through the night. Humans were coming and going near the Caboose at all hours. He was getting increasingly desperate to staunch his meat hunger. We can be sure, given the fact grizzlies can smell food several miles away, that he found the aromatic culvert traps that were set in several locations just inside the area. We can picture him circling those forbidding iron tubes carefully, for his memory of encounters with this kind of metal stinking of fish were strong; in other words the thing aroused his suspicions based on past experience – cause and effect. To his nose also, the area around the traps reeked of men, and that triggered the phylogenetic memory, some might call it instinct, to avoid contact with such creatures whenever possible. So he did not step on the nearby patches of disturbed ground that had been scraped down to the mineral soil (to capture at least his track if not his hide). At one of them, being downwind, he would have caught the stink of three different men in one crashing cadenza of odour. There was just too much funky stench of man, too much hither and thither to suit the black grizzly. Although they had not found one track of his, he found every track they left as he cut their trails, every place where a man had urinated, or spat, or stood for a few moments staring into the bush, even if no trace was visible in the long grass.

What set him in motion at last we cannot know for certain, but once he engaged his muscles his appetite urged him to hunt for not only food but solitude. Based on the ultimate events, based on the attractants that would be employed the next day in an effort to lure him close, and based on the signs of grizzly that were later detected along the riverbank beyond the edge of the perimeter, I believe that Sticky Mouth broke out of the Whiskey Creek Area sometime before dawn on August 26 when the sentries, widely dispersed and tired, had lost their edge and needed replacing. He may have waded under the Forty Mile Creek bridge; he may have glided across the Norquay Road like a black ghost when clouds obscured the moon.

On the morning of August 26, the *Sun* held amusing news for the warden service under the heading "Restaurant Bears Fine." The Kentucky Fried Chicken outlet had been fined $350 for failing to keep their greasy delights out of reach of bears. But the *Sun*'s reporters that morning had also fixed the Whiskey Creek bear in the public mind with an ominous new name – the Bad News Bear. As it happened, in newsrooms from Vancouver to Ottawa, journalists were preparing to depart for Château Lake Louise to cover the Liberal government's cabinet conference. At the same time stories filed in Calgary and Edmonton, such as "Rogue black bear eludes air hunt" and "Bear still elusive; victim recovering," featuring a "vicious" bear terrorizing the town of Banff and making the local bear police look stupid, caught the eastern reporters' attention. Bear stories were always fascinating to the public, this editors knew, and here was an opportunity to cover a story with some real drama and blood and guts in between the scripted press conferences at Château Lake Louise. So the Bad News Bear was now ranging through newspapers like the *Ottawa Citizen* and the *Globe and Mail*, papers that were read by park panjandrums in far-off Ottawa. The imminent departure of Minister John Roberts for Château Lake Louise, just up the road from Whiskey Creek, was a heads-up to nervous bureaucrats. One more slipup now, with the minister looking over their shoulders, and the Bad News Bear could gobble up someone's career in the regional office or the Banff administration building.

The bear was, similarly, bad news for the powerful tourism industry in Banff National Park, some of whose members were believed to have a direct pipeline, via the Liberal Party, into the minister's office. The *Sun* alarmed local hoteliers with its headline "Campers flee bear scare," and the story was worse: "Tourists fled campsites as forest rangers [sic] and RCMP searched to no avail for a vicious bear near the Banff townsite yesterday," it began. "Meanwhile, campers were faced with no-vacancy signs as they tried to check into hotels." After leaving the impression for its Calgary readers, who are a major source of revenue for Banff businesses, that there was absolutely no room at the inn, the *Sun* related how "one family of four from Toronto headed for Calgary when they couldn't find accommodation. 'I'm not taking any chances with my family,' said Roger Croan." The Mounties threw oil on the fire with their account of Muskett and Cohoe's ordeal and Cohoe's injury: "An unprovoked bear stumbled on to them and grabbed him."

The *Sun*'s account was a self-fulfilling prophecy. Tourists were in fact fleeing the area, especially after reading news about other tourists fleeing the area. Campers eyed their bear warning pamphlets, entitled "YOU are in Bear Country," which are still handed out today at the park entrance gate when one enters by vehicle. (Incidentally, those entering by bus or by train are left to their own devices.) The section, in caps, headed "DON'T LET YOUR CARELESSNESS CAUSE THE UNNECESSARY DEATH OF A BEAR" with its instructions about locking up food and cleaning up dirty cooking utensils did not kindle the imagination nearly so much as the words "ALL BEARS ARE POTENTIALLY DANGEROUS" and the advice "If you notice fresh bear signs, choose another area." The fresh bear signs in Banff's major campgrounds at Tunnel Mountain and Two Jack Lake included not only bear scat containing bits of bread bags and bear tracks in wet spots but often also the disturbing sight of actual black bears climbing onto picnic tables to scoff down someone's picnic lunch, while the family huddled in their station wagon. Another eye-popping bear "sign" that offered a clue was the warning on the park's culvert traps, which read: DANGER. BEAR TRAP. KEEP AWAY.

Ken Preston, reluctantly riding herd on public relations by remote control, felt Anderson was not communicating effectively with reporters. He called up the chief warden and suggested Anderson should concentrate on what he was good at, trapping bears, and he, Preston, would concentrate on what he was good at, dealing with the press. Anderson had a tendency to emit a nervous chuckle – *kee-hee-hee* – through his omnipresent pipestem when people irritated him. He also chuckled when people pleased him, so it was hard to tell what he was thinking sometimes. He saw things a bit differently from the public relations officer; in fact he would attempt, unsuccessfully, to get Preston reassigned and off his back. After hectoring Anderson, Preston demonstrated how a media expert deals with issues that can be damaging to the image of Parks Canada by providing this helpful tidbit, according to the *Edmonton Journal*: "Chances of finding him are no better than finding a needle in a haystack" (August 26), and "If we lose the track we might as well give up because it's a hell of a big park." In the same story the *Journal* reported: "The hunt was to resume today, because wardens fear that once having tasted human flesh, the bear will attack again." The statement, whoever the source was, had more to do with *Jaws*-type sensationalism than with what a warden actually thought about a bear's dietary preferences. Preston veered back on track by adding that the wardens were not about to give up on the hunt despite the difficulties. He suggested that the bear might be old and unable to hunt its own food. "Maybe it's got a toothache," he suggested.

At the time, I was following the hunt for the bear by calling former colleagues at night to get their firsthand information. I found it difficult to concentrate on the mundane life of freelance writing while friends were risking their necks to catch up with the mauler. The newspaper accounts provided a somewhat amusing, if irritating, diversion. I read Preston's suggestion about the toothache and cast the paper aside, thinking of other bizarre scenarios. Perhaps the bear had a case of lover's nuts; perhaps it had found some kid's stash of LSD and had freaked out. Perhaps it would find a stash of pot next and chill out. There was plenty of pot out there to be found, incidentally. As I recall, the warden search dog found dope in Whiskey Creek every time the dog master took it out there for a training exercise. The dog and its handler, Earle Skjonsberg, were trained by the RCMP to find narcotics and also human beings, be they lost kids, avalanche victims or escaped felons. They were extremely good at that. Unfortunately, the dog was not trained for sussing out grizzly bears, which requires a very different skill set, not to mention a different breed of dog. But, why not use trained hounds to find the bear, then? Well, hounds might flush the bear out into the town, or send it and other wildlife fleeing into the middle of the heavy traffic on the highway, with tragic results and a barrage of lawsuits, too. Then there was the public relations nightmare of harassing wildlife with hounds in the national park where all dogs must be leashed at all times. Hounds would be considered only if all other methods failed.

Campground staff reassured concerned campers that everything was under control, but many campers voted with their ignition keys. When campers left the park prematurely, they took hundreds of thousands of tourism dollars with them. The long weekend was only two days away, and what should have been a revenue booster was shaping up to be a financial disaster for the Banff hospitality industry. The bear must be found, the situation must be defused. Andy Anderson and his assistant chiefs heard these concerns firsthand. They bore the brunt of the public's demands to deal with the problem.

At ten o'clock that morning, the park radio system came to life with news that offered a bit of hope. Lance Cooper and Perry Jacobsen, hunting in the Fenlands, had found the track of a large black bear entering the area from the west. The tracks appeared to be that of the bear Keith Everts had seen on the 24th. Others, like Monte Rose, who had spent some shifts in the wetlands just shook their heads: from what they had heard and sensed in the bush, they were convinced the real mauler had never left.

On the periphery of events was warden Doug Martin, a recent transfer from Waterton Lakes National Park. I had travelled with Martin on fall boundary patrol. He was the kind of guy who would ride horseback all day through a blizzard for a thousand-to-one chance at catching a sheep poacher, a guy whose idea of a luxury lunch was two ounces of half-frozen kippered snacks eaten off the back of a Swiss Army knife.

As a newcomer to Banff and one of the new generation of university graduates, Martin hoped to play a role in the specialized wildlife management group that Anderson was organizing within the warden service. Instead, he felt excluded from the group and believed some members felt threatened by his academic credentials; he held a BSc (Hons) in wildlife management. A genial and good-natured young man for the most part, the tall dark-haired warden was impatient with the Outfit's unwillingness to embrace change and didn't mind telling people about it either. In Waterton, he had worked with warden Keith Brady and provincial wildlife specialist Dennis Weisser, capturing bears using the Aldrich snare trap, a spring-loaded noose made of airplane cable that snared the bear by one leg without causing injury – if properly monitored, that is. Dennis Weisser had captured many bears, both black and grizzly, using the snare, and Brady, who made his own improvements on the method, used the technique to capture bears that had wandered outside park boundaries to prey on local livestock.

Martin confided that he was frustrated spending his time in Banff on duty warden patrols where law enforcement and public relations dominate the day, rather than on working on wildlife issues that he was educated and trained for. When culvert traps failed to capture the Whiskey Creek mauler, the newcomer approached members of the wildlife group and suggested that a snare was the best option. His suggestion was rejected. Perry Jacobsen was part of the new "wildlife shop," as it was known. He told me that he does not recall Martin promoting the snare idea at the time, but does remember that advice and wild ideas were coming from all directions.

The problem is typical of large organizations that are slow to accept advice from "outsiders." Those in the wildlife shop had caught scores of bears using culvert traps or tranquilizer guns, or by means of a lead pill when all else failed. They had no experience using snares, though these had been in use in other parks, notably Yellowstone, for many years. They were reluctant to try an untested technique – untested in Banff, that is – and not inclined to put their trust in a new guy during a crisis situation involving a dangerous predator.

Instead, they decided to take a page from the oldtime bear killer's book and bait the bear into range with a ripe carcass. One thing a bear loves to eat is sweet-tasting horseflesh – when it gets a chance – and it just so happened that a dead horse was available and ripening nicely. Having broken a leg far from town, the horse had been put down Monday night in the very heart of grizzly country, on the Panther River north of Banff. The grizzlies out there had not yet discovered it. The helicopter was dispatched with Warden Larry Gilmar, to hook up the carcass for slinging to the Banff abattoir where it could be dismembered.

The Tuesday evening shift, August 25, found Perry Jacobsen, surrounded by a swarm of amorous flies, wiping his case knife off on a rag, before lashing a bloody haunch of horsemeat to a tree. Some crackling and popping in the bush, with a few curse words thrown in, marked the progress of wardens Cooper and Kunelius, also on duty that night. Each dragged a chunk of horsemeat into the swamp on a rope, laying down a scent trail to lure the bear to the bait. As darkness fell they staked themselves out on the roof of the Unwin Hardware storage shed next to the railroad tracks that offered a clear line of fire toward the bait tree. The bait was slightly upwind from their position. The weather was promising: it looked as if they would get through their shift without sitting out in the rain.

Keyed up from too much overtime and lack of sleep, the three young men, all in their thirties, stared into the bush, willing the bear to come out. The moon sailed its galleon through rifts in the clouds, lighting up the scene of ambush from time to time, then plunging it back into darkness. At one point a furtive coyote followed their scent trails to the bait. Just the click of a safety catch on a rifle was enough to send him fleeing. An hour crawled by, then the snapping of dry branches on the forest floor spoke of a large mammal on the prowl and one not too particular about who heard it. A pair of fiery red eyes floated in the dark. The men heard a huffing intake of breath, which might mean the bear had caught their scent after all, and they flicked on their lights simultaneously. In their sights was a juvenile black bear, perhaps 125 pounds soaking wet, up on its hind legs and tearing into the bait with hungry teeth. It paused to stare into their radar lamps like a worried burglar, its ears perked up and trained in their direction, then dropped to all fours and scuttled off into the night. They took their fingers off the triggers and eased the safety catches back on.

Time crawled by, and drowsiness had eyes drooping. At last there came the telltale noise of claws on spruce tree bark again. Off went the safeties and on came the lights. It was the young bear again. It definitely had a sweet tooth for horsemeat. This time it scowled into the lights, reluctant to leave, and insisted on first tearing off a good-sized chunk for a private picnic before darting into the bush, the meat gripped firmly in its jaws.

It was near the end of the shift, and they had been talking quietly about the mauling and what was known about Cohoe's injury. He had already spent six hours under the surgeon's knife with a lot more surgeries sure to follow in the months and years ahead. They were blinking off sleep with bleary determination, helped by the cold night air bathing their faces. (The temperature that night fell to 1° C, this after a balmy high that day of 19° C.) And then just when it seemed that the shift would end with no useful result, something else was moving in. Up went the guns and on went the lights.

But it was only the young burglar bear again. This time the little bear was huffy and determined to get himself on the outside of that entire haunch of horseflesh. The cheek of the little devil noshing down on their bait aroused umbrage among the wardens. Hunting on double shifts for a ghost bear that could rip your face off was getting on everyone's nerves, and this was the last straw.

"The little prick is actually grinning at us!" came an irritated whisper, as they lowered the weapons again.

"He'll be grinning on the other side of his face in a moment," promised another.

"Let's kick his ass."

Wriggling backwards, the three eased themselves off the edge of the shed roof, unseen by the bear. They dropped to the ground. There were some sticks lying about at the forest edge, which came quickly to hand. They rushed into the forest after the youngster with a whoop and a yell. Startled, the bear huffed a threat as it turned to face them. This was but a moment of bravado. Confronted by three dangerous looking wing nuts, it turned and crashed off into the pitch-black woods, broken branches flying. The three plunged in after the quarry, sending willows springing into each other's faces with accompanying profanity. Flashlights flickered in the darkness, lighting up the enveloping forest with an eerie glow.

"Where did he go?"

"Dunno. It's black as hell out there."

This banter went on for a while until they suddenly stopped.

"Listen."

Something was moving through the dewy brush. Branches popped and they felt the cold layers of air seeping through the wet-lands. Was it the juvenile black bear or a wandering moose – or was it the Whiskey Creek mauler?

That's when somebody remembered they had left the shotguns back on the roof. There was an embarrassed silence as their action sunk in. Their boots and gloves were soiled with horse blood. They smelled like ripe bear bait and the bear in question could be watching them, from literally a few yards away. But looking on the bright side, being gunless in the dark while hunting bears with a stick meant they could not accidentally shoot each other if Bruin suddenly attacked. They eased backwards through the net of branches to the forest edge, then turned and sprinted for the safety of the roof once again.

The juvenile was the last bear seen on Perry Jacobsen's shift that night.

On Wednesday the 27th, Anderson conferred with his team of experienced wardens. Jacobsen suggested that they should pull all the hunters out for a while and let the area cool down so the bear had a chance to move more openly in its search for food. Lance Cooper also felt that the bear was more likely to come to the bait once all the human noise and odour were dispersed. The hunting teams pulled out of Whiskey Creek early that afternoon. They were glad to take a break, to head back home briefly to hose the mud off their boots and try to forget about the bear for a few hours.

Black bear 054 had meanwhile returned to a forest rife with the smell of men. He had spent the time foraging for berries on the outskirts of the town and he had found the pickings very slim. Now he watched covertly as men came and went around the hoard of fat and sugar. The gamy odour of restaurant scraps wafted over the forest edge, but he dared not approach. And something held him back, for his nose found what men could not, the spoor of the black grizzly, prowling around the vicinity in a righteously irritated mood before he pulled out of the area to find peace and quiet elsewhere. The sign he left in the long grass would have been fresh enough to raise the hackles on B054, nonetheless. He sought his most hidden bed that day, perhaps a thicket under some blow-downs near Forty Mile Creek, to avoid being seen, feeling the gnawing ache of hunger in his belly as the day wore on.

The lack of human presence in the wetlands that afternoon and evening was a balm to the black bear's nerves. After dark he left his bed and moved toward the great hoard of flesh with eager anticipation. But a strange, exciting odour was on the night breeze, a rhapsody of horse blood as a counterpoint to the symphony of beef and fish odours wafting over the swamp. He could hear the sound of black bears moving in the bush that night, moving in the same direction, but paid them no notice. They would get to the cowfish hoard before he did, but just then he found the odour of fermenting horse blood on the awns of the long grass too enticing to ignore. He paused to lick up exquisite slivers of meat of a kind he had not tasted before, but which his stomach ached to gorge on. He followed the blood trail, enthralled by its promise. There was so much blood and raw meat on the breeze that he caught no whiff of human odour or any scent from the weapons held in the hands of Paul Kutzer and David Cardinal, who were waiting for him just east of the garbage enclosure.

They had their patrol truck located so a flick of the switch would illuminate the bins and the bait station, the latter set up at a range of some 50 yards. The sky was overcast, the moon and stars hidden. Three times that night the wardens heard the sound of black bears scaling the wire at the bins, and flicked on the lights only to discover the bears were too small to be the mauler. These were bears that would have to be live-trapped and moved. At 10:30 p.m., they heard the sounds of black bears scrambling away from the bins and fleeing back into the bush.

"Then this big guy came in," recalled Paul Kutzer. "We heard a commotion, we looked and we could see the outline of a pretty big bear. So we got out of the truck." They saw his hazy form moving forward against the backdrop of trees, then taking more definite shape in the backlit glow of the nearby town. He was headed straight toward the bait tree, his breath steaming in the chilled air. As he approached in that less-than-twilight with his head down, the bear's back appeared to be more prominent, so he looked more like a medium-sized adult grizzly bear, with the characteristic humped back, than a large black bear. Kutzer estimated his weight at around 400 pounds.

Kutzer had his 12-gauge shotgun, tapered to full choke and loaded with SSG (heavy buckshot), and Dave Cardinal had a .270 rifle. The black bear had a set of claws and wicked-looking teeth. Thus endowed he could easily kill any man who got in his way, but he wasn't going to get a chance to employ those weapons tonight. This was not a sporting event, it was an ambush pure and simple. "We turned on the lights," recalled Paul Kutzer, "and he made a couple of lunges towards us, just trying to figure out what it was. He was the biggest bear we had seen down there, and I decided we should take him. So Dave fired one shot, knocked him down. He came up and whirled around and took a couple of steps toward us and then I blasted him with the shotgun." Both the .270 round and the heavy buckshot made fatal hits to the heart and lungs and one shotgun pellet tore through the bear's brain.

The sound of the weapons echoed like a double thunderclap from the side of Stony Squaw Mountain and rebounded from the encircling peaks. The big male black bear, which had ruled the swamp for a good part of that summer, and had passed his genes on in the late-spring breeding season, reeled from the impact of the double blow, toppled and died with no inkling of where his death came from, or why. His bright blood seeped into the duff, his legs twitched with released, nervous energy and then stretched, slowed, and grew as still as dead wood lying in the forest. The shooters stepped forward warily, guns trained, but there was no need. What lay before them was a very dead black bear. They were not surprised to note the prominent genitals of a male bear when they put up their guns and rolled him over, but they were startled by his unusually broad head, which gave him a grizzly-like aspect. Even his battle-scarred nose seemed less convex than in most black bears, but there was no mistaking the shorter, black claws of the black bear species. Peeling back his lip, they saw what they had hoped not to see – a tattoo. It was hard to read the faint blue numbers and identify the bear. It might be one they had tattooed, it might be one tattooed by a neighbouring national or provincial park in Alberta or British Columbia. A closer inspection in the lab would reveal his identity, but the mark of man was on him, that was certain.

Paul Kutzer called in the news. They had shot a bear that seemed a dead ringer for the one that had attacked Ernest Cohoe, and the one that Keith Everts had seen breaking out of the swamp. Kutzer was elated, "over the moon" as one warden put it, as they winched the heavy carcass into their truck for delivery to the park abattoir. There it would be weighed, photographed, and measured, and prepared for necropsy. The two men returned to the depot area to finish their shift, but no other bears came near, which was not surprising considering what had transpired. The hour was late, but Kutzer proposed a celebration over dinner downtown. He was convinced that the hunt was over; the Bad News Bear was dead.

— TWELVE —

BUSINESS AS USUAL

"Parks are for people"

POPULAR SLOGAN IN BANFF NATIONAL PARK, CIRCA 1980

HALLE FLYGARE IS A well-known author of works on outdoor topics, in both Swedish and English. In 1980, he was a temporary warden with an abiding scientific interest in wildlife physiology. Flygare, who spoke English with a rapid-fire Swedish accent, was occasionally impatient with the understated, go-slow methods of the oldtimer wardens – part of the cowboy way. Because of his interest and skill, he was sometimes called upon to necropsy dead animals or to skin and preserve specimens that had died of natural causes in the park or as a result of losing arguments with King Automobile or its death-dealing rival, King Diesel Locomotive. One of the things that intrigued him were "coydogs," coyote–domestic dog crosses that resulted from the my-dog-must-run-free philosophy then rampant in the Bow Valley. One of the wardens' duties was to shoot these pariahs on sight; they were contrary to the stated purpose of a national park. I first learned of his interest one day in the warden office lunchroom. A large pot of something that smelled like wolverine fur stew spiced with dried skunk glands was boiling away on the gas range. The lid was dancing merrily up and down. Holding my nose with one hand, I lifted the pot lid gingerly with the other and peered into the steamy depths. A pair of eyeballs peered right back, and they did not belong to a lobster. This thing had long white canine teeth fixed in a snarl. I dropped the lid and leapt back in alarm. Halle was boiling the flesh off a coydog skull to preserve it for his collection.

At 1 a.m. on August 28, the excitable Swede got a call from an excited dispatcher, at his home in Canmore, informing him that he must drive into Banff immediately and cut the head off a dead black bear. Roused from sleep, Flygare suppressed a choice Swedish folk expression. "Cut the head off a black bear? What they thinking the dead bear running away before morning? What the heck!"

"It has to go to the lab, for a rabies test."

"Rabies? Okay, but now is the lab in the middle of the night so they closed it. So what time they for sending it?"

"Sometime tomorrow. Bob Muskett has to come in and ID it first," the dispatcher replied.

"Well, for Pete's sake, the abattoir they cold enough to keep its brains fresh. At 6 a.m. I'm coming in, so I cut the head off then."

"Okay, then. I'll let them know, in the morning."

"Well, sure, what the heck."

Halle Flygare arrived at the abattoir at the appointed hour and was soon joined by wardens Vroom and Jacobsen. In Flygare's memory, the bear had already been decapitated, but according to the *Whiskey Creek Report*, the head was on the animal but the brain had been removed the previous night and frozen in preparation for a rabies test. At any rate, the bear Bob Muskett had seen had had its skull intact at the time, and Muskett was coming in to try and identify this one.

Anderson meanwhile had imposed a total gag order on all staff, including himself it seems, because news of the bear killing would not be released to the media until later that afternoon. The shooting death of any bear in the national parks generated scores of angry letters from the public to Parks Canada headquarters in Ottawa: this had better be the right bear, at least. Anderson had asked Ken Preston, in Calgary, to keep a lid on the unpleasant details of how the bear had been baited and shot. So instead of hearing about a bear being shot, the townsfolk woke up to the *Calgary Sun*'s report telling them how afraid they still were: "Bad News Bear Still at Large: Banff parents fear harm to their children." There had been in fact some cause for alarm, and some alarmed parents. Who was to say that the bear rummaging in one's trash barrel for scraps was not the same bear that had destroyed Cohoe's face with one bite? What had become a mere nuisance (albeit a source of amusement to local residents when showing off the local bears to friends and relations from the big city) was now seen for what it represented all along: a threat to their children. Now they were of a mind to see the bears stay in the bush instead of around the trash bins. But the bears would not return the favour as long as garbage was accessible, and as long as garbage bins were still of the type that a bear could knock over, thanks to some careless residents and a lack of initiative by Parks Canada.

All the ruckus in the swamp had not deterred bears from raiding the town; in fact, it probably stimulated them to keep moving out of cover at night. A local resident, Bruce Johnson, age 29, told the *Edmonton Journal* that he had "often smelled the musty presence of bears in the darkness around his home" as he prepared to go to work, at 5 a.m. "It sort of worries me," he continued, "because the attack occurred only about 500 metres from my doorstep." There were times that Johnson felt trapped in his house by bears rummaging around his door. To leave his house, he would jump from his second-floor balcony into the front yard and make a run for it, leaving the bears in temporary possession of his property. How he managed to sneak back into the house later was not reported.

One key phrase in the news on Thursday morning brought worried frowns to the brows of Banff hoteliers and restaurateurs. "Park wardens are optimistic they will hunt down the animal before Labour Day weekend tourists hit the park." The business people smelled a spin doctor at work. The long weekend was one day away, and they needed those tourists to start filling up hotels and restaurants right away. How badly did they need the money? In 1998, by way of comparison, it cost $3.4 million a month just to pay expenses at the famous Banff Springs Hotel, the town's grandest. There was very little time left to kill or capture the Bad News Bear and get the good news out to the public. Besides, those in the know suspected that the park wardens quoted by the newspaper were not the gun-toting grunts wading through the Whiskey Creek bogs but rather their supervisors, Andy Anderson and Peter Whyte.

Later that morning, Anderson and Whyte stood in the abattoir, staring down at what was left of the terror of Whiskey Creek. He smelled like old potato peels, ash tray, and dead dog coated with dish detergent and pine sap. He was a large boar and his muzzle and flanks were branded here and there with the white scars of many battles, inflicted by the claws of rival males during the mating season. He would soon be identified positively as a Banff park resident, B054.

It was a sad spectacle for all concerned. Bear 054 had been degraded by his contact with our waste, then laid low in the game preserve where he was supposed to be protected. Robbed of the vital force, his rigid carcass looked more like a taxidermy project than the bad news terror of Banff. His excised skull cap of fur and bone had been pressed hastily back into position; his brain had been put on ice.

Anderson was hoping that he had the mauler at last. Keith Everts had already come by early in his shift to view the bear. He had taken a long hard look, and he believed this was probably the one he had seen crossing the road on August 24. The size and dark colour seemed right. He measured the lengths of the dead bear's feet and its pad widths; later that morning, he reported that the tracks found re-entering the area on August 26 were a good match for B054's feet. All this was good news to Anderson, yet he was startled by the atypical features of this big male, who weighed in at 350 pounds, unusually large for a black bear on the east slope of the Rockies. His broad head, bushy-looking nape, and scarred, dished-in muzzle gave him the look of an immature male grizzly. Of course, his curved black bear claws gave him away, while his dirty-brown to black colour matched what Muskett and Everts had described.

"The bank manager [Bob Muskett] showed up," recalled Halle Flygare. "Talked to him. He didn't say it was a black bear; a black-*coloured* bear, he said. He said, 'Well, it had a bushy head.'" Those words immediately caught Flygare's attention. "'A bushy head?' I said." Flygare frowned at the description. "Had to be a grizzly," he'd suggested to Muskett. But it seems nobody acknowledged this remark, possibly because the bear in question had an atypical bushier look to the fur around the head than other black bear specimens. Muskett explained then, and maintains to this day, that he was focused mainly on the attacker's teeth, not its chest and the lower part of its body. Then there were the words Muskett had written down just after the attack to consider. "When I turned around and looked up, a large bear was standing on his two hind legs looking down at me. From that laying-down position, the bear looked very large and did not at all look like the usual black bear that is often seen in the townsite of Banff. The bear was very dark brown in colour and had no distinguishing marks on him. It looked much larger than the normal bear, but from laying down anything would likely look large." Those who saw B054 recall that he had a white chest patch, a small one but still indicative of the black bear species, a distinguishing mark, in other words, which Muskett had not seen. Why not? Because at that moment he was focused on the bear's head, and he was terrified. Also, the paws, held at chest height, might have hidden the patch from view. I have to assume, for lack of other information, that Muskett's not seeing the chest patch was explained away by the above factors, which the investigators were all aware of. Later on, Anderson's as well as other wardens' memories must have played a trick on them when they claimed Muskett mentioned the patch.

But the other unanswered question is, What else did Muskett not observe? In retrospect one has to wonder why Anderson and his team put so much import on Muskett's testimony. The man was a good witness, in that he stuck to the facts of what he had seen and refused to speculate further, but he was a bank manager after all, not a full-time outdoors man and not an expert on bears. Muskett may have looked cool and collected to the wardens, but he told me that he was traumatized for at least a month after the attack. Flygare recalls Muskett saying something like "It's lying dead on the floor there. When I was looking at it, I was the one lying down and it was standing up looking down at me."

As Muskett was looking at the carcass of B054, there came a noise overhead and the bear suddenly jerked into motion, as if risen from the dead. It slowly came to a sitting position, with one of the wardens holding the skull cap on as Muskett took a nervous step back. Now it rose, in a jerky pantomime a few inches at a time, coming slowly to its feet to the squeal of a steel pulley overhead, rising up toward the shadowy ceiling like a macabre puppet, as wardens hauled on the pulley chains attached to the bear by meathooks. The bear now hung, or stood weightlessly at full length, swaying gently on the chains.

The silence was broken by the sound of an argument at the abattoir entrance. Warden Tim Laboucane was blocking the door as several curious civilians demanded the right to come in and view the dead warrior. Laboucane told them that B054's corpse was not a tourist attraction and sent them packing. Muskett turned back and stared up at the bear, at its glassy eyes, at the pink tongue lolling out between its gleaming white teeth. The room was very quiet. According to Perry Jacobsen, Muskett then stated: "Boys, I think you got the right bear." (Superintendent Paul Lange recalls Muskett said something very similar at a meeting of the Rotary Club they both attended.) The bear swayed from his chain as if it, like the wardens, was hanging on Muskett's words echoing from the cold walls. They lowered the bear down to the concrete floor, hoping to trust in the welcome news. For a warden, getting some time off on the Labour Day weekend was usually just not in the cards, but with the mauler put to rest, and Anderson looking happier by the moment, anything seemed possible.

Anderson was relieved at Muskett's certainty. He left the office with two of his hunters and hiked into the scene of the Cohoe mauling to take one last look for any signs that might militate against the black bear being the attacker – or confirm it – but there was nothing else to be found; the ground had been thoroughly covered.

Anderson ordered the carcass and brain to be shipped to provincial laboratories for necropsy. The veterinarians would look for any signs of abnormality or disease process, which ranged from rabies to hidden wounds from a poacher's bullet to mundane conditions like abscessed teeth that might account for the bear's aggressiveness. Then the carcass, along with Cohoe's hip waders, would be sent on to the RCMP crime lab in Edmonton for further analysis to tie the bear to the actual victim.

Sending off the waders was an iffy decision. It was essential that B054's bite pattern match the marks on Cohoe's waders if he was truly the attacker. Yet the marks were not measured in Banff, before the waders were sent off, as far as anybody recalls now. Steve Herrero discussed the waders in a telephone call with the chief warden. "Sometime before September 2," Herrero wrote in an e-mail to me, "and, as I recall, after the black bear was killed . . . I remember mentioning to him that there would be little to no overlap between the canine spread measurements of adult male black and grizzly bears and suggesting that this [measuring] be done. Measurements for canine spread for both species were well known from museum collections. I never saw the waders, nor did I make any measurements at the hospital."

Perry Jacobsen has offered this explanation to me by e-mail: "I do recall a group of us wardens, plus Herrero, examined the waders before we sent them to the lab, and everyone agreed that because of the stretch of the rubber it was difficult to measure the bite marks without the help of forensic assistance." (Herrero participated by telephone at this discussion.)

The measurement decision might not have been crucial if the area had been kept closed while awaiting results from Edmonton. But at the meeting that followed the last search, several senior wardens were startled when Anderson announced that he wanted to open up the area to the public by noon that very day. He gave his reasons in detail in the *Whiskey Creek Report*:

> Based on composite descriptions given of the bear that was first spotted near the mauling site by various wardens, and the tracks made leaving the area, and again seen re-entering the area by the same route, there was a reasonable certainty the bear shot was the same bear. The squeals the bear made during the mauling were considered more in keeping with a black bear rather than a grizzly. The probability of a second large dark brown black bear without any chest markings,* and with a large grizzly type of head, being in or returning to the same area seemed unlikely. These factors, along with Muskett's description of the bear and his confirmation the bear that was shot was the same bear that attacked Cohoe and him, indicated that we had the right bear. On this basis, the Chief Park Warden ordered the closure signs removed. As other black bears had been seen in the area during the hunt, and the tracks or sign indicated bears were frequenting the area, warning signs were posted. The wardens will continue going over the area for any indications as to what caused the bear to attack.[34]

Some felt the decision was hasty and said so, but one had to be diplomatic in dealing with the chief warden. The speed and power of the attacking bear and the damage he had inflicted did not fit the profile of a black bear attack and that made the experienced hands very uneasy.

Perry Jacobsen later recalled: "I advised Andy not to do it [reopen the area]. I asked myself a question: 'Would I walk through there without a gun?' And I said no, I wouldn't. So I wasn't totally convinced, you know – and there were other bears in there as well."

---

* Here Anderson is in accord with Muskett on the lack of a white chest patch. However, Anderson told me (October 2003) that the bear had "a very faint white mark on his chest. It wasn't a prominent one."

Warden Rose reminded his supervisors of the grizzly bear tracks he had found in the swamp. Grizzly bears were obviously frequenting the area, despite the lack of grizzly bear tracks at the mauling site itself.

"We have the bear," said Peter Whyte at the time, dismissing those who wished to keep the area closed, according to Halle Flygare's memory of events. During our interview, Whyte confirmed that he supported Anderson's decision at the time and, based on what was known back then, still supports it. Assistant Chief Park Warden Paul Kutzer also backed his boss at the time.

"I was overruled," Monte Rose recalled when I interviewed him in Pincher Creek, Alberta. His voice held a sardonic edge that I remembered from days of yore. "I had trapped many bears over the years, looked into the eyes of a lot of black and grizzly bears, but our wise leaders knew much more than I."

Today, when Parks Canada gives such good phone on the theme that protecting the ecological integrity of the parks is its first priority, we look back at 1980 with 20/20 hindsight and shake our heads – "What were those guys thinking?" It is pleasant indeed to judge the past by the light of current knowledge. It allows us to forget, to give one example, that CP Hotels' multimillion-dollar convention centre, built on the shores of endangered Lake Louise and in grizzly bear habitat, was built during the current era of ecological integrity. Bragging about ecological integrity doesn't help the grizzly bears killed while feeding on the railroad tracks in Banff in recent years because the CPR can't plug the leaks in its grain cars. In 1980, one seldom heard of ecological integrity: what we heard was "Parks are for people." Of course they are, but the implication of this mantra was that people's needs for access trumped wildlife protection in Banff. The advocates of that idea also pushed for expansion of the park's three ski resorts and the opening up of park fire access roads to private vehicle travel and of the hiking trails to snowmobiles and dirt bikes. The political climate of the 1980s meant that any decision that denied access to the public was met with controversy, and the policy was to reopen such areas as quickly as possible. When politics messes with public safety, it is like mixing blasting caps with dynamite in a steel bucket and giving it a good shaking.

In this case, closed areas and the reason for the closure – a dangerous bear roaming the back alleys – was hurting park businesses on the last long weekend of the summer. Banff was basically a small town and nearly everyone was affected by decreases in tourism revenue, including park staff who might have family members either running a business or working in the industry. Anderson was well aware of the campers fleeing the park. Both Perry Jacobsen and Paul Kutzer believed their boss was under pressure, particularly from town business people and from at least one politician (whom Kutzer declined to name). Paul Kutzer told me, "We could always shut it off by saying, 'Well, we don't make the decisions.' But Andy couldn't do that. I know that I heard it said numerous times that 'these maulings aren't good for tourism' and this kind of stuff. There was some urgency to get this thing resolved. You got people with interests from different angles on this."

As for the park brass, Anderson told me that it was not really pressure from his superiors that influenced his decision. If anything, he said, they were more intent on backing away from the problem, happy to let him step into the breech. It was the fear and paranoia about bears in the town that he'd found most troubling. "The one thing I wanted to do," he said earnestly, "when we got the black bear and everything, was to not have the fear factor amongst the townspeople [anymore]." Anderson explained that he wanted his message to the public to be very definite that they had the right bear and that the problem was over and therefore the area could be safely reopened.

Perry Jacobsen knew Anderson well and says he was not the kind of guy to admit when he was under pressure. "There was so much pressure coming from the regional office, and even right from the Ottawa level 'cause the townspeople thought it was ruining all their tourist attractions," he recalls. Jacobsen believes the media coverage made some townies hysterical. "It got crazy in town. We got a call one day from a woman who was scared to leave the bus depot." The bus depot was in the centre of town.

"What the media played up," he recalls, "was our incompetence to be able to shoot a bear. That was their storyline more than anything else; that's where a lot of the pressure came from: that we were just incompetent." The media interest was so intense, with photographers anxious to get pictures of the dead bear that Kutzer decided to throw off the press by loading the carcass into the trunk of his private car and driving it to the lab at Airdrie, Alberta, dressed in his civvies. It was a hot day, and the ripening bear carcass soon developed a wicked pong as Kutzer idled his car in a traffic jam in Calgary, getting some alarmed looks from nearby drivers who frantically rolled their windows up. Arriving at the lab, Kutzer found the media waiting at the entrance, tipped off but expecting a government vehicle to arrive with the bear. He assured them he was only a humble turkey farmer with a trunkload of dead turkeys for the vet to analyze. One whiff of his car was enough to satisfy the reporters.

In Banff, the decision to reopen the area, effective immediately, was supported by Anderson's superiors, Superintendent Paul Lange and Operations Manager Tom Ross. Yet, as if hedging his bets right to the end, Anderson decided to replace the closure signs with bear warning signs, before reopening the area. These signs read "Bear in Area Travel with Caution." In 1983, Anderson would be asked to explain his decision as part of a legal action. He wrote, "Bears were frequenting the area primarily attracted by the garbage from the Caboose Restaurant. I considered it prudent to maintain bear warnings in the area until such time as we could persuade or force the clean up of the garbage."[35] If being prudent was his only aim, then keeping the area closed would have been the safer choice but, as I have suggested, prohibiting access was politically unpopular in 1980; it remains unpopular today in some circles.

There is an obvious irony here: one can argue that national parks by their very nature contain potential hazards. Gravity aligned with rock falls, loose footholds, avalanches, and waterfalls kills many more people in these mountains than are killed by bears. One of these victims, rescued by Tim Auger's crew on August 18, 1980, was

Montrealer Charles Goymour, who died a day later, at age 19, in a Calgary hospital. Even as I write this book, news comes of a Calgary couple who went for a walk in Kananaskis country, slipped on some wet rocks while crossing an avalanche gulley, and tumbled down the mountain to their deaths. Such tragedies are annual occurrences in the Rockies. The mountain parks are not theme parks, they are wilderness preserves. A physically fit and dedicated fool can get sprayed by a skunk, forked by a bull elk, beaned by a boulder, and swatted by a bear, all in one fun-filled day in Banff park.

Anderson left the office in a buoyant mood, and why not? The press had yet to skewer Parks Canada for its negligent handling of garbage in the park for decades, which was the reason for the ensuing tragedy. Instead, it had bought into the official position, that this was a case of a rogue bear, whose motives for the attack were "completely unexplainable"; as Anderson put it to the *Edmonton Journal*: "The answer lies in the bear itself." Now this inscrutable and definitely ungrateful brute, fed from our own tables in a manner of speaking, would be sent to the lab so specialists could dissect and explain the mystery.

The chief warden was relieved to have the sad affair over with. He had successfully managed a major hunt for this dangerous predator, involving both wardens and police, many of whom were inexperienced in such a business and had never worked together on such a large scale before. His men had worked hard in hazardous conditions, the quarry had been clever and elusive, and the papers had been full of criticism, either direct or implied, about the competence of his people. Nevertheless, in a matter of 96 hours since the mauling of Ernest Cohoe, the bear had been destroyed and the area was, at least in essence, open again to the public. The birdwatchers and the colour photographers, the hikers and the fishermen, were free to come and roam. If parks are for people, well, this park was open to the people; the problem had been solved and he had the support of his supervisors in a job well done.

As the word spread via the media that day, people hurried home from work to pack their RVs for the Labour Day weekend. By Friday morning, the cash registers in Banff would resume playing the merchants' favourite tune as the good news spread far and wide: the Bad News Bear was dead.

In the forest, the black grizzly was not content to bide his time, waiting for the influx of humans in the wetlands to end. If he had been given to wishing, he would have wished to be left alone. As if looking for a sign that the season of usurpers might be over and the season of solitude and white silences was at hand, that welcome time of dreams and oblivion, the great bear stalked out of the forest on the night of August 26, the same night, according to the *Whiskey Creek Report*, that B054 returned from his meandering.

Tracks found later indicated the black grizzly forded the Bow River west of town and headed south. No one knows how far he roamed south or westward. Wandering is an adaptation for survival in this species, particularly among males, who require on average 542 square miles of country to survive in this semi-arid habitat of rock and forest. Hunger was the prod that could push him beyond the known limits of his range, looking for the red buffalo berries that were scant that year north of the Bow River. The need for calories, the need to find enough of them to store as fat, had kept him in the wetlands but, when not sated, it had driven him finally out and across the river. Soon it would draw him back to that man-haunted place for another attempt upon the cowfish prize; it was in his memory, its coordinates of scent, colour, and sound are locked in his brain.

A network of well-used trails may have led the black grizzly between the arms of two mountain ranges to the high country along the Great Divide, on the edge of Assiniboine Provincial Park in British Columbia. There were fewer people to hem a bear in if he wandered up Brewster Creek to Allenby or Fatigue Pass, feeding on whatever berries he could find in the meadows along the way, keeping clear of the trail used by hikers and outfitters (for this bear was a dodger when not a stalker). Perhaps he circled around through the Valley of the Rocks or looped back over Citadel Pass and made his way down the seldom-travelled Howard Douglas Creek. It's likely he sought out the high, moist avalanche slopes where the vegetation was thick. Here altitude retarded the season, snow melt was delayed, and plants that had already dried out in the valley still held some succulent stems. So his route likely became a subalpine traverse, feeding on grouse berries, which were ripening then until, frustrated by their tiny size and scarcity, he climbed higher to dig up the corms of hedysarum or the bulbs of the avalanche lily in some drier patch where the earth was as much shale as dirt. Then he angled upward again, side-hill-gouging on steep slopes with the taste of starch and dirt in his mouth, never seeming to run, moving in a kind of rambling shuffle unfazed by height or, in the gullies, by the shintangle of fallen trees and thick slide alder. His ambling gait ate up the miles and he crossed the sky-lined ridges where nobody was there to witness his silhouette as he went on over the mountain to see what he could see. And the other side of the mountain was all that he wanted to see, turning his course again northward, until he found himself sitting on one last ridge line, his rump on a pile of frost-riven limestone, his great front legs and paws lying in his furred lap.

Idle and at rest, Our Brother-Across-the-River sat gazing down at the blue thread of familiar water, blinking in the mountain sun. If you had seen him sitting there, as I have seen others of his kind, you might have concluded that he was simply admiring the scenery that swept away from his rocky seat to the toothed ridges of the Sawback Range across the Bow River Valley. The heat of the day soon made him sleepy. He rocked backwards and rubbed his back vigorously on the rough edges of rock. He rolled over onto his feet, backed into the rocks, and gave his behind a good scratching, swaying back and forth, sending some loose rocks clattering down the steep slope, his mouth agape at the pleasure of relief. With his circulation thus stimulated, he went rollicking down into the forest seeking a place to rest. There he raked together a bed of conifer needles and twigs and lay down with his head on his forepaws to wait inspiration from the up-slope breeze and the setting sun.

THIRTEEN

COUNTING COUP
LIKE A STONE MONUMENT

Take time to connect with nature here. Let its patterns, its
rhythms and its life forces inspire you . . . Take a moment to reflect
on the memories you will take away with you.

PARKS CANADA
"Self-Guiding Brochure for Fenland Trail" (2006)

THE HUNT FOR THE Whiskey Creek mauler was over, the armed
sentries and flashing police lights were gone from the roadside and the
railroad right-of-way. A tenuous calm visited the beaver ponds and
forests of the wetlands, as if the creatures there had been shocked
into silence not by the scale of human intrusion, but by its sudden
withdrawal.

As the town moved into holiday mode, the wide-eyed days of fear
began quickly to recede from popular memory. The cool weather put
the thought of autumn in the air, autumn and the coming winter,
when the bears would be sleeping under the snow, and Parks Canada
mandarins would sink blissfully into their annual amnesia on the
subject of bears. But the warning signs posted around the wetlands
were rude reminders that the bear season was not quite over. Later
in September, the comings and goings of a large grizzly bear would
be conned from its signatures printed in the muddy banks of the

Bow River, but for now, no patrols were being maintained at that site.

The bear control teams had no time to celebrate the end of the hunt: they just shifted their focus from Whiskey Creek to the so-called "bear problems" (meaning human food-management failures) elsewhere in the park. In the busy season, resource management was really crisis management. The warden's life was basically one damn thing after another. He might be hanging from a helicopter in the morning and chasing elk off the golf course or fighting a runaway campfire in the afternoon. There were also hours of stupefying boredom spent report writing. Thankfully, we tend to forget about those hours as life goes on.

On August 30, when things should have been settling down after the death of the Whiskey Creek mauler, there was a flurry of excitement involving a "tan/grey-coloured" grizzly bear "with large hump" that was intent on raiding the garbage bins at the Rimrock Hotel. Unable to gain entry, he moved up the mountain toward the Upper Hot Springs swimming pool, to vacuum the picnic tables situated there. En route he was entertained by some tourists who stopped their car and rushed out to take his picture. Feeling playful, he turned around and chased them back into their vehicle. By 5 p.m., he was back at the Rimrock, where Constable John Evans of the RCMP spotted the bear and was startled to see a young man following it around, on foot. "The man said he was from Switzerland," states the *Whiskey Creek Report*; he was otherwise unidentified. The Mountie gave him a lecture about the dangers of harassing bears and let him go. Meanwhile, Warden Earle Skjonsberg hitched his patrol truck to a rusty old culvert trap and hauled it up to the Rimrock, banging and clattering every foot of the way.

The grizzly retired to the woods to digest his stolen picnic lunch but came in again at 10:30 p.m. to look for dessert. Unimpressed by the bait Skjonsberg had provided, he took out his frustrations on the trap, bending the plate-steel door so that it malfunctioned. The wardens repaired it later that night, using a sledgehammer and pry bar. The bear was a subadult and was probably wandering around in confusion, trying to establish a home range and figure out how jam sandwiches and Colonel Sanders – he of the jolly KFC bucket – fitted into his survival needs. They found some better bait, and the bear obliged by trapping himself the next day. He was flown out to the north end of the park and released, and did not return – at least not that season. Perhaps they dropped him in the middle of a buffalo berry patch; perhaps he wandered beyond the park boundaries, and wound up as a bearskin rug in some hunter's rumpus room.

With the Bad News Bear destroyed, Warden David Cardinal, acting as Crown prosecutor for the service, busied himself drawing up some long overdue charges against a number of restaurants, including the Caboose, for improper storage of garbage. One of the managers he talked to was at the Clocktower Mall in downtown Banff. According to CBC Television's "Calgary News Hour," that gentleman told Cardinal to "stick his ticket where the sun didn't shine."[36] In the wetlands meanwhile, hopeful yokels wandered about on the edge of the area as if they were visiting an action-flick set, eager to glimpse a martial arts celebrity. From the window of the RCMP building, which then abutted the forest, secretary Geri Friesen watched in disbelief as people ventured past the warning signs, thrilled by the menace they promised. When challenged, they said they only wanted a picture of the bear. The Mounties Friesen worked with would not even let her walk to her car without an escort, because of the bear scare. Other tourists settled for ripping down the signs as souvenirs. The duty wardens diverted themselves, as time permitted, chasing down the offenders and nailing the signs back up.

Remy Tobler, from Switzerland, and his countryman Andreas Leuthold, of Banff, were not concerned about warning signs when they left Leuthold's home at Number 6 Whiskey Creek Condominiums and crossed the tracks into the Whiskey Creek wetlands on August 31. In fact, Tobler, age 29, would later assert, in court, that he never saw any warning signs. Leuthold, age 25, had moved to Banff a year earlier and was employed as a mechanic at the Husky service station near his condo. Tobler was a machine parts designer by trade but was then working as a delivery man in Zurich. He was on a holiday tour of North America and had come to Banff to see the sights and visit his old friend.

I travelled to Carlsbad, California on a sunny February day in 2007 to interview Andreas Leuthold. Sporting a brush cut of thick brown hair, Leuthold is now 52 but looks younger. He is a suntanned six-footer with the physique of a pro tennis player. As we talked, I learned that the two Switzers were boyhood friends in their native country. Both enjoyed the outdoors, but "we were not outdoors men as that term is used in Canada. I was not into backpacking for five days at a time, in the mountains." Young Tobler was a skier and also liked to race stock cars. He didn't know it at the time, but his racing days would soon be over.

Leuthold recalled the summer of 1980 as a happy time. The sister of his then fiancée was also visiting, so they made a cheerful young foursome and were out almost every evening walking the local trails, cycling, or sightseeing.

It was one week to the day after the Cohoe mauling. The two men had followed news reports of the attack, the hunt for the bear, and the eventual reopening of the area. As far as they were concerned, the threat had been removed and the area was now safe again. "Remy wanted to see the beavers," Leuthold remembered with a chuckle. It seems Tobler was fascinated by the dam-building skills of the little beasts and the way they slapped their tails on the water to warn each other of danger. He wanted to get some pictures to take home. "You don't see that in Switzerland," Leuthold explained to me.

Leuthold knew that Whiskey Creek was one of the best spots to view beavers in action. He had been there a few times for a walk. Leuthold's memory was vague on the subject of seeing warning signs posted. "There was some kind of sign there," he conceded but he emphasized that the "Closed" signs had been removed; the area was open.

He found a game trail near the railroad Y and the two men followed it into the bush until they came to the first large beaver pond. It was a coolish day, but the waters of the pond were still. The cold air held the edge of coming winter in its breath: there would be frost that night. The beaver kept out of sight, though the dam showed their webbed footprints in muddy sections. Perhaps all the human activity in the wetlands had made them more retiring than usual. It was disappointing, but the two friends had a bright idea. "We kind of damaged the dam a bit," Leuthold admitted. "We let quite a bit of water out of it. It was hard to pull it apart, however."

I have often used old beaver dams as natural bridges while hiking in the bush. Once built, they last almost indefinitely and are visible for decades after their impoundments have dried up. (Of course it is illegal to tamper with these or any other natural objects in the parks.) "We wanted to see how quickly they would repair it," explained Leuthold. Beavers are sensitive to changes in water depth because they need to keep their lodge entrance submerged to ward off predators, such as wolverines — or bears. In this case, the beavers were too coy to play the game. It turned out that repairs would be made by the night shift.

Though wet and muddy, the two friends headed home for supper in good spirits. Gabriella Schmitt, Leuthold's fiancée, was startled to see them arrive home splattered with mud and water. "*Warum seit ihr so nass?*" (Why are you so wet?), she greeted Remy. Remy saw a chance to pull Gaby's leg. Feigning fright, he exclaimed, "*Ein Bär haf uns verfolgt!*" (A bear chased us!) The men were delighted by Schmitt's shocked reaction.

Indeed, Andreas Leuthold was not overly concerned about the danger of bears that summer, despite the recent attack. According to Tobler, the two had never discussed the bear situation in Banff, strange as it seems. "I don't think I had ever seen a grizzly bear before," Leuthold confided, but he had seen "a dozen bears that summer, some close up." He had witnessed a mother black bear calling her cubs down from a tree while people were moving in for pictures:

she showed no aggression to the humans. He had seen people feeding black bears on the highway without any problem. Once he had looked up and found a black bear staring through his patio doors. None of the bears had ever posed a threat.

I asked Leuthold about his own attitude to bears – did he take them seriously? I asked him about a run-in with Assistant Chief Warden Paul Kutzer that summer, referred to in the *Whiskey Creek Report*. "There's more to that story than what they said," Leuthold responded, then gave this explanation of what happened that day. "In Whiskey Creek where I lived, there were a lot of young families and the kids played all over the place. Near my place was this big garbage dumpster bin. There was a kid playing a few feet away from it. I looked out and saw a bear walk right past the kid and climb up on top of this bin. Then it reached its claws under the lid and flipped it open, and jumped down inside it. Everybody came running to see the bear. The bear jumped down and started coming between our house and the next building. He passed quite close to me and did not seem upset. I followed him just between the buildings, I was there with my camera, between the buildings, and the bear was about 35 feet away. That's when the warden and a Mountie arrived. The warden [Paul Kutzer] came over and said, 'This is really stupid what you are doing.'"

Kutzer's comment riled Leuthold for a couple of reasons. For one thing, he was not impressed with the local *gendarmes*. A neighbour that summer, witnessing a thief ripping off Gabriella's bicycle, had phoned the police, but they were three hours late in arriving. "I was kind of insulted by [Kutzer's] remark," said Leuthold. "I said, 'Why weren't you here before when there were two or three kids playing near the bin and that bear was right with the kids?'" Leuthold chuckled and shook his head. "The cop was with the warden, and I think I said something like 'And where were you when our bike was stolen?' or something like that. So they said I was arrogant."

Paul Kutzer also later reported that Leuthold stated, "Bears don't hurt people." Leuthold's experience with bears, based on one year's residency in Banff, had convinced him that these creatures were not a threat. Leuthold was wrong, but his was an attitude shared by some long-term residents of Banff: it was circular logic, relying on their limited experience with garbage-habituated bears in an artificial urban setting.

The bear Leuthold described may have been black bear 953, which, as it happened, met its end the very next day. Though this male black bear tolerated kids playing near his food source and put up with Leuthold following him, he could not tolerate "a mob of 100 people," according to the park's 1980 Bear Summary, who cornered him near the Sundance Mall in downtown Banff on July 5. First he took refuge by climbing a tree. But he was a big bear, and fat. After a while he got tired of clinging to the tree and came down, sending a few broken branches down ahead of him. When he hit the ground, his ears were back and his muscles rolled and rippled under the fur. He suddenly charged out at the people who had crowded him in, scattering them amid shrieks and shouts of fear. Perhaps they had cut off his escape route, which would have frightened him. He was subsequently captured and put down by the bear control team, who described him as a "large aggressive male." As I have said before, concern for public safety predisposed the warden service, over time, to select for more docile bears in Banff National Park.

Alberta's seventy-fifth birthday was another cool day. The smell of fall, the pungent scent of damp aspen leaves was in the air. In Banff, Remy Tobler felt the chill and went shopping for a warm "Canadian jacket," by which he meant a down vest. Later that afternoon, Tobler and Leuthold decided to hike back into the beaver pond, hoping to view the inhabitants at work repairing the damage done the previous day. Tobler's only experience with bears at that point was in seeing one from the safety of Leuthold's car earlier that summer. He never saw a copy of the Parks Canada pamphlet entitled "You Are in Bear Country," co-authored by Andy Anderson.[37] (Tobler travelled to Banff in Leuthold's car and as a resident, Leuthold did not have to stop at the east gate when he entered the park, so no pamphlet was issued to his party.*) But the young Swiss did learn a few relevant facts about avoiding a bear attack from the papers, which were full of advice that summer. He later testified that he knew "if you ran into a bear or confront a bear, you shouldn't run away, and if you have enough time that you should climb a tree, and that one should kind of slowly retreat, not running, but slowly retreat and maybe talk or something. And that one should also lie down and play dead." What Tobler knew turned out to be just barely enough to save his life. Had he read the bear pamphlet, he would have learned a good deal more, such as "All bears are potentially dangerous," which was the opposite of what his friend Leuthold believed in 1980. The pamphlet warned readers to stay out of thick bush where there are food sources, to carry a noisemaker, to be aware of wind direction – all calculated to avoid surprising a bear at close range, thus triggering an attack. The pamphlet gave more detail on what to do when confronted by a bear, including how to "play dead," face down, hands clasped over the neck, knees drawn up to the chest. It is possible that if Tobler had read the information and acted upon it that he might have escaped serious injury on September 1. But no one really knows with certainty exactly what he will do when attacked by a large predator, no matter how well informed or experienced he is. Too many variables come into play.**

Tobler and Leuthold left the house about 6 p.m. and hiked down the path that led to the ponds, about 300 yards into the wetlands. Tobler, dressed in blue jeans and sneakers, was wearing his new down vest over a sweater for the chill of evening. They came to the pond but it held no beavers, only a reflection of trees and mountains. They were intrigued to see how the industrious beasts had worked hard to plug the breach in their dam overnight with a welter of sticks, mud, and the occasional stone pried out of the bottom mud. The beavers were keeping out of sight.

---

* The gate by-pass lane was still in effect in 2007.

** For advice on dealing with bear attacks, see endnote references for Stephen Herrero and James Gary Shelton.

"There was a wildlife trail there," recalled Leuthold, "and we decided to follow it. I used to love walking in the woods back in Switzerland. So we walked along but we had to go single file. We went through stands of pine, and then through thick bush in other places." Their general direction was toward the Banff Recreation Centre, which sits on the Norquay Road. About 45 minutes after they entered the wetlands, they came to a small clearing in the forest. The spot where Cohoe was attacked was 150 yards northeast. A clearing is always a welcome interval in thick bush, a place to stand upright with no branches in the way, with only the sky overhead. The two men were just five or six yards apart as they moved into the open. Leuthold took a look around at the trees and the mountains, thinking it might be a good idea to be able to recognize landmarks when it was time later to find their way back to the railroad.

Daytime dodges through shadowy forest edges and night moves by starlight bring Sticky Mouth back into the wetlands, his fur soaked from river wading and bog-busting. He finds the underlings more numerous now, bedding in the forest but closer to the great cowfish kill, far too bold with the cold nights firing their resolve to feed. His inclination is to ignore them. He is the lord bear and they are mere impersonators. Men are moving at times around the kill, or standing on the serpent's trail of wood and metal that passes by it. He watches from the forest edge, then he stalks deeper into the bush to rest and wait for them to go away. But another disturbance soon catches his attention, two husky dogs decide to make nuisances of themselves. See them rousing Sticky Mouth out of a pleasant nap on his day bed with a sudden volley of hysterical barking that puts his hair up instantly. See him coming out of the shadows, the gleam of one eye growing eerily closer in a tunnel of willows like the glint of a bullet leaving a gun barrel, branches popping at his shoulders like firecrackers in July, coming as fast as a grizzly bear can move, which is fast enough to catch a horse in the first hundred yards. See the dogs, astounded at the monstrous bulk they have rousted from cover, bending every inch of sinew in their bodies to get clear of his furious, relentless charge. And see them flee, thrilled and grinning, across the bog and back into town.

Sticky Mouth's blood is up now. He will turn back to sort out the underlings next. Grim with purpose, he pursues them on every fresh trail he finds, treeing them, or if they won't tree, sending them flying to the outer edges of the wetlands, away from the central attraction.

The siding is deserted when he comes in to feed at last, and he eats his fill of prime rib scraps. He snaps up piles of crab legs, crunching them down in a slurry of melted butter, so they stick out of his mouth like pink antennae, the mallets of his jaws whack bones and shells open. Food is his religion and eating is his way to worship. So he guzzles and gorges, then before the dawn, he drags his heavy belly back into the woods, 600 yards northeast of the Caboose and downwind. He will sleep most of the day until it is safe to go back for more gut-stuffing. He is too full to bother scratching together anything recognizable as a bear-bed. He lies down with his nose into the wind.

Tobler was in the lead now as the pair left the small clearing and pushed on, heading northwest into a thick forest of shrubs and conifers, some 500 yards from their starting point. The humans were between the bear and his jealously guarded food cache. It might seem to the bear that they had come to steal his grub, but the grub pile was some distance to the southwest. More important is the critical distance a dominant male demands for himself, his space, and it varies from one bear to the next. This male had been constantly disturbed by the coming and going of people, by dogs, and also by the white noise of town and highway traffic. And the black bears stealing "his" grub probably kept him in a jealous mood. Tobler stepped across that invisible line, treading, metaphorically speaking, on the black grizzly's shadow.

"Suddenly, we hear this noise – something big was coming, it was crashing through the bush. We kind of stopped and looked at each other. I didn't know what it was, but whatever it was, I knew it was attacking," Leuthold recalled.

An approaching wave of energy flattened the willow bush; a dark vortex expanded from its centre. The two men turned around to run. Leuthold remembers Tobler running toward a tree and assumed he would try to climb it. Tobler remembers no tree. In 1983, at a discovery hearing for the lawsuit he launched against Parks Canada he told the court, "I was totally blocked off to get anywhere. I think I said, 'Something is coming, or what's there?' I can't quite remember. And about three seconds later that bear came from the right-hand side out of the bush." The bear was only 15 feet away when Tobler caught sight of it. "Mr. Leuthold ran away," Tobler testified, "and the bear chased him."[38]

Tangled willow roots snared the younger man's feet and had him staggering, trying to keep his balance, trying to make some headway. Leuthold sensed the beast was right on his heels. By this point he assumed it was probably a bear though he had not actually seen it. When he later testified, Tobler recalled urging Leuthold to lie down. He said, "Myself, I was totally paralyzed . . . I think I stood there like a stone monument."[39]

Leuthold dropped to the ground. The bear was over him in seconds and he froze, terrified of what would happen next, and played dead. "I felt a sharp pain in my left shoulder. That's where it bit me." The bear's canines went in deep, but fortunately did not break any bones. "I also was clawed across my back below the shoulder blade, two claws went quite deeply in the fleshy area, with their scratches getting shallower on the spine."

At our interview, Leuthold told me, "I remember hearing heavy breathing. By then I knew it was a bear, but I didn't look at it. The bear's mouth must have been right by my head, then I kind of felt it moving away." Time was suspended. Leuthold couldn't recall whether the attack lasted for 30 seconds or for minutes. But he had, perhaps inadvertently, done the right thing, which was to drop to the ground and curl up, face down, protecting the vital organs, and hope the bear would not press the attack.

At the discovery hearing Tobler said, "What I really can't

remember at all is how the bear got from Mr. Leuthold back to me. I just felt that he bit me in the head, that's the first thing I felt." He recalled the bear coming at his face with its jaws open. "I fell down and the next I noticed was that he bit me in the leg. I think I wanted to protect myself so I think I turned around to my stomach. I'm not quite sure if he was sitting right on top of me, but I heard quite close breathing and grunting."[40]

Tobler remained conscious, trying not to move. As for the bear, "I only saw . . . it was big and dark, nothing else."[41] As the noises made by the bear faded away, Tobler realized the creature had left as inexplicably as it had arrived.

"Then I heard more noises," testified Leuthold, "but this time coming from Remy." Not sure of what he was hearing, he remained motionless, listening. "I lifted my head, very slowly," Leuthold told me: "I couldn't see anything. So I stood up, very slowly and looked around for the bear. Then I found Remy, about 15 or 20 metres away, lying face down. I went over there, still watching for the bear. 'Remy,' I said in a hoarse whisper, 'are you okay, are you all right?' He said, 'No. No I'm not.' His voice sounded strange, that was because of the injuries. So I turned him over and his eye was out, it was hanging on his cheek."

Leuthold gasped at the shocking sight. It was hard to estimate all of Tobler's injuries; blood covered his mangled face and scalp. Tobler had been bitten on the legs and groin and was unable to stand up, let alone walk. Leuthold knew that he had to get help immediately if Tobler's eye was to be saved. He stared into the woods, listening intently for any sign of the bear's return. He tried to reassure his friend as best he could, then headed for town at a run.

Eventually, he came crashing out of the wetlands to the tracks, where a moving freight train blocked his path. Desperate, he wondered if he should jump aboard and slip between the cars to reach the other side. It was a dangerous idea: suppose he had an accident; nobody would know about Remy lying back in the woods. Then he remembered the big culverts where Whiskey Creek flowed under the railroad. He sprinted down the tracks to the creek bed, then, moving at a crouch, he splashed through an echoing cement tunnel to the other side. He charged through a belt of forest and came out behind some condominiums. Panting for breath, he raced to the first house he saw and pounded on the door. His jacket was ripped and blood stained, his clothes were wet, and his eyes were wild. An elderly lady answered the door but recoiled in fright at his crazed swamp-man appearance. "She panicked even more than I did," recalled Leuthold. "'My friend and I were mauled by a bear,' I told her. 'Please call the wardens, we need help!' She went, 'Oh my God, my God! I don't know what to do!' and closed the door in my face. She was terrified. I went to another place, it was a young family, the Keller family. The wife came to the door and she had it all together. It didn't take long before someone showed up."

The RCMP called the warden service dispatcher at 6:40 p.m. and reported the new attack and requested assistance. The phone rang not long after at Chief Warden Anderson's modest government bungalow on Elk Street. Anderson's first reaction was "Oh no, not again" as he listened to the dispatcher's voice. But at least this time it was not a fatality. (The sound of that phone was to become annoyingly frequent in the days ahead as word spread among the media of another bear attack.) "Get hold of Peter Whyte and Paul Kutzer," he told the warden dispatcher. "Tell them to meet me at the office. And get started calling the guys out, everyone you can find. I'm on my way." Anderson grabbed his Biltmore hat and car keys, bid his wife, Barbara, a hasty adieu, and headed for the operations room, determined to get a handle on events as quickly as possible. He knew that the next call would probably be from the park superintendent – or the CBC.

Wardens Dave Cardinal and Halle Flygare were patrolling Area 1 when the call came in. Cardinal immediately flipped on his police lights and siren and hit the gas pedal as he headed for the Whiskey Creek subdivision, not knowing what he was up against. A CPR freight train was on the tracks. Cardinal saw a man with ripped clothes in animated conversation with a police officer. He jumped out

of the truck, turned, and yanked his .308 carbine out from behind the
seat. He saw the two enter the culvert of Whiskey Creek. Flygare
jumped out, packing his personal 7 mm hunting rifle and took off
running to catch up. They charged through the tunnel shouting for
the Mountie to stop. A brief confab took place beside the moving
freight train, over the squeal of brakes. "We have to wait for the train
to pass," shouted one of the officers. "Let the paramedics catch up."

"No, no!" cried Leuthold, thinking of his friend lying in the
swamp, terrified and bleeding. "We have to go right now. I know the
way, let's go!" Cardinal decided they could guide the ambulance party
and other armed wardens in by portable radio, with one man hanging
back to act as a guide. But Leuthold was not waiting. "You've got to
stay behind me," insisted Cardinal as they started down the path. "If
the bear comes at us, I won't be able to shoot with you in front."

"Okay, okay," said Leuthold. "Let's get moving." The ambulance
and more armed wardens pulled up across the track as the party
headed into the bush.

Remy Tobler lay prone on the boggy ground of the wetlands,
holding his wounded face in his hands, terrified at the damage to his
eye and the pain of his other wounds, unable to get up and deeply
afraid that the bear was going to return any second and attack him
again. He told Leuthold afterwards that this 20-minute interval of
agony in Whiskey Creek, during which he prayed for rescue, was the
most horrible time of his entire life.

Sticky Mouth is not far away from the injured man. His retreat
from the scene is only temporary. He stands well back in the
willows, listens for sounds or movement that present a further
threat. His encounter with the Twolegs had confused and unnerved
the black grizzly. Their blood tastes of hazard. He pictures a toad-
stool, recalls the tar flavour of the Meatmaker under the entrails of
its kills. Once a Twolegs falls down and "dies," he feels no urge to
press the attack home. What makes him retreat he does not know;
he just feels safer when he retreats. He remembers their eyes, their

strange light. Stop it. When they stare at him and there is no place to go. Stop it. Attack.

He listens intently to the sounds made by the two left lying in the bush. One is moving, fading away; one groans in a bearlike way that makes his hackles rise. It is not moving much, it is not threatening much. Sticky Mouth lies down on his stomach with his great chin resting on his paws and his round ears tipped up. Under the branches of the trees he sees farther into the bush. He sees things like tree trunks moving among tree trunks. He listens hard, he reads the wind.

The moaning noise is like a lullaby to Sticky Mouth. Now the noise stops, the creature is still. The bear's heart slows to normal, the adrenaline washes clear of his nerve ends. Now his eyes droop, droop and close, for he is still digesting a massive bolus of fat and flesh. But after a while his nose twitches, and his eyes suddenly open wide, gleaming like fireflies in the gloaming. He smells their weapons before he hears them coming, and staring into the bush he sees the thin green tree trunks walking toward him, the upper parts of them hidden by leaves and branches. Some come from the sun-up side, some from the sun-down side. Were he able to wonder about any motive, other than hunger, he might have wondered why they would not leave him be.

Leuthold remembers that he kept wanting to get by Cardinal, impatient at trying to lead from the rear. The warden ordered him to stay back. "We came to an opening at last. The warden wanted to go a certain way where he thought Remy would be. But I recognized the landmarks and said, 'No no, it's over this way.' It was a good thing I had taken a look around before I left. We heard Remy moaning then. He could not talk anymore because he was swelling up from the injuries." Leuthold charged through the bush into the tiny clearing where Tobler lay, shouting for the others to follow. "He was mumbling something but I couldn't make it out," he recalls. In a few more minutes, the paramedics arrived with several armed wardens who spread out to guard them while they worked. Leuthold reassured the injured man in his native tongue, translating for the paramedics.

They were worried about moving Tobler over such rough terrain. The meter was running to save his eye; it had to be reimplanted as quickly as humanly possible and the light was rapidly fading, which could slow them down even more.

The helicopter offered the best chance for removing Tobler quickly. Cardinal checked with dispatch at 7:10 p.m.: yes, the helicopter pilot was at hand and wardens Kunelius and Vroom were already suiting up in the flight-rescuer harness. Tobler would be in good hands: by 1980 all mountain wardens were qualified emergency medical technicians. Cardinal turned to the paramedics as they worked on Tobler. It was their call on how Tobler was to be extracted. "We can sling him out to the hospital a lot faster and smoother than packing him out," said Cardinal.

The paramedics agreed. In the distance, they heard the reassuring sound of the Jet Ranger's turbine revving up. They would concentrate on stabilizing Tobler in the meantime. Leuthold himself was feeling a good deal of pain by that point, but felt he could walk out of the swamp. Stiff from his injuries, he bent down to talk to his friend. "I told Remy 'I'm going to leave now. The bear won't come back. There are lots of people here, trained to help you and I'm just in the way now.'"

Leuthold left with an armed escort. As they made their way through the bush, Leuthold, still deeply shocked by the experience, kept saying, "I don't understand why it attacked us. I just don't understand it." Nothing anybody said consoled him. Bill Vroom later questioned Leuthold on the details of the attack. All Leuthold could tell him, based on the brief glimpse he had before he fell, was that it was "a large black-coloured bear."

"People said, 'You were stupid to go back there,'" Leuthold recalled on that warm California day when we met over coffee, his voice revealing an edge of irritation. "But I thought it should be safer than ever. How can it be stupid? They shot the bear and opened the area up again. So to me it should be safer than ever."

Back behind the barrier of trees and willows, Sticky Mouth rises from his stomach, unseen as the rescuers descend on the fallen man. He stretches his limbs, doglike, as if not at all concerned about what is happening in the clearing. But the great piston of his heart speeds up slightly and his senses bristle from brisket to backbone. He gives a low, gurgling rumble of warning. He listens a bit longer, turns his head, stares up at the sky. The giant insect thing is approaching again. Suddenly it comes into sight for a few seconds above the treetops. He can see it has captured two Twolegs this time, which hang under its shiny belly. It is coming closer, the noise rides over everything. Will it pounce on the one he had left in the clearing? He feels no sense of jealous loss.

The rescue party heard the Jet Ranger approaching their position and watched it come into sight, as a warden hailed it on his belt radio.

"Helicopter, six-two."

"Go ahead," pilot Geoff Palmer replied.

"Swing left to about 11 o'clock and we're about two hundred metres west, copy?"

"Roger that – okay, I've got you."

"Copy. Six-two clear."

Palmer, checking the site and the approaches for hazards such as transmission lines and tall trees, did a circuit above them. Kunelius and Vroom, secured in their webbed rescue harnesses, were suspended 60 feet below the machine on the nylon rescue rope. They looked as small and bright as a pair of flags in their orange rescue anoraks, trailing out a bit behind the machine on the end of the rope and facing backwards for stability. Kunelius's crazy grin was visible under his shiny plastic helmet as they rode the slipstream. A minute later Palmer turned and came in on final approach to their position. He slowed to a hover, lowering the machine so the two could sit down, guided by Kunelius via portable radio. (Due to the terrific engine noise and rotor chop, the radio microphones were in the warden's helmet liner and actually picked up his voice through contact with the top of his head.) They touched down and unclipped their harnesses from the rope. The waiting medics shielded their eyes and crouched under the onslaught of rotor wash. The Jet Ranger rose, turbine roaring, trailing the weighted sling rope, and turned away to fly circuit until they had secured Tobler in the folding helicopter rescue stretcher. Once loaded, the stretcher's straps would be clipped into the main rescue rope so that it would be suspended in front of Kunelius at waist height. This would allow him to monitor Tobler's breathing during the flight, a vital necessity in any first aid situation. Meanwhile, Vroom would stay at the mauling site, gathering evidence.

Tobler was conscious. He could hear the rescuers talking, but although he knew a few English words, his injured jaw and mouth made it impossible to speak. They wrapped his head with gauze bandages to cover his lacerations and to protect his eyes. And then he heard the thrumming of the helicopter rotors as if at the far end of a tunnel. He felt the down-wash wind and he was suddenly weightless, flying.

From Kunelius's vantage point beside the stretcher, it looked as if the bear's canines had plunged in like giant pincers below Tobler's right eye and through the lower jaw. But the bear had then released the victim without tearing his flesh away, as had happened to Cohoe. Fortunately the flight would be very short. In a few minutes Remy Tobler would be landed at Mineral Springs Hospital and rushed into the emergency ward. The next thing he would see would be the doctor's face looking down at him, the first of many doctors' and nurses' faces that he would be looking up at in the coming months.

Sticky Mouth will not leave the wetlands now until it is time to go to his den. He has found nothing in the surrounding mountains to equal the cache of fatty flesh and sugar heaped up here. Now he will fight to keep it, he will fight anything that comes near it. Like the shadow of a cloud that flows across a mountain and is lost under the wing of a canyon, he fades into the bush.

FOURTEEN

THE TRACK

That we do not know you
is your perfection
and our hope. The darkness
keeps us near you.

WENDELL BERRY
from his poem "To the Unseeable Animal"

THE EVENING OF SEPTEMBER 1, two hunting teams probed the wetlands looking for bear sign and also for illegal campers, but they found no fresh evidence of either. One team, led by Earle Skjonsberg, reported hearing something moving through the bush, but was unable to catch up to it in the failing light. Skjonsberg believed the bear had circled away and wound up behind them before slipping away. Peter Whyte ordered them out as night fell. Meanwhile a cordon of police and wardens surrounded the area. Andy Anderson was fairly confident that this new attacker was within his cordon. The highway and the Norquay Road were lit up by warden and police vehicles and extra cars provided by Parks Canada. But the cordon was thin: there were only five men for every 15 vehicles. Anderson has said that at this point he did have some misgivings about his decision to reopen the area, but chief wardens in that era tended to keep self-doubts to themselves. Like oldtime cattle ranchers, they were territorial and self-reliant, and took pride in solving their own problems using their own resources. Nevertheless, Anderson was wise enough to know that an operation like this required more men than he had available, and he had put out a call for help to both Yoho and Kootenay parks. More wardens would arrive in the morning. Meanwhile the entire area was once again closed and barricades were set up around the railroad station, with signs forbidding any passengers, transient campers, and hobos from venturing into the woods.

Having caught up with the first attacker fairly quickly by using bait to draw him in to the guns, Anderson and Whyte were inclined to employ that trick again. Bill Vroom, Earle Skjonsberg, and John Wackerle knew the area well and could be counted on to set up bait stations in the most suitable areas. These hands directed a few of the younger men where to lay down scent trails, dragging some road-killed elk meat and horseflesh between the Caboose Restaurant and the Banff recreation centre, which was now closed to the public. The bait was fastened to trees where open ground offered a clear line of fire. Doug Cardinal and Ian Pengelly set up their bait station east of the Caboose and watched it from the roof of the Unwin Hardware shed all that night.

The soft-spoken, bespectacled Ian Pengelly had hit the ground running since his recent transfer from the seascapes of Pacific Rim National Park to the towering peaks of Banff. When the call came on the Tobler mauling, he was off-duty and in the midst of filling a feed dish for Mr. Brown, his chocolate Labrador. He had rushed back to work, forgetting to give the dog its dinner. All night long, as he stared into the dark woods with the rifle close to hand, he kept picturing Mr. Brown, alone in a strange house, sitting on the kitchen floor and gazing mournfully up at the counter, smelling the food he could not reach.

In the forest, bears were also smelling food they could not reach. Several smallish black bears approached the bait, but they were nervous and easily frightened off by the hunters flicking their six-volt lanterns on and off. At 2:25 a.m. the RCMP called in at Banff dispatch to report on Remy Tobler. He would survive, but he had lost the injured eye. He had suffered a severe bite to the left thigh and groin; the wound was deep but without complications. He was in serious to critical condition but was expected to recover. Tobler had also lost a number of teeth and suffered a broken jaw, a comminuted fracture in the centre of his face, and permanent nerve damage that would make it difficult to eat, as well as lacerations and contusions to the face and body.

Surprisingly, the first plastic surgeon who worked on Tobler believed that the main facial damage was more likely caused by a swat from the bear's paw than a bite. "We see this kind of injury from just a bad beating from human beings sometimes" he commented, "so the animal could not have been very serious about what it was doing." Tobler told Leuthold the injury was definitely from a bite, however.

Leuthold went to visit his friend in hospital where he found him in serious condition, with his jaw wired shut. Tobler could only communicate by writing, and he knew few English words. He had a foolscap sheet and a pen to write with. Leuthold remembers the two words that were written on that sheet, over and over: "Much Pain."

A rigorous schedule of surgery in Canada and Switzerland lay ahead of the injured man, to repair the damage of being hit by an animal with the striking power of a small backhoe, and bitten by jaws that could break horse bones. It would leave him scarred, numbed, subject to chronic pain, and handicapped for life.

At 7 a.m. the shift changes came in; there was no real news to report as dawn came to the valley.

From Canmore, I followed events in Banff via the news media and occasional calls from former colleagues. As the latest chapter in the debacle unfolded on September 2, I was in between calls concerning yet another long-distance argument with my Toronto publisher. The phone rang and I heard my wife, Myrna, answer it upstairs. It was the wife of a warden friend. Listening, I heard an edge in Myrna's voice that sounded like trouble. I went upstairs as she was hanging up. She stared at me a second and ran one hand absently through her long strawberry-blonde hair. She is the kind of wife that a husband spends a lot of time admiring. "You're not going to believe this," she said.

"Try me."

"The first guy who got mauled?"

"Yes, Cohoe – what?"

"He died in hospital. There's a rumour going around that he pulled out his airway."

"Jesus H. Christ! On purpose, or was it an accident?"

"I don't think they know the whole story in Banff yet," she answered. "But that's not all. There's been another mauling. A tourist. And the same place where Cohoe was attacked."

I gaped at her. "Another –?"

"That's right."

"Good grief. There's no way this is a black bear."

I hurried out and got a newspaper. The headline read: "Two More Mauled; Earlier Victim Dies." The details on Ernest Cohoe's death were sparse. He had been transferred to a Texas hospital for extensive plastic surgery, but he had died of "head injuries suffered in the August 24 mauling." He was 38 years old, just two years older than me. And like me, he had a family that needed him. There was no mention of him pulling any tubes out. (That aspect of his death would not be confirmed until some days later.) Something about this story did not ring true (in fact, Cohoe died in Calgary, not Texas), but more alarming was Andy Anderson's description of the attacker in this latest case, once again, as a black bear. A "typical" black bear, "smaller than the first" reported the *Calgary Herald*, "but wardens will be attempting to get a more detailed description." Based on past experience dealing with both species of bears, I took that news with a grain of salt. As for Cohoe's attacker, the *Herald*'s Bruce Patterson reported: "They were unable to immediately confirm with medical tests that they had killed the right bear but Chief Warden Anderson said Sunday he is sure they destroyed the right animal. 'We're positive on the first one,' he said."

Andreas Leuthold had gotten only a glimpse of the bear that attacked his friend Remy Tobler. In other words, I said to myself, reading between the lines, most of the wardens, despite what the boss says, are probably *not* sure they got the right bear before, haven't got a clue what bear they are looking for now, and are hoping that Tobler, severely injured and traumatized, might shed more light on the mystery. Good luck.

The blood, sweat, and tears visited upon my former workmates reminded me of what I disliked about the writing business: the part where you hide away behind a desk while real life goes on all around you – the writing part, in other words. I clumped back down to the brooding pen, as a friend had named my office, to ponder events. I reminded myself, yet again, that I was a civilian now. The bear problems in Banff were no longer any of my business, yet I knew that the "Yellowstone redux" disaster (as described in Chapter 3) unfolding there was one that I and other wildlife workers before me had long predicted. It was ridiculous really. I had been out of the warden service for two years. But the warden service was not just a job: to quote an old cliché, it was a way of life. The best of life there was lived as if in a dream dreamt by a mountain. Days of sun or days of rain, bleached or soaked by turns in the saddle, and days in the powder snow. Days when we literally risked our necks to help others, days to tell stories about. Despite everything, the Outfit was still so inculcated in my sense of identity that in a very real way I had never left; its concerns were still my own. I sat thinking of the dedicated staff and the price they had paid: Wilf Etherington had paid with his life, suffering the same kind of attack as Cohoe. I thought of Eric Langshaw, his career now effectively over for trying to do the right thing: enforce the law without fear or favour. I thought of a day on Stoney Creek back in the mid 1970s. John Wackerle and I had been ordered to set a trap for Four Toes, a big grizzly that was raising hell all along the northeast boundary. Four Toes had laid claim to any kind of food found in his domain, and that included any canned goods or other comestibles cached in our patrol cabins. He had been smashing into warden cabins, busting open paint cans, burglarizing grub, and generally wrecking the place. In *Wilderness Essays*, preservationist John Muir wrote about a grizzly that tore a hole in a cabin roof then hauled a bed out through the hole, dragged it under a tree, and took a nap in it. At Barrier Cabin, Four Toes played his own riff on that theme when he came calling one night. He'd forced two guys to chin up through the attic hatch opening *tout de suite* to escape him, then he'd bent their iron bunks into junk, leaping up and down on them in a frenzy of fun and fury.

There were no culvert traps available except one that had been waiting for repairs at the park shop long enough that we had almost forgotten about it. We drove in to check it out. Its tires were flat, and I jumped out and grabbed an air hose to inflate them while the mechanics, on coffee break, watched with interest. The steel pin on the latching mechanism was broken. The last warden to use it had put a nail into the latch pin opening as an improvised repair. A rusty nail. The nail was still where he had left it, the head just big enough to keep it from falling right through the opening.

The shop foreman had trucks and graders and white-line painting rigs to keep running. The park had highways that needed attention and the town of Banff, where most of our budget was spent, had a huge demand for motorized equipment of all kinds, from sewer snakes to jackhammers, all of it needing upkeep. Maintaining some silly bear trap came low on the list in Canada's first national park.

It seems Four Toes had not seen a culvert trap before, because we caught him in fairly short order. I can't find the records, but as I recall he was over 600 pounds. His head had filled the whole round end of the culvert and behind the steel bars his eyes were full of fire. Then he'd disappeared into the dark trap as if he were an apparition we'd only imagined, and everything went silent; the whisky-jacks in the spruce trees held their breath and the red squirrels froze, holding their pine cones up to their lips like rosaries. That's when the trap bounded on its springs like a live thing as Four Toes backed up and charged the gate, trying to get at us. He hit the bars so hard the whole trap rang like a gong. All that kept him from breaking the latch and tearing us to pieces as we rushed to hook the trap to our bumper hitch was that rusty nail.

The area manager decreed that Four Toes must be put down. Thinking all these years later about that bear gave me the blues. If it had been my call, Four Toes could have gone on trashing cabins till hell froze over. Cabins were our intrusion, for administrative purposes, into his home. Bearproofing them was the proper solution (and this was actually underway at that time). At heart, I hated meddling with these big carnivores and thanked my lucky stars they had not managed to work out their frustrations on my hide. I thought of my former comrades crawling through the willows in the wetlands, and I hoped they had a mere black bear on their hands, as their witnesses had indicated, and not another Four Toes. I myself had not seen a black grizzly bear before, though a quick check in A.W.F. Banfield's *The Mammals of Canada* revealed "almost black" was a possible colour phase. These thoughts made my flesh creep. What was really going on in that swamp?

I opened the basement door that led to Myrna's garden and checked out the cloudy sky for a moment. The smell of rain was in the air. In one corner of the basement, my old rucksack hung from a peg alongside skis and other outdoor gear. It held extra socks and a sweater, along with a first aid kit. I now tossed in a six-volt lantern and a police-issue flashlight and stuffed my old yellow slicker in on top. The oilcloth slicker made a good cagoule when you were bivouacked in the rain waiting for a bear to show itself in the middle of the night. I got the rifle, a pump-action .308 out of its locked cabinet and put it in its travelling case. Myrna was not surprised to see me stomping up the basement stairs in my mountain boots with a greasy Stetson on my head and rifle case in hand. My sons Paul and Nathan, then ages eight and five, ran for their own boots and coats when they saw me coming. I was glad to let Myrna break the news that they would not be going with Daddy on this trip.

"I'll make you a thermos of coffee and some sandwiches," she offered. "I take it we won't be seeing you until the morning?"

"Well, that's assuming that they want my help."

"I wouldn't worry about that," she said grimly, over the loud protests of the kids. She bent down to pry them off my jacket hem. "I read that piece in the *Herald*," she added. "It sounds like they need all the help they can get." I nodded, though in truth I was not at all certain of my welcome. My resignation from Parks Canada had not ended on a happy note. I knew full well that one of several aspects of my first nonfiction book, *Men for the Mountains* (1978), that had annoyed park managers was a chapter entitled "Killing Bears So They Won't Die." Then there was the article about Eric Langshaw, published in April 1980 in *Today* magazine, which had poured more vinegar on open sores.

Half an hour later I was parking my battered GMC pickup in front of the Banff park warden office, a squat, ugly building resembling a tire sales depot in the industrial area of Banff. As I got out, the office door opened and out stepped Chief Warden Anderson in the flesh, car keys in hand with his Biltmore at the usual jaunty angle. Like me, he tended to wear a pipe under his mustache in those days. The pipe emitted a smoke-ring challenge when his eyes fell on me, and out came one of his involuntary chuckles, *kee hee hee*. A chuckle should be happy but it didn't sound that way on this occasion. With one victim dead and two more injured, Anderson no doubt had a world of trouble on his mind, including, I suspected, his decision to reopen the Whiskey Creek Swamp area. He was a man who tended to shoulder his burdens without showing outward signs of strain, except for the nervous chuckle. But knowing what he was up against, I felt a pang of sympathy for my old boss.

With my own pipe, a Peterson bent, clamped in place, I puffed out an answering signal, a request to parley. The chief warden grimaced with distaste as if someone had slipped a wolverine turd into his pipe bowl – a rare but not unheard of practice in the Outfit, though not one usually directed at our superiors. Frowning, Anderson listened to my offer but he surprised me with his response: "Yes, we can definitely use you." I watched his well-seamed poker face for traces of irony; to him, I must seem like the black sheep returned to the fold, but the foxy chief warden seemed sincere. "If you could work some

evening shifts for us, that would help." I saw the value of his suggestion, it would mean at least one guy who was pulling double shifts,
hunting in the swamp all day then guarding part of the night, could
get some sleep, and hence be more alert. "No problem," I offered.
"I'm glad to help out any way I can. I can start tonight."

Armed with a note from Anderson, I went to report to Assistant
Chief Peter Whyte and draw a portable radio, while Anderson headed
off to another meeting at the Kremlin. It was strange to walk once
again into the warden office, where there were several new faces I
didn't recognize, including one who was now holding the position
number I had vacated. Peter Whyte gave me a perplexed smile, read
the note, then thanked me for volunteering. I had worked for him
before and we knew each other pretty well. I learned I would be
posted to the railroad tracks near the Caboose early that evening.
Whyte suggested I draw some ammunition from the gun locker.
"Hopefully, you won't have to use it, but you never know. I take it
you've been following this situation."

"Yes, some of the guys have kind of kept me informed. I heard
about Cohoe. Goddamn!"

"Yeah. He's got a wife and family."

"What about pulling the life-support stuff?"

Whyte leaned back in his chair and shook his head. "It hasn't been
confirmed. We heard he pulled it out, but it could be an accident."

"Man. That is harsh."

I glanced out the office door. Grim faces were going by. Some
wardens were in their green uniforms, others wore jeans or coveralls
more appropriate for setting traps or hiking through the bush. Their
pants were soaked; an afternoon hailstorm had caught them out in the
open. In a 2006 interview, Dan Vedova, who is today an operations
manager at Pacific Rim National Park, but was then a young seasonal
park warden, described those days for me. "Until we set up the baits,
we are going in there every day hunting for this bear, and I was with,
I believe, Perry [Jacobsen] and Billy [Vroom]. We were walking
through those willow thickets; for the first time in my life I really had

a visceral fear. Like a gut fear. I mean, we had done a lot in the warden service, right? We had hung under those helicopters and had our asses kicked up cliffs [during mountain rescue training] that I never even thought a human being should consider going, and I had never felt fear like that. Because I knew that that bear was probably going to go for my face. There was just something very, sort of, very primal about that. You're hunting for an animal in willow thickets and you don't have much room to move. And you're wondering, Do I have the right weapon for this?"

The three men had set up the flying trap (a large cage-style live trap) close to the mauling site, then hunted the area in an expanding circle trying to cut the bear's tracks. Once again, the high grass had sent them off on a wild goose chase. One of those trails would have been the bear's, but it was lost in the willows where it wasn't hammered flat by the hailstorm. The area was not large, so the bear's ability to elude them was as frustrating as it was uncanny. Cohoe's death, coming on the heels of another attack, had hit them hard. This operation was going from major to mega disaster.

Back at the warden office, Whyte's phone was constantly ringing. Glancing out the window, I saw a few men and women in media jacket-and-tie milling around a television camera, waiting to buttonhole anybody in authority, so I left him to it. I had been planning to ask him what was known about the Swiss tourists and this new attacker, but I knew I could get that information lower down the food chain.

Out in the hallway old friends greeted me about the way I expected. "Took you long enough to get here," and "So you just had to come back and look for more trouble, eh?" – the usual male camaraderie disguised by machismo bullshit. Having recently spent many days hunkered in my basement office, surrounded by visiting kids and young moms making the coffee rounds, I had to admit that I missed the male environment badly.

I learned that the results from the necropsy of black bear 057 were not yet known. Some other disturbing news had people shaking their heads with disbelief: the black bear's jaw had been burned in error at the Alberta Agriculture lab, so it could not be passed on to the RCMP crime lab to be checked for confirmation against the canine punctures in Cohoe's waders. The crime lab would still examine B057's paws for blood and look for human tissue, hair, and textiles in the bear's stomach, but completion of that work was a week away. It seems the only luck that week was bad luck, and when you've got a run of bad luck going, never assume it won't keep on getting worse.

People were scratching their heads and asking each other, "Didn't we just solve this problem?" Dan Vedova summed it up in our 2006 interview: "The 'holy fuck!' factor was really high. Everybody was racking their brains for an answer. There was a lot of second-guessing going on. We did not have a strong protocol to rely on back then like we do these days. We were winging it. And then there was the politics of the office to deal with and intense media coverage; it just mushroomed. We were just not ready for that attention and distraction, like we are nowadays. And there was the pressure from Ottawa. They wanted to see some dead bears and they wanted this thing to be over with."

According to Doug Martin, who was then new to Banff, office politics more than slightly hindered operations. "That's when the 'circle the wagons' occurred, you know, on the second mauling. I got involved with that, and that's when we had the big pissing contest going on, everybody saying what we should be doing, bring in infrared heat sensors to try and find [the bear], that sort of stuff." For his part, Martin remained convinced that snaring the bear was the answer. Someone else agreed with him: bear expert Steve Herrero, who had some influence with park management.

Anderson, I learned, had just held a meeting with Whyte, Kutzer, and his lead hands. They had decided to ask for assistance from Herrero (who had by now returned from the Alaska inquiry) and his colleague Dick Russell of the Canadian Wildlife Service, and worked the phones to make it happen. Herrero suggested they should call in Dennis Weisser, a problem wildlife expert with the Alberta Fish and

Wildlife Division. Anderson made the call and his request was immediately granted. All these experts would be on hand by the morrow.

The wardens' common room was like a stirred-up wasp nest, people coming and going and telephones ringing as callers reported on every bear seen moving in Banff park, or just wanted to know if it was safe for the kids to play out of doors. Some had words of advice or encouragement, but by no means was every member of the public on the side of the wardens. Somebody reported seeing a T-shirt on Banff Avenue that referred to the four men who had so far been bowled over by the attacker. It bore the charming slogan "Bears 4 Wardens 1."

One of the most singular pieces of advice came via the *Calgary Herald*, in an interview with the late Derrick Rosaire, an animal trainer who gained fame in 1960 after starring on the "Ed Sullivan Show" billed as "Rosaire and Tony the Wonder Horse." Rosaire was the trainer of Gentle Ben, a 725-pound "Canadian" black bear. Rosaire thought that the bear victims in Whiskey Creek might have misunderstood the grizzly's "playful advances." Grizzlies, he told the *Herald*, males in particular, like to "play" with humans but they don't like it when we resist their advances. "And then they don't know how hard they are biting," explained Rosaire. No one so far had been resisting the bear, nor had they found his advances playful.

The Outfit was a bit shellshocked at the time with the various unsolicited theories rolling in. Rosaire's was the "Give me a hug or I'll rip your head off" theory. "Speaking of bullshit," said one sun-wrinkled veteran, rolling a smoke from a pouch of tobacco like a cowboy "to the manner born," which he was: "You hear about Anderson's beaver theory?"

"What's that?" I wanted to know. "A sex manual?"

"Ha ha! I don't know what he smokes in that pipe. He thinks the bear has learned how to catch beaver. The beavers are fat and sassy in that swamp. Bear loves this beaver meat so much, he figures anything coming in there is coming to steal it from him."

"Any of these beaver making their home in a garbage bin?"

"That's kinda what I was wondering. Maybe we should do another study on it."

"More studies are needed, that's a given," I agreed.

Bill Vroom meanwhile had another novel idea. The flying trap had been hoisted into the swamp by helicopter but so far the mauler had not deigned to visit it or the two culvert traps still set in the area. Vroom wanted to strew the flying trap site with some horsemeat bait, then lock himself, no doubt smelling like a dead horse at that stage, in the trap for the night and ambush the bear. He would let it get as close as possible and then he would blast it with his .30-06. According to Maureen Vroom, nobody shared Bill's enthusiasm for this project (their attitude still puzzles her today). As for the beaver meat theory, beaver meat, and especially beaver castor, would play more of a role in this incident than we naysayers could foresee.

In those early days of September, the Theatre of the Absurd came to play the Whiskey Creek wetlands and many are the bizarre tales that have been told of that time.

The absurdity began, as Dan Vedova recalled, with the sudden materialization, in the warden common room, of bearded PR man Ken Preston, clad for the occasion among these mud-splattered mountain men in a dapper trenchcoat, à la New York City, the city mouse come to take charge of the country mice. With his British accent, hauteur, and urban attire, however, he smacked more of *Monty Python* than Parks Canada.

The reporters were milling around the entrance, demanding action. Perhaps Preston felt he needed some raw meat to feed these hounds. He had an idea for a photo op. He rounded up some wardens on their way out to relieve the perimeter guards. Some were not keen on helping him, but he got a few to jump in the back of a pickup truck. In an interview with Noah Richler of the BBC, warden Tim Auger, the mountain-rescue team leader, recalled the scene: "When it was happening, you couldn't help but sort of see yourself in a movie. And I can recall driving into my familiar parking lot at the office, and as I'm parking my car a pickup truck goes by with several wardens sitting on the edge of the truck, with rifles slung on their shoulders or standing up like a bunch of Mexicans going off to the civil war. And looking for all the world like they're loaded down with ammunition, shooting jackets, and the works. And you go, 'Get a grip!' Normally you don't sit up on the back of the truck and go off army fashion to do anything."[42] Wardens recall this spectacle, reducing the outfit to some trigger-happy good ol' boys turned loose in a game preserve, as "the stagecoach routine."

Dealing with the press was not easy by any means, and it kept Preston crazy busy that day. He dealt with 89 media calls, including 12 radio interviews and four television interviews. Dennis Weisser, for one, was very impressed with the way Parks Canada handled the media. Perry Jacobsen was also impressed, but in a different way. Scouting around on the edge of the swamp earlier that day, Jacobsen had left the road and dropped to his knees to crawl into what looked like a bear tunnel in the willows. There was a CBC Television crew nearby. Jacobsen paid the television crew no notice: that was Preston's department. With his nose to the ground, he was watching for bear tracks among the willow roots when he felt something nudge him in the butt: he nearly jumped right out of his skin. A cameraman was trying to crawl in behind him and goosed the warden with his camera lens. Jacobsen advised the crew where they might put their camera next and ordered them out of the area. "Take my word for it," he told them sternly, "you definitely do *not* want to be where I'm going."

Jacobsen was already nervous about working alongside younger men who had no firearms training. "I was really afraid somebody was going to shoot somebody else. Everybody had a gun, but we weren't sure what their qualifications were. It was not long after Whiskey Creek that we started the gun schools, and everybody got some training. We got the right calibre weapons after that, we got the .375 bolt actions, the shotgun slugs we used more. The .308s we had at that time would not have stopped that bear. I remember somebody was packing a .243 [a light weapon more appropriate for coyote hunters than bear hunters], so everybody brought their own private rifles. We had .30-06 and .270, which is dynamite. You can interchange the cartridges." He made a wry face at the memory. "It's lucky we didn't get somebody wiped out. You can imagine, shooting that big guy with a .243."

A grizzly bear, as I mentioned earlier, will turn and hunt people who have injured it. But what counts more than a gun's calibre is the calibre of the shooter in any given situation. It was not just armament, it was professional firearms training that was needed.

Jacobsen remembers another funny incident: "We were teamed up with people around the perimeter, and they teamed me up with a young Mountie. He had this shotgun with a fold-away stock like they use as a man-killer. And he kept telling me, as we walked along, 'Boy, I sure hope that bear comes out of the bush, I'd sure like to blow him away,' and he's going on and on about it. Finally I said to him, 'What have you got in that gun for ammunition?' He said, 'Oh, powerful, I can blow a car door off.' I said, 'No, what weight are they?' 'Well,' he said, 'I don't know.' 'Well, are they SSG? [8 mm buckshot].' He says, 'I dunno.' I said 'Well, give me one.' So he gives me one – they were bird shot! They were number 7 bird shot! And I said to him, 'I tell you what. If that bloody bear comes out of the bush, just turn the gun on yourself. Because if you shoot him with bird shot you're just gonna piss him off.' And I went and got another partner. I was not gonna partner with that."

When darkness fell that night, I headed the truck down to the Caboose Restaurant. As I drove, I looked, without success, for a pickup belonging to a character known as the Man in Black. "If you see the Man in Black," I'd been warned, "don't encourage him."

"How will I know him?" I'd asked, redundantly.

"We don't call him the Man in Black for nothing," came the terse reply. One of my regrets in this account is that I never actually met the Man in Black in the flesh. The MIB (unfortunately no one seems to remember his real name) was the flipside of bear trainer Derrick Rosaire. He'd come from Texas in a 10-gallon hat not to hug bears, but to blow them away. Having heard about the maulings in Banff, the story goes, and being by his own account the killer of many a man-eating bear, he had thrown his gear and an assortment of death-dealing weapons into the pickup and pointed its nose north. Once in Banff, he wasted no time in offering his services as a professional bear hunter. Apparently his idea of the professional bear hunter uniform was to dress up like Paladin the gun fighter in the antique television series "Have Gun, Will Travel." His hat was black, his clothes were black, and he wore black cowboy boots and dark sunglasses. Dan Vedova claimed he drove a jet-black pickup truck with a black camper on the back. He could be seen, according to Dan Vedova, sitting in his truck, dressed for combat and waiting for the call that never came. "I'm ready to go in, and I'm ready to go in now," he said to anyone who asked. Perhaps he was parked in a shadow and I missed him. He would definitely have been a road hazard if he'd stepped out on the highway at night.

Chief Warden Anderson quickly sized up the Man in Black as "a bit of a nut case." "A few questions," recalled Anderson, "showed his knowledge of Grizzly was limited. I asked him several times to give me the names of any wildlife persons or biologists he had worked with that I could call. He tried to evade the question, then when pressed said he always worked alone. I told him we didn't need his help and to stay away from the area. I don't remember him being around after that and didn't see him after the bear was shot. I don't recall any of the wardens mentioning him being a problem, just a harmless nut."

Other wardens do recall the MIB hanging around the Caboose area, however. According to Jacobsen, Anderson brought him down to the abattoir later, after the smoke had cleared, so to speak. Jacobsen took his boss aside and asked, "Andy, who the hell is that?"

"I don't really know," said Andy, *sotto voce*, "But he was just too good not to share."

There was a boxcar on the siding behind the railroad depot and the Caboose Restaurant; this was my assigned position for the watch on the swamp. The garbage enclosure for the restaurant was across the tracks and nearly a hundred yards east. I walked down the tracks and waved to the next sentry down the line. I found the ladder and climbed up the steel rungs to the roof. There I sat down on the edge of the roof with the .308 in my lap and loaded four rounds into the magazine, then eased the action closed, depressing the rounds into the magazine with my thumb, letting the bolt slide over them as I closed the forearm. An empty breech is the best safety for most situations. I figured I would have enough time to ease a round down the spout if the bear showed up; he wasn't going to climb that steel ladder. I favoured the pump-action rifle back then because, as a long-time grouse hunter, I had fired hundreds of rounds using pump-action shotguns, which are almost as fast as an autoloader.

As for the .308 (*pace* Perry Jacobsen) I had seen what it could do to flesh and bone; I had no doubt that it would kill any poor old bear God made, given a clean shot in the open like this.

Now some 14 feet off the ground, I had a view overlooking the station yard and the forest edge. The radio, strapped to my chest, came alive and I adjusted the squelch control and turned the volume down low. I heard that a subadult American black bear had been spotted crossing the Trans-Canada Highway at a dead run, as if something had put the fear of god in it. You could hear the edge in the speakers' voices, tinged with disappointment. The bear was the wrong colour and wrong size for the attacker, so they let it go. It was reassuring to know people were keeping their cool, especially when handling firearms in a high-traffic situation.

A strong odour startled me and I turned to check it out. Behind and below my position just 10 yards away was the loading dock of the restaurant, illuminated by an overhead light. On it was a Chev half-ton truck. The truck box was full to overflowing with restaurant scraps, and this restaurant featured prime Alberta beef and seafood on its menu. Some of the stuff was tantalizingly ripe, from a scavenger's point of view. I was downwind of this olfactory treat; I smelled the ocean, I smelled the feedlot; I smelled a grizzly bear's wet dream. It was just this type of situation that had motivated Eric Langshaw to prosecute Château Lake Louise one year earlier.

Later on, I learned that the Caboose's manager had stopped using
the garbage enclosure soon after the Cohoe attack and was hauling
Caboose garbage to the transfer station, as he would testify under
oath on February 9, 1981. Furthermore, the warden service had asked
him "not to go over there and not to take out any garbage because
they were trying to catch a particular bear."[43] So the surf-and-turf
leavings were piled up in the truck, waiting to be hauled away.
According to Warden Jacobsen, bears raided the truck box on at least
one occasion, which would not be surprising. Unaware of these
arrangements at the time, I just had to shake my head at this bizarre
and, from what I knew then, illegal situation. I pictured the Whiskey
Creek mauler sitting out in the bush inhaling the enticing odour of
that grub pile, waiting patiently for darkness to make his move. It
would have to be a cautious move; he had five sets of busy railroad
tracks to cross and some 18 to 20 trains a day to dodge.[*]

The light breeze snuffled around the station like a hound dog
unravelling a rabbit trail. Occasionally, I caught a whiff of roasting
prime rib wafting from the restaurant's exhaust fan but, next to
ripening flesh, the default odour was *eau de* railroad, a unique blend of
human ordure, creosote, and spilled diesel fuel. I glanced again at the
grub pile on the platform and grinned sheepishly. Here I was, back in
the same situation I had experienced before writing *Men for the
Mountains* – waiting for a bear that I accused Parks Canada of failing
to protect, with a gun in my hands, fully prepared to shoot it dead.
Yes, the chief warden had placed me in a very strategic position –
between the Whiskey Creek bear and its grub pile. You had to hand it
to the guy, he had a unique sense of humour. *Kee-hee-hee.* Touché!

A shadowy form suddenly drifted between me and the trees; I
tightened my grip on the rifle. The shadow lifted up to the sky; it was
only an owl hunting along the forest edge. I pondered Anderson's
beaver theory. Certainly it had more romance than just blaming the

---

[*] Louis Kovacik told me he was "very hurt and upset" about the loss of life and injuries
that summer but felt that no one person was to blame for the tragedy. "Whose fault was it
really?" he asked. "Who can you point the finger at?"

whole disaster on poor garbage management. Beavers — bears love 'em, they will fight to defend them, and there's not much we can do about it. It even fit nicely with the beaver emblem on our hat badges, in some vaguely metaphysical way. Although Anderson was running the operation mainly from an indoor office, it occurred to me that he was still just another perplexed and troubled warden, deeply saddened by the blood that had been shed, staring into the dark and telling himself a story that offered some kind of consolation.

As darkness settled on the mountains, I taped the flashlight to the underside of my rifle barrel, a crude but sometimes effective method for getting off a night shot. The wetlands were quiet, no sound of ducks or rambling moose disturbed the stillness. From time to time, the station yard was lit up by the powerful beams of CPR locomotives, hauling freight through to the west coast. We were an eye-popping sight to the engineers as the headlight lit us up; train robber–like figures spread out on top of the boxcars every hundred or so yards, sporting cowboy hats and "dusters" (oilcloth saddle coats or slickers) and each armed with a rifle or shotgun.

Later that night Halle Flygare and Perry Jacobsen came in to set up a bait station at the old Caboose garbage bin, which had lured bears with its mix of fish and beef scraps until recently. They would use a hindquarter from a road-killed elk for bait, lashed to the heavy duty fence with rope. This new enticement seemed a bit redundant to me; the bait was already set at the restaurant's back door within good smelling distance. With two wardens close at hand and so few to guard the track elsewhere, I was asked to move down the line to the railroad Y, several hundred yards east, to tighten up the cordon a bit.

We were there to watch for the bear, but also to keep a sharp lookout for railroad hobos who were known to camp in the nearby forest. This danger was highlighted in an encounter Paul Kutzer and Dave Cardinal had around this time. As Kutzer remembers it, they had set up their bait station east of the depot behind Unwin Hardware's shed, not far from the garbage enclosure. First they had heard a heavy-sounding animal moving around in the bush behind their bait. They had been using their lights to scare off snoopy black bears. Now they kept the lights off and waited for the mauler to come in. Instead, the silence was broken at about 3:30 a.m. by a freight train that slowed to a stop on the siding for a short time then moved on. The night got dark and quiet again. As they sat listening, they heard something rustling in the bush to their left and pointed their rifles that way, waiting for the bear to emerge, but once again the sounds soon faded away.

At 7 a.m., they gave up on the vigil and began to pack up for the morning shift, but sounds in the bush had them grabbing for their rifles again. There was a crackling noise and the willows were shaking; something was thrashing around in there. The wardens cycled rounds into their chambers, checked their safeties, and stood waiting. "And then out comes this fellah," Kutzer recalls, "not too clean, long hair just a real mess and dirty clothes. He comes stumbling out of the bush to the left of us. And I'm wondering, 'Oh, my god! How the heck did he get in there?' Because we made darn sure there was lots of barricades all along there; there were signs and police tape and everything. We didn't want anyone coming through the bait station.

"So, I went up to this fellah and I said, 'What in the world are you doing in here!' I guess he had pitched a camp in the bush off to the left of us. And I said, 'When did you get there?' And he said, 'It was about three o'clock or so in the morning.'"

Kutzer was horrified at the possibility of hitting somebody with a stray bullet. "'God,' I said, 'don't you realize what this is all about? Do you remember going through barricades?' The guy was quite put out with me. 'Well, yeah. You shouldn't leave those things there. I had to climb over those at night.'"

Trying to calm his frayed nerves with a joke, Kutzer had told the hobo it was a damn good thing for him that he hadn't tried to steal any meat. Apparently the humour fell flat. Riding the rods, though romantic, is of course illegal, so Kutzer checked the man's ID and had the police dispatcher run it through the Central Police Intelligence Computer (CPIC), in Ottawa. It came up clean, so Kutzer let the bum off with a warning to buy a ticket or stay off CPR property.

Ten millimetres of rain fell on September 2, and the night was cool and wet on top of the boxcar, where I huddled under the horse slicker in the misty dark. Snow would be falling on the mountain tops – whitecaps at dawn flushed to a salmon red. Aspen leaves would soon be turning gold; the smell of autumn was in the air. My sector was pretty quiet, and I was too far down the tracks to be involved when the mauler finally made his move in the early hours of September 3, and left Tim Auger with a story to tell.

Tim Auger retired from the warden service in 2004. A compact, dark-haired man, he is one of those ageless outdoors types blessed with great skin, a white-toothed grin, and a modest and unassuming manner. He was liked and respected as a warden, but in 1980 he was from the new school of hires and by his own admission he had little experience in hunting. As he told the BBC's Noah Richler: "I'd hardly ever had a gun in my hand but I was wearing the uniform and we needed bodies, so you handed the trooper a rifle and said, 'Go out and keep your eye on this stretch of the road.' Basically I'm saying, not everybody that was working here then was born with a gun in his hand."

It was around 3:45 a.m. when Perry Jacobsen radioed Banff dispatch and requested that somebody should spell him and Halle Flygare off while they went in search of some hot coffee. Tim Auger and Keith Everts, who had been patrolling Area 1 as duty wardens, heard the radio call and drove over to the depot to relieve the shooters. They pulled up where the other team had been parked and turned off the engine. They had their rifles to hand and radar lamps ready to flick on, just in case. The night was dead quiet. Even the traffic on the Trans-Canada was at a temporary standstill. The two men sat quietly, letting their eyes adjust to the darkness. It was now 4 a.m.

After the attack on Remy Tobler, Sticky Mouth stays back in the forest, made cautious by the comings and goings of men near the railroad station, constrained to subsist on green shoots and a taste of scant berries, forced to gnaw the mere bones left by coyotes and black bears. Any colony of ants he found in a honeycombed log, any wasps' nest dug out of an abandoned squirrel midden was like a vein of caviar on his tongue in comparison.

Late at night, he prowls out of the forest to the fringe of trees where the silver tracks left by the great broken-back snake that often roared through here shine under a mystic light that is neither moon or sun. He stops well back in the dark forest. There he smells the enticing odour of the new cowfish kill that is piled next to a big Twolegs den on the far side of the tracks. But he also smells the Twolegs that are lying in wait for him nearby, and he retreats back into the depths. He comes again the next night; the cold rain and the fall of hail that day still prickle his hide, still nip at his cracked footpads with a warning of colder weather to come.

He glares at the rows of tracks he must cross. They glisten and seem to writhe with life on the wet gravel under the station lights. He has raided this new kill before these Twolegs came back again, but now he is warier because it is open ground and dangerous. As he prowls eastward within the safety of the trees, a pungent odour of well-ripened elk flesh flares in his nose, ripples through every nerve end, and thrills him to the roots of his stomach. The old cowfish kill, where he drove off the underlings before, has turned into an elk kill. So be it. It is all his to claim, yet he is careful to stay out of the light and walks cloaked in the forest dark. The elk kill is much closer to the woods; he senses it as safer. The smell of the meat makes him tremble; his stomach leaps up against the heart and he is dripping drool on the duff as he moves forward. The faintest smell of the Twolegs comes, but he blinks at it as if brushing flies from his sight. To feed now is everything.

He flows out of the woods low to the ground, his feet shying from anything soft, seeking the gravel, but closer and closer, the ground is wet and soft and cannot be avoided and now he is there and the kill is his for the tearing. He rears, towers up onto his hind feet to embrace and seize it, his long yellowed claws stab deep to rip it loose, rattling the Frost fence as if it was hit by a runaway car. The Twolegs are coming out from their hiding, but the kill is in his salivating jaws, and he falls to all fours again, turning for the woods. In a few heartbeats, moving at an awkward run, gripping a leg bone in his teeth, he drags the carcass behind the buildings and into the woods. He has left them a set of tracks; he will hide the rest.

"So we are now in the seat of the most important part of the operation," recalled Tim Auger in the BBC interview, "and we're talking in really hushed tones, just in case, and it's dark. There's no moonlight, there's just a little bit of light filtering over from the town. And damned if I don't look straight out through the window down at this fence arrangement and realize that there is some large black form there. It's so indistinct that I must take a second to check my eyes – am I just imagining it, but I go, 'Uh, Keith' like this, and he's talking and I'm trying to make him stop and I'm pointing. And I quietly open the door and look ahead – there's nothing there. The meat is gone.

"And we're talking the hindquarter of an elk. Something that probably would have weighed 75, 150 pounds. Whoever put it up had tied it up with polypropylene – that's a yellow plastic rope – and wrapped it around the chain-link fence a bunch of times. And the rope was just hanging there and the meat gone. Something's definitely been here . . . And as we come walking up we're shining flashlights on the ground. And here, in a recently dried puddle, is the perfect track.

"And it is the print of a mega grizzly bear."

— FIFTEEN —

THE SNARE

"He was not hunting people, he was hunting peace. But it's a funny way to get it, whacking people."

STEVE HERRERO

IN 1980 WILDLIFE TECHNICIAN John Taggart was but 25 years old, but he was not a complete rookie in the bear business. He had had experience capturing black bears while working for the Manitoba provincial parks before he signed on with Alberta Fish and Wildlife in 1979. Based out of the Calgary office of the division, he was involved in live-trapping black and grizzly bears for a bear study prior to the development of Kananaskis Country and Peter Lougheed Provincial Park, in the mountains adjacent to the southeast boundary of Banff National Park. Black bears Taggart knew, but grizzlies were exotic and enigmatic prowlers that would not step in the snare traps his supervisors were employing that year. These were unspoiled bears, not habituated to feeding around visitor facilities, and culvert traps did not work well on them either.

I met with Taggart on an April morning in 2007 at the Fish and Wildlife offices in the sagebrush city of Medicine Hat, where he now works. "I miss those days," he admitted with a grin. The events of that September came alive again as he consulted his log books and his memory for the details.

In 1979, Taggart's superiors had asked for trapping assistance from Dennis Weisser. Weisser showed young Taggart how to build cubbies for grizzlies using the Aldrich leg snare trap, how to set snares in locations that were safe for both bears and humans. He baited the traps with a bear delicacy – beaver meat – and lured them in by smearing the bait with castor, the waxy and pungent substance excreted by the beaver's scent glands, a smell that is like catnip to a bear. Weisser taught the art of patience, the foremost ally of wildlife workers, and learned from his colleagues' experiences as well as his own. He related how officer Jan Allen, another skilled trapper, had dealt with a grizzly bear that used his nose to deliberately trigger the spring-activated leg loop. (Allen had read the story one morning in the tracks left in a fresh fall of snow.) The bear had simply let the snare slip harmlessly off his nose, and then entered the cubby and stole the bait. "Grizzlies," said Weisser, "have a bad habit of thinking they're smarter than you. And maybe some of them are," he allowed slyly, "but they won't quit you. They'll keep tryin', they'll keep coming. They say, 'Oh, this dumb human is going to feed us more beaver.' Ha! So its kinda fun; you're workin' with them and they don't quit. They just say, 'Well, hey, don't worry about this guy, he's got nothin'.'" Weisser showed his apprentice how to hide a second snare, where the bear would have to step while approaching the original trap. "They're watchin' one and walk into the other one," he explained. "They've done that a couple of times. You have to have the traps pretty close together and smell will bugger things up, so you have to keep your equipment and snares clean."

Weisser became a mentor to the five-foot-eight, sandy-haired Taggart, who had a genial disposition and a love of the out-of-doors. The younger man was a keen angler and hunter, as was Weisser, and was a steady hand when things got edgy. Although the division's trainer preached the virtues of the 12-gauge shotgun, which was the weapon issued to officers for bear control, Weisser still kept a .30-06 to hand. The younger man had a .300 Winchester Magnum and was proficient in its use. Weisser noted that in his favour.

After Weisser agreed to Andy Anderson and Steve Herrero's request to consult with them on the bear attacks at Banff, he immediately arranged to have Taggart assigned as his assistant. Taggart told me he was "quite impressed that [Weisser] asked a young kid to accompany him . . . basically he trusted his life with me." Of course, that trust worked both ways.

On the morning of September 3, the men loaded their truck with snares and beaver meat stored at the division's warehouse in Calgary, then drove up to Banff for a 10 a.m. meeting with the panel of experts convened by Andy Anderson in the superintendent's office. The day was cloudy and marked by showers. As they neared the town, they saw the cordon of official vehicles ringing the outskirts and armed men watching the woods. It looked as if they'd been called in to a major operation, indeed.

At the office, the panel of experts was welcomed by Superintendent Paul Lange, who introduced Ken Preston, explaining that the latter was to handle all media contacts for the group. Anderson went over the events up until then: the attacks on Ernest Cohoe; the shooting of the black bear that he still felt might be the attacker in Cohoe's case; the current hunt for the bear in the Tobler mauling, and the discovery of the first large grizzly bear track. He explained how the witnesses' description and the lack of grizzly bear signs had led them to focus on a black bear attacker. Anderson believed that they had shot the right bear, but now another attacker had replaced that dominant male; it could be a grizzly, it could be another big black bear.

Dennis Weisser listened with some skepticism. As he explained to me, "We found we couldn't rely on a victim's testimony in a bear incident. They are traumatized something terrible."

Scientists Steve Herrero, John Gunson of Alberta Fish and Wildlife, and Dick Russell of the Canadian Wildlife Service were asked for their opinions. Herrero, who had a bear habitat study underway in the park at the time, cut to the chase. According to Superintendent Lange, whom I interviewed again in 2007, Herrero said, "I think you got the wrong bear the first time. The one that's causing you trouble is still out there." Turning to Anderson, he added, "I think we should get Dennis to set some snares right away." Herrero was concerned that the bear might slip out of the cordon. He suspected it might have done that after the Cohoe mauling. Anderson and his assistants readily agreed, as did Weisser. Meanwhile, the experts would visit the latest mauling site to see if anything else could be learned there. Herrero's colleagues David Hamer and Tim Toth would survey existing study plots and then move in to the wetlands with an armed escort to evaluate the natural bear foods in the area, particularly the berry crop.

This was an opportunity for the wardens, each of whom had captured many bears with culvert traps or tranquilizer darts, to learn some new methods from a snare expert. Bill Vroom, tired from pulling all-nighters, opted for rest instead. Perry Jacobsen and Monte Rose were assigned to assist and guard the trappers while they worked. The superintendent was reassured by the presence of so many well-credentialed experts, according to Andy Anderson.

The trapping team drove down to the Caboose Restaurant to begin operations, and Steve Herrero rode with them, keen to look over the general area. The first order of business was to examine the grizzly bear track left the night before. Seasonal warden Alan Westhaver was examining the tracks, hoping to make a plaster cast. The prints proved too faint for that purpose. Westhaver measured the front right paw print at six inches wide and five inches long to the tip of the third toe pad. He could not get a total foot length; the round front heel print typically does not register on hard-packed soils, as in this case. The size of the tracks indicated an adult grizzly bear, but were not a good predictor of its weight or sex. Adult grizzly bear females, despite being hundreds of pounds lighter than adult males, may leave front pad prints that are only marginally smaller. Westhaver, schooled in biology, needed more evidence than tracks to link this grizzly to the attack on Tobler.

A grizzly was what Rose and other wardens had suspected all

along, but the fact that it kept giving them the slip seemed to indicate a smaller bear was the attacker. Then Westhaver pointed out the rear footprint left by the bear, where the ground was softer, and conversation stopped. The sight turned Rick Kunelius into a believer: "Holy shit!" he gasped reverentially. "The back foot," he recalled in a BBC interview with Noah Richler, "which is always bigger than the front foot measured 13 inches from the heel to the end of the toe pad. Which, uh, really gave everyone cause for a sphincter pucker right there on the spot. We said, 'Oh my God! We are looking for something a little bit bigger than we all imagined as we wandered through the woods.'" Kunelius meant hundreds of pounds bigger.

Dennis Weisser and Steve Herrero also viewed the track. A bear's foot length is measured from the back of the heel to the end of the middle toe pad. Kunelius may have been remembering the length from heel to claw points. Weisser, whom I interviewed at his home in Coronation, Alberta, said the foot was 11 inches long. A young seasonal warden who was thrilled to be near the famous trapper, asked Weisser excitedly, "Do you figure it's a grizzly, Dennis?"

"Well, if it isn't," replied the trapper in his laconic baritone, "then it's the biggest black bear on Earth." The bear that had left that track promised to be a bigger grizzly than most wardens had ever seen before. Yet it had come out of the night and snatched away the hindquarter of an elk in mere seconds before anyone could so much as lift a rifle to stop it.

From the scuff marks and blood on the gravel, Weisser read the bear's route. He left young Taggart to sort out equipment with the wardens while he and Herrero donned waterproof jackets then followed the bear into the bush. In his hands the trapper carried his .30-06 rifle. In a few minutes the sombre woods closed them in and they had to hunch over at times to dodge the wet overhanging branches. The dragged carcass had made a furrow; bent grass and flecks of blood marked the bear's trail. Herrero, who had spent a lot of time studying the natural foods that bears ate in the wilds of Banff National Park, noticed immediately the main food items that were attracting bears to the area were imported. "There was a trail of Alaska king crab legs and prime rib bones leading away from the dumpster way back into the swamp," he recalled in a conversation with me. "It didn't take a genius to see what the attraction was for bears."

The two men worked their way through the bush, stopping to look and listen along the way. Weisser was watching for a good place to put a snare set. "It was nerve-wracking going in there where he'd dragged that elk in," Weisser recalled. It got even hairier when, after they were several hundred yards into the bush, they parted the branches from their faces and found themselves looking at a big pile of dirt and brush that had been scraped over the remains of the rank elk haunch. The musty, gamy stink of bear was also in the air. They were staring at a grizzly bear's food cache, its most jealously guarded prize. (Next to a sow with cubs, a bear's food cache is just about the most dangerous thing to get close to in grizzly country.) "I looked at Steve and Steve looked at me," recalled Weisser. "I said 'I'm pretty sure he's watching us.' I can tell you we didn't dilly-dally backing up out of there."

The team of Monte Rose, Rick Kunelius, and Perry Jacobsen led the trappers back into the bush early that afternoon. All were armed and also loaded with the snares and a plentiful supply of beaver meat. The wardens did not know Weisser, except by reputation, but his quiet, watchful way of moving through the bush soon assured them that he was at home there. With one man standing guard at all times, Weisser began by setting a snare near a bear-rubbing tree the hunters had found earlier in the hunt. Game trails radiated out in all directions from that point. Warden Earle Skjonsberg had heard a heavy animal moving in the bush near that location the previous day. Weisser explained why it was a good site; obviously bears frequented the spot, but more importantly there was a safe line of approach to the captured animal and a sturdy tree to anchor the snare cable. The first task was to build a cubby of sharpened tree branches. They were pounded in to the ground with the back of an axe to form a V shape,

the bait being placed in the narrowing of the V. The walls of the
cubby would direct the bear toward the bait. The snare was set where
his front foot would naturally set down as he stepped forward. (The
majority of bears, 99 percent in John Taggart's experience, are right-
handed and are caught by the right front foot.)

The Aldrich trap consists of a spring-activated snare loop that is
triggered by the bear stepping on a metal pan. The loop and pan are
set into a depression the trapper scoops out in the soil and a step log
is typically placed in front of the snare so that the bear must step over
it and into the hidden depression. The undersurface of the pan is
fitted with metal stakes that anchor it to the ground. The snare wire
is aluminum aircraft control cable. It has a locking device and a swivel.
When the pan is depressed, the spring arms fly open and tighten the
noose above the bear's foot; the pan and spring remain on the ground.
The bear has limited freedom of movement, which doesn't mean it
won't fight to get loose, and it risks injury in doing so. The use of a
padded snare loop or of a modified snare trap, where the snared
animal is tethered to a spring device that softens impact on the leg, is
said to prevent most injuries. The key to humanely snaring the bear
depends on the trapper monitoring the trap and either tranquilizing
or destroying the bear as soon as possible, depending on the situation.

As he worked, Weisser entertained and informed his audience
with anecdotes about bear captures. Although the snare trap is an
efficient capture method, some bears are too clever to play along
with the plan. By keeping all human scent off the bait and equipment, you may fool them once, but the next time they might elect
to break in through the back of the cubby and steal the bait. You
might have to place another snare right on the main trail near the
cubby. You have to be patient, try different setups. Weisser
recounted for me the lengths his partner Jan Allen went to to catch
a cattle-killing grizzly. Allen boiled and cleaned his snares to erase
all human scent, but nothing seemed to help. "He had a helluva
time," recalled Weisser, "spent two weeks on it. Then he literally
covered himself and his traps with cowshit from one end to the

other." That finally hid the human scent and the clever bear stepped in the snare one day and was caught.

Then there are the pluckers, the rare bears that will worry the snare with their teeth. Given time, they will unravel enough to get started on biting through a strand at a time, or they will work the lock loose and slip their foot free. It happened that Weisser caught such a bear one time, south of Pincher Creek, Alberta. He was out at dawn that day, checking snares he'd set the night before. One of them was down in a draw, and the trapper was on a knoll up above when he heard the bear roaring down below as it fought the snare. "I could see that he had chewed the anchor tree right through and knocked it over," said Weisser. "He had chewed up and knocked over four to six other trees there that were eight inches through, but they tend to chew them off fairly high up, so the snare was still anchored." The bear sat on his haunches and glared up the slope to where the trapper stood, and he was huffing and chopping his jaws together in threat. He was an adult grizzly bear, and a big one.

Weisser decided to radio his partner to bring in the tranquilizer equipment and a culvert trap to move the bear. They planned to relocate the animal to a place where there were no range cows for him to molest. Weisser had to drive to a new location to get a radio signal. He wasn't gone long, but when he came back and peered down into the gulch, the bear was gone. He had managed to slip the lock off and escape. The grass on that hill was wet from dew. What caught Weisser's attention were the fresh tracks coming up through that wet grass, coming at a run, coming right to where he had been standing when the grizzly had last seen him. The sight made him turn quickly to make sure the bear was not behind him. "I guess he wanted to get even," was how Weisser summed up that hair raising moment.

While Weisser and company set the first of seven snares they would deploy that day, Andy Anderson and the biologists were working their way into the Tobler mauling site, to provide Parks Canada with some scientific explanations for the bear's actions, though the most obvious reason was strewn all around them, filling their nostrils with its fetor. The biologists would survey the plants for signs of bears grazing on them, and find some scat to analyze back at the lab for protein sources.

"After mauling Tobler," Anderson recollected in an e-mail, "the bear showed no inclination to leave the area. The wardens hunting him in pairs were very much aware of his presence, and at times wondered who was doing the stalking. I myself was leading Herrero and a couple of other biologists to show them the site where Tobler was mauled, when it came close enough in the thick bush, that I could smell him. I signalled the others to stop and stepped back a couple of paces to where I could see Larry, who was ahead of me and had the only rifle. He had stopped and was peering into the bush at a point opposite me. He later said he had heard it, but could not see it. The grizzly backed off and so did we."

Actually, there was another rifle along, according to Monte Rose, who was carrying it. Rose is hard on his old boss for not packing heat in such a dangerous spot. "If the griz had come out and somebody's gun jams, our chief warden might wish he'd brought a weapon," sniffed Rose indignantly.

Rifles have an amazing ability to jam when they are confronted by a grizzly bear – it's almost a syncretic relationship. This incident had quite an effect on Anderson's thinking: "If that bear was in the area at any time during the first hunt and displayed such characteristics we would certainly have been aware of it. Also there was never any of its tracks found in the area until after the second mauling." ·

Perhaps, but we have learned since those days that for every bear seen by a person many more people are seen by the bear. Researchers have watched bears leave hiking trails to sit in the bush, unseen, and wait for people to pass. In some of our crowded North American national parks, and 4 x 4-riddled forest lands, bears have no choice but to adapt to our comings and goings through their living rooms.

Andy Anderson got dealt another bad hand in the form of a call from Bob Muskett. Muskett had left Banff just after the Cohoe mauling to go out to Victoria, where his mother had passed away.

When he returned, he had the tragedy of his buddy's death to contend with. Cohoe's death was ruled to be an accident. He had pulled out his life-support tubes because he was choking, according to Muskett, and it was his bad luck that his nurse was out of the room and came back too late to help him.* In the wake of that event, Muskett learned something that might have been of real importance to the investigation, had it been reported earlier. After the shooting of the black bear 054, the radio was on in Cohoe's room and his doctor was present when it was reported that the wardens had shot the black bear responsible for the attack. Cohoe, unable to speak, had grabbed a pen and paper and written for his doctor, "No way! It was a grizzly bear," or words to that effect. Cohoe was adamant on this point.

No one reported this information to Parks Canada at the time. Would it have made a difference? Anderson would have had to balance the circumstantial evidence and Muskett's description against Cohoe's assertion, and weigh Cohoe's knowledge of bears against Muskett's. But in my opinion, had the senior wardens heard about Cohoe's statement earlier, they would have insisted that their boss keep the area closed.

Another man was listening to the radio that week during his travels away from Banff. His name was Alden Brososky and he was the Texaco bulk-fuel dealer in Banff. It was he who had spotted the black grizzly on August 24. When he heard about the first mauling and the description of the bear, he wondered if the black grizzly had anything to do with it. But soon after he heard in the media that a large black bear had been shot, and that Parks Canada was "positive" they had the right bear, he saw no need to come forward with his information.

Weisser and his crew pressed on, Weisser convinced they were looking for a grizzly bear, and Perry Jacobsen suspecting that to be the

---

* Brian Patterson reported on Cohoe's death on September 5 in the *Calgary Herald*. Cohoe had been on the way to recovery, according to hospital spokesman Dr. Robert Lampard. That had changed at 6.40 a.m. September 1. The patient became very "'. . . agitated and disturbed,' said Lampard. 'Quite unexpectedly, he grabbed and ripped out everything. Hospital workers tried to save him, but failed,' he added."

case but still looking for further confirmation, despite the track at the Caboose. They would set a total of seven snares that day, most of them at places showing the most frequent use by wildlife. Around 4 p.m., they were placing the fifth snare about a hundred yards from the Trans-Canada Highway, along the Calgary Power right-of-way, a route that wildlife found convenient to travel after dark. One of the belt radios was squawking with news about a car theft in the industrial area. Nobody on the crew suspected this news was of consequence to them.

It seems that while most people were content to stay out of the swamp during that dangerous time, there was a stubborn minority determined to rush in where wardens feared to tread. Earlier that day, two young men, Joe Dodge and James Jamb,[*] were attempting one of the dumber car heists in the history of Banff National Park. They were trying to steal a car from the government compound parking lot. They were observed by a government worker, who called the police, but the two men fled the area, apparently on foot, before the cops arrived.

Later that day, the two were spotted south of the industrial park on Cougar Street. Constable Sandro Parillo was closest to the scene and responded. The description he had was of two men, one with a cast on his leg and accompanied by a dog, the other riding a bicycle. In 2007, I reached Parillo by telephone in Regina, Saskatchewan. His voice was gruff but friendly as we talked over those days. "I remember the second bear mauling, too," growled Parillo, "because my car got totalled in a hit-and-run."

My ears shot up, "What happened?"

"That ambulance driver, I can't recall the name just now. Think he was from Ontario. While I'm coming out of the bush, he backs right into my cruiser. Did $5,000 damage. Then he just takes off." Even over the phone I could tell that the sergeant had not forgiven that one.

---

[*] The names Joe Dodge and James Jamb are fictitious. I used them because I could not locate and interview the real people involved. (In 1980, these two men were the subjects of a police investigation for a relatively minor offence.)

"Anyway, I remember I took the call on this theft, headed over to Cougar Street. There were the two guys. So I jumped out and collared the guy with the cast. While I'm talking to him, his dog is acting up, and it bit me on the right kneecap, a serious bite. So now I arrest this guy and handcuff him to the lockup in the back seat. I got the dog by the scruff of the neck and tossed him in, too. Now I want to talk to the second guy, but he jumps on the bike and takes off. The knee is bleeding badly, I chase after him as best I can on foot: he heads for the railroad tracks, the taped-off area. I'm yelling at him 'Don't go in there, Don't go in there!' But he dumps the bike and keeps going. I get to the tracks, I look down the tracks, I see a warden coming with a rifle." The suspect had gone out of sight. Parillo needed medical attention, so he got on the radio, reported what had transpired and headed back to the office with his prisoner, James Jamb.

When I worked in Jasper National Park in the early 1970s, I heard a story about an oldtime warden who went out one night to put a halter on one of his horses and wound up trying to halter a grizzly bear. They say he lived to tell the tale. I thought it was a good story with maybe a shred of truth in it somewhere. Then one night, up in the Moosehorn country, I went out in the dark to check on my horses, and found that I had somehow accumulated one more than I had when I left Jasper. I moved closer, talking softly to reassure the animal. I was just thinking that I should have brought a flashlight with me when I suddenly got a good whiff of grizzly bear coming off the dew. At the same time the bear let out a *whoof* – it sounded more like a conversational utterance than a threatening one – so I started backing away, slowly. But the grizzly bear, which was grazing on grass within a stone's throw of my horses, did not stop eating. It was pretty obvious that my horses didn't see the bear as a threat.

I shared the valley with that old male grizzly all that summer. I believe the reason he did not charge or flee was that he had already been watching me and checking out my scent for some days before I noticed him. He knew the cabin was my den, knew that I wandered around that vicinity, and he was not unduly alarmed when he heard or smelled me approaching.

Similarly, though he was no friend to humankind, I think the black grizzly of Whiskey Creek had become familiar with some of his pursuers as he followed them through the woods with his sensitive nose. According to researcher Dr. George Stevenson, a grizzly bear can smell seven times better than a hound dog, which in turn smells 300 times better than we do.[44] Sniffing at a spot where a man had urinated, or just following a human trail through the bush with his nose until he was close enough to look at the man he was following (bears see in colour), helped him later to picture the man associated with that particular smell; perhaps one had more garlic in his urine, one had more fat cells. Perhaps one had inadvertently stepped on a coyote dropping stale enough that the man himself didn't even smell it. The black grizzly would appreciate the virtues of dung piles; with his inquisitive nose he could read them like a book. (Perhaps he was the ursine version of anal retentive about where he left his own ordure, incidentally, because none of it was ever found, as far as I know.) So I think the black grizzly might have come to know Rick Kunelius, Monte Rose, Perry Jacobsen, Dan Vedova, and the other wardens by their scent trails. Maybe he even got close enough to see the man that went with the scent, and came to know him as Fat, or Sweet, or Smells-Like-False-Wolf.

They have a way of moving through the bush these Twolegs, and Sticky Mouth is curious about them. Being curious is how he finds food, and identifies threats. He has followed other beasts that live by blood, big cats, little cats, and real wolves, and he sometimes finds good things to eat at the end of their trails. But these ones never take Sticky Mouth to food and he is losing interest in them. He waits for them to go back to their dens, then he will go out to feed. By late afternoon he is less patient, anxious for the darkness and for feeding time. He gets cranky on an empty stomach; he feels mean.

The presence of so many new humans in the swamp has the big bear agitated and on the prowl. Two come to his meat cache as he lies in a day bed downwind of the prize. He rises and listens; they move like hunters through the bush. But as he hesitates, they turn and fade away again. He barely settles down and more come, a bit farther off. He rises again, stalks them, circles, and prepares to strike, but there are too many coming where he had fought them off last time. The ones in front have the weapon-stink; he sees a red cloud in his head and remembers pain.

And now his hold on this place is being tested again by a pack of Twolegs moving around by the rub tree. These ones smell of beaver musk and beaver flesh – enthralling scents rushing up his nostril bores. But he dares not approach. These Twolegs are now hunting in packs like wolves. He sits in the shadows on his hunkers, nodding his head back and forth as if there was an idea in there too weighty for the balancing. Pouting as only a bear can pout, he stalks off to the northwest corner of the wetlands, shaking his head at a coterie of noisy magpies and announced by a relay of red squirrels. He will seek a place thick with doghair pines on the north bank of Forty Mile Creek. There he will wait in ambush.

Constable Parillo's warning shouts to the fugitive had fallen on deaf ears, and the young man soon vanished into the forest at the east end of the Whiskey Creek swamp. Joe Dodge moved quickly through the forest and bog and went around the end of the railroad Y. He came to Forty Mile Creek and crossed it on a fallen tree. There was a narrow trail above the creek, hemmed by the encroaching forest. He had followed the path downstream, keeping close to its north bank to avoid the heavy bush. It was around 4:30 p.m., but the day was pleasantly warm, so he took off his leather jacket and sweater and carried them under his arm. The purling rush and rumble of the torrent masked the sound of his approach from the black grizzly lying in the timber close to its bank. There was an abandoned squatter's cabin on the far side of the stream, and Dodge stopped briefly to look it over. He had the impression that somebody had been camping in it of late, and he shouted a hello just in case someone was there. There was no response, so he stepped down from the creek bank to a sandbar where the walking was easier, to resume his journey.

In the bush, the black grizzly suddenly woke up with the echo of a human voice in his ears and the smell of man in his nose once too often. There was no smell of metal weapons mingled in the odour of sweat and new leather coming off this new trespasser.[*]

Joe Dodge had not gone far on the sandbar when he heard an ominous growl. Turning, he saw a bear coming quickly toward him, down on all fours and about 10 feet away. It was dark brown or black, big in the shoulders and wide, and it was moving fast. Dodge dropped his jacket and sweater, turned, and sprinted for the opposite bank. The stream channel (including the sandbar) was about 10 yards wide here and the bank perhaps three feet high. Dodge went splashing into the stream, thinking he would put the water between himself and the attacker. He was a good runner but now he was running for his life. In a few strides he reached the opposite bank, slipped on an exposed tree root, recovered, scrambled up again, and made a sharp turn to the right to the nearest tree, one with a twin trunk. (Freshly broken tree branches later showed that he attempted to climb out of harm's way.)

The bear caught up to him just as he began climbing, reared up and, according to Dodge, swatted him on the head from behind, knocking him out of the tree. He landed on his backside, sustaining a puncture injury near the rectum. The bear, still behind him, then cuffed him on the head, half scalping him, and the blow tumbled him over onto his stomach. (From this point on, Dodge, very wisely, attempted to stay face down as much as he could.) The bear then

---

[*] Dodge told the wardens two differing accounts of what happened to him that day. To give two examples, in version 1 he looks for a tree to climb but can't find one; in version 2 he finds a tree and climbs about six feet up it. He told Rick Kunelius the bear gnawed on his head; he told Paul Kutzer the bear clawed at his head. These examples support Weisser's point, made earlier, that bear victims are too traumatized to give accurate accounts of events. I have tried to corroborate Dodge's statements by referring to evidence found at the scene by wardens or by Dennis Weisser.

pounced on him, bit into his back over the right scapula, picked him up bodily off the ground, shook his whole body violently, then dropped him on his stomach. According to Dodge, the bear was now intent on trying to turn him over, using its muzzle and paws, but he had his arms spread out to try and prevent this. Finally it got him over on his back briefly. He raised his left arm to shield his throat; the bear bit into the forearm and shook its head back and forth before letting go.

Dodge immediately tried to get onto his stomach again, but the bear was now biting at his injured head. He later told Rick Kunelius that he sat up at this point, unable to lie still under such torture. He had not cried out when he first saw the bear, but now he was "saying things," as he put it. What he said was not recorded; we can probably imagine. The bear must have released its jaws, because Dodge then dropped back down and buried his face into the moss and branches like a gopher trying to get to safety. "Like I was laying down face first," Dodge related. "He kind of put his paw on me and sat there and he was breathing really heavy and I was breathing really heavy too . . . I could smell his breath. . . . It smelt terrible . . . Just maybe five or six seconds he hung over me and he was breathing really heavy and then he ran away." The bear must have been satisfied that Dodge was not a threat. If he had intended to kill the young man, he could have done so with the first blow he struck.

The exact time of the attack was not recorded, but it probably occurred around 4:40 p.m.

· Dodge played dead for a few minutes, fearing the bear would return. Then he got to his feet, blood pouring down his face from the head wound. He took off his T-shirt and held it over his mangled head to try and stop the bleeding. All of his wounds were covered with dirt. At this point, Dodge would have been wise to start cautiously moving out of the bear's space. Instead, dazed and in shock, he lay down in a shallow backwater pool, his mind fixed on the notion that he must clean the head wound first. He lay still, his upper body white as driftwood except where the puncture wounds to the forearm oozed blood. His shoulders, pressed against the shelved gravel of the stream bed, kept him stationary in the current.

The black grizzly had counted coup on Joe Dodge. His scalp was torn from the back of his head above the nape forward to the forehead, where it was still attached by a hinge of flesh. The washed-out pink fascia, homely layers of flesh, sebaceous glands, and granulated fat at the vertex of the skull shone in the clear water as the current tipped his scalp-hat up in a mock salute. He felt his head with a trembling hand. He forced his frantic digits to reach *in*, finding bone where his scalp should have been, to reassure himself that his brains were not, in fact, coming out.

The bear was gone – wasn't it? He must have wondered where his assailant had gotten too. He recalled later that it had ran off not straight, but in an arc. He stayed in the stream for a few minutes, weakened, shocked, not knowing which way to turn, seeing the grey autumnal sky pooled overhead where only a circle of evergreens leaned over to attend him. His hair streamed from his mangled scalp, wavering to the whim of the current, red tendrils of bright blood feathering and curling out in the crystalline water. It was cold, that stream, as cold as the stone heart of a mountain, but it washed his wounds with its cold comfort and cleared his head.

Behind the tree boles, Sticky Mouth watches the Twolegs floating there, and he gurgles a low growl that can not be heard over the lap and chuckle of the stream. Emanations play like a magic lantern show over the screen of his cognition, triggering emotions, untapped energies, warnings to retreat, inciting aggression or watchfulness or curiosity. Even the potential for playfulness lurks there, of the cat-and-mouse kind.

Comes a wailing, crazy noise, the Meatmaker calling. Twolegs keens an answer, lifts its head, hearkens. Sticky Mouth pictures the floating Twolegs as a water thing, swiftly finning away. No. It struggles, flails, rolls. That picture fades. What is it for? Red blood spills from the Twolegs beast and it flops down. On its knees it claws at its head and moans, stares down at its red paws. The eyes flip around, why can't they stay still! Get away, eyes! Now it tears its hairless skin off and shows a raw slug skin underneath. Sticky Mouth gapes, stares, almost charmed by this magic. So much blood on its head and the white fat there – is it food? In his mind he remembers a Twolegs with a burning stick. Pain. No. Not food, not yet.

Look out, it rises. Lie down, Twolegs; stay put. With his small eyes narrowing, his round ears trained up, he watches and listens as it staggers and splashes its way to the stream bank. It slips and falls back into the water; it gropes out with its naked forearms and pulls itself out of the creek, streaming red water and slime. It crawls into the willows and disappears, moaning again like a bear, now on all fours. Another underling bear thing? Maybe. No. It is Twolegs. Sticky Mouth lifts his huge head and listens to the creature retreating until he can hear it no more; he raises his brown muzzle and tracks its further progress with his nose.

He rises to all fours and silently sets forth one great, parlous foot: he follows.

The trapper team were in the bush about 100 yards from the recreation centre, about to place the last snare of the day. There had been some radio traffic earlier about somebody running across the tracks pursued by the police, but that was at the east end of the wetlands, and other wardens were handling that situation. The team had to keep moving and get their own work done before night fall.

At 5:08 p.m., Perry Jacobsen's radio came alive again, with a report that made them straighten up and gawk at each other in disbelief. The Whiskey Creek mauler had counted coup once again.

And the mauling site was just 400 yards northwest of where they were standing.

SIXTEEN

LAST STAND

God bless the bear,
arthritic as me, doing its death-clown act
on two legs, ready to embrace, saying
I'm just you in funny clothes.
Your clothes are funny too. Let's wrestle,
my little man, my little son, my little death, my brother.

JOHN NEWLOVE
from the poem "God Bless the Bear"

DIZZY AND WEAK FROM LOSS of blood and blinded by blood running into his eyes, Joe Dodge followed the creek bank for a short time then stopped to listen for the bear, terrified it might be following him. Faintly, he heard the sound of vehicles somewhere to the west. He turned to the right and regardless of the thick forest in his way, staggered forward toward that sound, the sound of salvation.

At five o'clock on Wednesday, September 3, a 19-year-old hitchhiker from Oak Ridges, Ontario, named Chris Allen was hiking out along the Norquay Road to thumb a ride on the Trans-Canada Highway. As he drew abreast of the Vermilion Lakes turn off, he heard somebody scream for help from the bush on the east side of the road. This area was known locally as the Echo Creek Transient Camp. It was intended at one time to house the multitudes of would-be

Dharma bums hitching across the country in the sixties, but it was no longer in use. A picture of Allen in the *Calgary Herald* shows a hirsute young man with a pack on his back, a guy that would fit the above category. Allen later told reporter Bruce Patterson that the victim had come staggering toward him crying, "I was mauled by a bear, I'm hurt, I'm hurt."

"He was drenched in blood," recalled Allen, "His scalp was torn, his arm was ripped open. I pulled my jacket over his head and flagged down a car. He said he was looking for the highway when he was attacked."

The two young women that Allen flagged down took one look at the victim, bundled him into the back seat, and drove him straight to the Mineral Springs Hospital.

A few minutes later, the warden service dispatcher was startled when she got a telephone call from the hospital, asking if more victims from the bear mauling would be coming in.

"Bear mauling? What bear mauling?"

"You didn't know you had another bear mauling?"

"No, I did not."

"Well, you know now."

Paul Kutzer immediately headed for the hospital. He recalled: "I got the call at the office that somebody had come out on the highway with his scalp torn off and hanging over his face, so I took off down to the hospital and he was already there. They were working to stop the bleeding." Kutzer confirmed that it was a bear attack and asked the attending physician, Dr. Sheppard, if he could come in the operating room to photograph and measure the wounds. The surgeon agreed on one condition; they were short-handed that day so Kutzer must put on a gown, scrub, and be ready to put down the camera and help hold the victim's scalp in place when it was time to put sutures in.

The victim, Joe Dodge, was conscious at this point; he claimed he had never lost consciousness, throughout his ordeal. The bear was at first described by Dodge as a black bear, but with considerably more questioning, Kutzer obtained the following description: "Not jet black; nose a little lighter than rest of bear; rounded ears; bear very large, big shoulders and fat."

Dodge later claimed he had not seen or heard the policeman on the railroad tracks shouting for him to stop. In fact, he claimed he never saw the railroad tracks, at least not the main-line tracks. He did see the railroad Y. The young man had only arrived in Banff a few days earlier. He claimed he had entered the Whiskey Creek Area around 4.15 p.m. via the Banff Construction Company woodlot in the industrial park where he had gone to look for work. Afterwards he decided to take a shortcut through the bush to reach the highway. The highway was in the opposite direction from town. In his report Kutzer wrote, "When asked why he chose that route to town, he did not answer (after repeated questioning).* When asked if he was alone in the area, he hesitated but answered that he was alone at the time of the attack."[45] Yes, he had heard about an area being closed due to a bear mauling, but he didn't know which area it was and, no, he hadn't seen any "Area Closed" signs, or heard people yelling at him. (Dodge, it turned out, was staying with Jamb at the Banff Springs Hotel staff residence. Witnesses had seen Dodge and Jamb hanging out together prior to the incident.)

In our interview, Kutzer recalled, "I asked him he was taking off from somebody. I don't know if I asked him specifically from the police or whoever. But I did ask him if he was running away. And he kind of sheepishly said that he was. I said, 'You probably won't do that again, will you?'"

Kutzer was able to get good measurements and photos of Dodge's wounds. There were scrape marks on Dodge's skull that might have been made by a grizzly bear's claws and canine-teeth puncture wounds in the scalp. He also secured some black hairs found in Dodge's scalp as the doctor was cleaning the wound. "I took a close

---

* On September 10, Dodge would tell Warden Kunelius that he went into the area because he was "checking out the fishing." (*Whiskey Creek Report*, p. 111.)

look at it and it had a dark body to it and lighter on the end." The lighter tip marked the silvertip phase of the adult grizzly bear. "Black bears don't have colouring like that," said Kutzer. "So then I got on the blower right away and phoned the office and told them 'We're dealing with a grizzly bear.'"

It appears, however, that Kutzer's findings were treated as just one more piece of evidence rather than as conclusive proof that the target was definitely a grizzly bear. A "large, black-coloured bear" was the description of the target, which meant another American black bear was not ruled out.

"So then [the doctors] put me to work," Paul Kutzer continued. "'Hurry up and get your pictures,' they said, 'because we are going to need your help here.'" By this time the anesthetist had put Dodge under, as they prepared to suture his scalp in place before transferring him to the specialists in Calgary. Kutzer had donned rubber gloves, ready to apply pressure to damaged blood vessels. "They were pumping a lot of blood into him, he was bleeding badly. There would be a big spurt and the doctor would tell me to grab hold of it while he was working. They had to send him in to Calgary because they were running out of blood in there, that was the biggest reason; otherwise I think they would have finished the job."

In addition to Dodge's head wounds, the puncture in his buttocks, and the bite marks on the left arm, Kutzer reported there was a bite injury with serious muscle damage across the lateral border of the right scapula, one puncture under the armpit into the ribcage, and one puncture into the upper arm near the armpit. These were consistent with the upper and lower incisors of a large bear.

At the sharp end of the hunt, those who began the day thinking that another American black bear was the perpetrator were in for a scalp-prickling awakening. When the attack occurred, Alan Westhaver and Herrero's colleague, David Hamer, were driving west to count buffalo berries at a study plot. They would find that the berry count was a fraction of what it should have been that summer. Their report reads: "Berries per plot in 1977, 1978 and 1979 averaged 151, 21 and

779 respectively. The 1980 average is . . . between 5 and 10." This scarcity of plant sugar meant the bears in Banff National Park were just as desperate to find alternative calories as the bears in northern Alberta were. No wonder they had moved in close to town.

Westhaver was monitoring the park radio and heard the news about the latest mauling. He pulled a U-turn and drove back to Banff – fast. He left Hamer with the truck and joined Rick Kunelius, who had been detailed to backtrack Dodge's route and locate the mauling site. "The ambulance had just taken this guy to the hospital to treat him. So Rick and I found out where he had come out of the woods and went to that point, saw blood, backtracked the blood trail into the bush. We'd gone maybe 50 or 80 metres into the bush when we came across a little tributary of Forty Mile Creek, white sandy bottom about a metre wide, and we could see where the victim had come out of the bush. His footprints were in the sand; we were just about to leap across the creek and carry on. We looked downstream about two or three metres and there's the biggest grizzly track that I've ever seen in my life, and our hair stood on end, 'cause that's when we knew that the whole equation changed, you know. There was a grizzly involved – and he was big."

But there was an even more chilling revelation of what they had been up against all along, for they found where the bear had stepped on one of Dodge's running-shoe prints. Weisser, who also checked those tracks, told me that Dodge was probably running as fast as he could, but the bear was moving at a leisurely walk. The grizzly had stealthily followed Dodge out of the bush, making sure, it seems, that the trespasser had really left. This was not only a big grizzly but it was a bear of mind and intense resolve. How big it actually was, however, remained to be discovered.

Kunelius led the way, rifle at the ready as they came out on the banks of Forty Mile Creek. A leather jacket and a sweater were lying upstream on a sandbar, looking very forlorn and out of place. They would leave these for Weisser's team, then approaching from the south, to examine. They gazed nervously around, keeping still, listening and sounding the air like bears themselves. It was the kind of moment when a person becomes all ears, eyes, and nostrils. "We crossed the creek and went another 20–30 metres," recalled Westhaver, "and we found the spot where the guy had tried to get underneath a young spruce tree. And you could see where the bear had been running around this spruce tree, and he had literally torn the moss up. There were clods of moss hanging two or three metres above the ground on the branches, where he had just been spinning around and trying to fish this guy out from underneath this conifer. And [Dodge] had been hanging on, trying to cover the back of his neck and do the right thing – at that point, anyway."

The two young wardens must have exchanged some shocked looks. It was another scary epiphany. They'd been dragging smelly horsemeat and elk meat baits around in those woods, laying down scent trails, but in effect playing cat-and-mouse with an adult grizzly bear, a bear intelligent enough to beat them at the game had he chosen to do it; one determined enough to follow his victims out of the woods to make sure they did not come back to bother him again.

The trappers had been monitoring events on the park radio system. John Taggart remembers them pausing to ask each other, "How the heck did this happen? And we didn't hear a thing! It had only occurred a few hundred yards from us, but the lodgepole pine is so thick in there, you couldn't hear anything. And then of course the whole place is cordoned off to begin with, so how the heck did [Dodge] get in there? We said, 'Well let's go right to where this kid was attacked, 'cause we know the bear's there, right?'"

The event impressed itself on Weisser's memory also. Someone, perhaps Kunelius, radioed to report what they'd found. Westhaver and Kunelius headed back westward, measuring the bear tracks as the trappers continued north to the site. Weisser and Taggart, who had not been on the hunt long enough to be sidetracked by talk about black bears, were not particularly surprised that a grizzly bear had now been officially confirmed as the target animal. Weisser remembered that they worked their way up the creek for several hundred yards, weapons at the ready, and sure enough there was the jacket and sweater right where Dodge had dropped them when he spotted the bear.

The trappers could read the story of what had happened by the tracks on the sandbar. "Well," said Taggart, "the bear had set off on the one bank, landed in the middle of the creek, at a bounce, and then pretty well had the kid on the other bank. Now it's getting dark, by the time we got in there . . . it's dense lodgepole pine in there."

Taggart beamed and chuckled at the memory of this darkening adventure. As he spoke, I pictured the scene as I had seen it at twilight, the old trees close to the bank draped with wolf lichen like old ladies in yellow prayer shawls, leaning over the creek to watch these supplicants setting out their offerings of flesh and incense.

"The creek is running," Taggart continued. "That's drowning out a lot of noise, and there's the four of us: Dennis and I setting snares, each armed, Dennis had asked me to bring my .300 Winchester Magnum with me. So anyways, we had set the snares, seven snares in six different locations and the mauling site the seventh location. It was getting dark. If you want feelings, it was a little eerie. I wasn't concerned, with Dennis there. He certainly knew grizzles more than I did; I was getting a quick education on grizzly bears, what to expect. I remember at one point I went to look for some forked twigs to set the snares and I stepped about three feet to the side of him to break a branch. I was out of Dennis's sight for a moment and I heard him say [Taggart's voice dropped to a hoarse whisper], 'Johnny! Where are ya?'"

Taggart laughed, a tender laugh at the unknowing young man he was then. That moment was when he'd first realized that Weisser was on edge. "If he was concerned, maybe I should be concerned, too. 'Cause it was getting that dark, eh? And we didn't have lights. So the tension was there."

Perry Jacobsen, tired and jumpy from lack of sleep over the last ten days, kept an eye on the woods while Weisser studied the ground ahead. "That was the first time that I saw his tracks," said Jacobsen, "in the sand of that creek, and I just about fell through the ass of my pants. I mean he had a *massive* foot, right? And there was blood and shit all over. There's pieces of clothes there, and blood. And this bear had roared through: there was some real doghair pine right there and he cut a swath right through it. I've never seen anything like that, he must have been in a rage. And I can still feel this today. I have never had my senses that sharp before. I could have heard a grasshopper fart at 400 yards. I've never seen anything like it. And that little .308 gun just turning in a 360-degree circle. I was sure any second this sucker's gonna come out of the bush at us. And I said to these guys, 'Get the damn things set, we've gotta get out.'"

It was at this juncture when they heard the helicopter approaching their position. Suddenly it came booming in and circled overhead, carrying Lord knows what curious park officials and/or newshounds wanting to rubberneck the scene. Dennis Weisser had not been overly worried before that moment. But he could feel the presence of the bear; he believed it was close by and in that thick bush; their safety depended on hearing the bear coming before it emerged from cover.

Crouching under the rotor wash, Weisser and Jacobsen exchanged worried frowns. "This is stupid," yelled the frustrated warden over the racket. The noise of the creek was distraction enough; the shadows among the doghair pines were deep, tombstone deep. Somebody grabbed a radio and gruffly asked Palmer to back off. It was a bad moment for them all; Weisser was glad to see the last of the helicopter. "I know how it seems," he said, "but this is going to work well; it won't take us long to set the snares. He's in here somewhere; he can probably see us or hear us. But we have enough here to handle him and it's not likely that we are gonna have to. Just keep a lookout and we'll get this done, get back to town, and crack a beer."

They set one of the snares right next to the tree where Dodge had tried to evade the bear. The smell of pungent beaver castor mixed with the funky mushroom scent of the disturbed moss melded with the smell of blood and the fish and pine scents of the stream. The creek chuckled to itself and lapped the blood from the stones. By the time they got back out to the trucks, the night had fallen.

"We went back to the office," recalled Weisser, "and everybody was there, shooting the breeze. There was a forestry guy they had brought in; he had brought an infrared camera unit. He said, 'In the morning, we'll find that bear with the infrared camera. No problem.' I said, 'I hope you do. But you know, I heard it doesn't work on bears: now I don't know anything about it, that's just what I've been told.' And the guy says, 'Oh no, we'll find him for sure.'"

Steve Herrero remembers something Monte Rose said on this occasion. They were talking about the attempted car theft, and the kid making it into the swamp, the one place nobody expected him to run to. And he should have gotten away with it, too. What are the odds – he runs right into the bear! Rose's face lit up with that sardonic grin he had and they all waited to hear how he would sum up this one: "Yes, victory was in sight," agreed Rose, "but then the long paw of the law got him." According to rumour, when a Mountie went to the hospital in Calgary to question Dodge, who was bandaged from stem to stern, Dodge had cracked his own joke: "Jeez, you guys have the biggest damn police dog I have ever seen."[*]

Herrero had to laugh, but not for long. He and the other members of the scientific panel had returned from the wetlands earlier that afternoon to discuss their findings on the earlier maulings. They had just sat down when they were stunned by the news of the Dodge mauling. Scientific objectivity was temporarily out the window: what in hell was going on out there? If a greenhorn kid could bypass the cordon and sneak into the area, what real hope did they have of keeping the bear from sneaking out?

That same night (September 3), John Wackerle and his assistant, Dan Vedova, were in the warden office preparing to go on shift manning the bait station down by the railroad Y. The day before, they

---

[*] Andy Anderson told me that he requested the RCMP not charge Joe Dodge with an offence, since he had suffered enough. It seems the police agreed with him. A source with the RCMP told me Dodge must not have been charged since he was not fingerprinted. James Jamb, however, was charged with vehicle theft at the Banff courthouse on September 4.

had run out of bait, but that was a trifling concern; God would provide. No sooner had Vedova mentioned the lack of it when the radio had interrupted with the timely news that yet another elk, a calf this time, had been slaughtered out on the highway.

The two men exchanged glances. "Chust what we need," said Wackerle. Wackerle was a natural leader of men, and a kindly mentor to young wardens. He excelled at everything from skiing to horseback work and could be plugged into any situation with confidence, so Vedova felt lucky to be his assistant. The two downed their coffee and headed out to the roadkill site in their patrol truck. There was the fatted calf and it sure was dead, born in the high country in June and smoked by a speeding truck in the Bow Valley in September.* They'd grabbed the calf by the hocks, dragged it out of the traffic in a swath of blood and muscled it up into the back of their pickup truck.

(While the confab was going on at the warden office that night, I was back on the boxcar with rifle at the ready once again, as shocked by the news of the days events as everyone else. It was a one in a thousand chance that I would have to use the rifle, but I had the magazine loaded. Winning this back-asswards lottery with an empty weapon would be just too embarrassing to live down.)

In a 2006 interview with me, Vedova related how he and Wackerle headed out to the railroad Y, out of sight in the woods, to set up their bait station for the night ahead. Wackerle, always thinking, explained to the kid that they would chain the dead elk to a heavy railroad tie he'd found. That way, if the bear came in, it would probably drag the calf for a while, rather than just ripping it free as it had done at the Caboose bait station. This would give them some time to get a shot

---

* Such collisions were an everyday occurrence prior to 1981, when the first eight-foot-high fences were installed to keep game off the roadway. Since 1981, wildlife fencing on Highway 1 in the park has reduced ungulate mortality by 95 percent and mortality of all wildlife combined by 80 percent, according to the Banff National Park of Canada website article, "Trans-Canada Highway Mitigation in the Mountain Parks: Are We Reducing Wildlife Roadkill?"

away, Wackerle reasoned. He asked Vedova to lay a scent trail down to draw the bear in.

"We had a pretty good little vantage point on where that elk calf was," Vedova recalled. "I remember we had the truck backed in there and we had the spotlights all set up. We were hunkered down and we had our rifles set up on sandbags so we could get a real good shot." Vedova had traded the 12-gauge for a bolt-action .30-06. He told me, "The whole thing had become surreal by this time, because there was the Man in Black, there were the media, there were the Ken Prestons, there were mystics calling in with tips on where the bear could be found.

"So it's getting dark, and Wackerle says, 'Danny, I think it's time you dragged that elk calf a bit. I cover you.' I'll never forget this. 'Yah,' he says, 'you open up, gut that animal. Yah, sure. I'll cover you, and you lay a scent trail.' There was a lot of things wrong with this picture! But you didn't argue with Wackerle. At that time, I should add, against the bureaucrats' wisdom, we all had sidearms. Cooper had gotten me a .357 Magnum, a Colt trooper model, a beautiful little double-action gun, and it fit in a shoulder holster.

"There's no way I can drag this elk calf through the bushes with my rifle along, but I do have that pistol. I take hold of the elk calf and I lay a scent trail down. Anyway, that spur goes right through the middle of the area. I'm in there and, remember now, I've got the rail-road tie to deal with and the elk calf and that fear; that gut fear. So I'm hyper-attuned to everything and suddenly I hear a movement behind me – and I know, I know it's that bear. And I wheeled around, and it's a double-action gun, and I tell you, I had my hand on the handle but I hadn't drawn it yet. And standing there is, a willow-thin guy with reddish-blonde hair, and he's all in white! I thought, I'm already dead, this bear took me out, you know? Like that notion sort of struck me instantaneously, the irony of it all, right?

"But I knew really I wasn't dead. I was like a nanosecond away from drilling six bullets through this guy. It was a cook from the Timberline who had a shortcut through there. Fuck the closure signs, he was taking the shortcut. And of course Wackerle was rolling a cigarette and didn't see him come through."

(We both chuckled. I too had seen Wackerle stop the world while he rolled a smoke.)

"Well, I said, 'What the fuck are you doing in here? You don't know what's going on, you haven't seen the signs?' And at the same time I was so angry I remember kind of grabbing him by the belt and giving him a half wedgie.

"That further amped it up in terms of how surreal it was."

On the last night he would be in this world, Sticky Mouth goes to feed again on the buried elk hindquarters he has left to sweeten in his food cache. After eating his fill, he wanders through the wetlands following the scent of the Twolegs pack, seeing again, behind his eyes, the shape of those his nose conjures: the Sweet One, the Fat One, the False-Wolf-Shit One. There is the Burning Grass One also: he sees that one in his head, going around with its mouth on fire all day long, leaving a trail of smoke. He pictures a forest fire when he recalls that one. And now there is the most enticing Twolegs he has ever followed. It leaves beaver anus smell everywhere so that Sticky Mouth is compelled to roll in the Twolegs tracks near one of the beaver kills, eager to imprint the smell into his hide so that he can have it with him always. But he doesn't go into that kill. There is a dog stench there where the beaver flesh should be. At another beaver kill he is distracted again because an underling bear has raided it first, scoffing down the beaver meat that should have been his and leaving a thin shiny looking thing that does not smell of the Twolegs hurt-me thing but reminds him of that because it does not belong there. After he has tracked that underling bear and set it running, bawling, out of the woods, he forgets about the beaver meat for a moment. Besides there is more of it to find; he can smell it coming from several different directions at times, making his nose dizzy.

He comes to the rubbing tree and stands up to scratch his back again. Turning and sniffing along the bark, he rises to his full extension and majesty to bite his mark into the bark higher than any bear has bitten there before. He catches a whiff of elk meat on the night breeze and he circles around to the east to get downwind and home in on it. He keeps on eastward until he comes to where the iron serpent's trail enters deep into the bog. He comes out of the bog and climbs up on the serpent's trail; the tracks are cold and dead on the gravel, beaded with the rain that fell that day, but he fears them not. The night wind is strong with the nose-candy smell of dead elk. Survival dictates that he must lay claim to any food source he detects, even though his belly is full. The fingernail moon is hidden behind the cloud and he follows the silver tracks toward the latest offering of flesh, half reluctant as he shambles along, an old man on an errand of blood kinship that must be fulfilled. He must come and take their offering – peacefully or violently.

"John and I had a system worked out," Dan Vedova recounted, "if that bear showed up, but it's late at night now, and I've been staring down that track and into those bushes for so long that I was wondering if I was imagining bears. And then suddenly I saw the bear coming down the tracks, ambling toward the bait." The bear was on the spur, and it was massive. Vedova could just make it out with the ambient light from the town painting in the outline. "We had set it up earlier," he continued. "Wackerle instructed me to take the shot and he was going to operate the lights. And I realized I was either going to be a hero or a bum. It could be worse, if I hit him [and didn't kill him]."

This was a real worry. Merely wounding the bear would make the situation even more dangerous for himself and for others who would have to go after the animal and finish the job. The bear, with his head down and humped back so prominent, was pure grizzly, of that Vedova was certain. But the town's light made it appear more an unreal, spectral silhouette of a bear than an actual animal. "He was moving so slowly, and again it was all so part of the surrealism of the whole event that I wondered if I was really seeing it. I'm not sure that John did; in fact, he didn't. And now that I think back, I realize that at my age now, my night vision is really only a fraction as good as it was then. But I said to John, 'He's there.' And I had the sights perfectly, just above his shoulder.

"I'll never forget it because the bear presented his right side to me. And it was a beautiful shot, like it was a dead simple shot, and at that time the whole world calmed, and I was there. And I remember thinking, you can shoot this animal but remember it's not just one shot. You've got to get another one in the chamber right away.

"Just as John went to turn on the light, there was a camera crew. I think it was CBC. They were actually setting up a scaffolding behind a railroad car, and they dropped a piece of scaffolding or something. And John turned on the lights and there wasn't any bear there.

"I was full of self-doubt after that."

(While Vedova was facing the grizzly, I was on top of a wet boxcar, close by. I don't recall the scaffolding incident. We did have two wardens working to set up stands and hook up emergency lighting that evening.)

In the morning, Dan Vedova would find the tracks of a massive grizzly bear in the mud of a beaver dam where it had veered away into the forest. Today he believes in his heart of hearts that it was a lucky thing that he didn't take that shot, clean though it seemed. He was right. A shot in the dark could have had dangerous consequences.

Also the young warden had been conflicted about his mission. He was not taking the bear for food or medicine, like a true hunter of old; he was there to punish it for defending its home against incursions. He was there, in essence, to punish the bear for being a bear, there to weed out its dangerous DNA. That is why he was fortunate not to get the shot: as someone devoted to protecting wildlife, he doesn't have to carry it on his conscience. Good for him. I wish I could say the same.

Punishing the bear; that's what we were all there for, and therein lay the root of our disillusionment. We weren't really hunters – we were managers of a wild animal that refused to be managed, an animal that was too wild to live in Banff National Park.

That night a sentry reported seeing two malamute husky dogs running across the tracks and heading into the swamp. It turned out later that they might have sprung at least two traps. Later that evening, one of the dogs came racing out and scurried across the tracks with its tail between its legs. The other one would be found by Monte Rose on September 4, caught in one of Weisser's snares and grinning sheepishly with relief and embarrassment at being rescued. "I turned him over to the welcoming arms of the domestic animal control officer," Rose would report. "Charges are pending."

A black bear crossed the road that night from the Fenlands and went into the area. An hour later what appeared to be the same bear dashed across the Norquay Road, back into the Fenlands. Another black bear, a bigger one this time, sidled across the Trans-Canada near the Norquay overpass and went tearing up the mountainside. Those of us on the cordon held our belt radios up to our ears, the volume muffled, and listened to these reports with building apprehension. The big grizzly was determined that nothing should intrude on his demesne this night. Weisser's bait was working its voodoo on the big bear.

On the boxcar that evening, I remember studying the sky. It would have been fitting for Orion the Hunter to be out but instead the summer constellations shone on the wet forest and the wet rails from the partly clouded sky. Ursa both major and minor had to do as bear signs for guiding whatever course events would take. And this was not hunting anyway, this was an ambush, but we were definitely not sure who was the ambusher, who the ambushee. That which we waited for also waited for us. I believed he was close to me; I believed he was watching me from the velveteen shadow at the edge of the woods. I had to believe that, or I wouldn't be ready.

Something rattled softly down the grade in the deeper shadows below the boxcars. It sounded like a bear's claws on gravel. The noise stopped for a moment, then as the night breeze came winding along the cars I heard it again, closer this time. It came again, and a dark form floated along down below my boxcar, a few feet above the tracks, and seemed to settle on the ties. I swung the rifle, tracking it with the trigger hand, and flicked on the flashlight with the other. A black garbage bag fluttered on the ground, the rattling noise pursued it. I swung on that, saw a pair of Styrofoam coffee cups rolling along the greasy railway ties.

An engine coughed in the dark, then caught and rumbled, and powerful construction lights flared into dazzling brilliance, lighting the tracks and the adjacent woods, burning the night out of our brains. But there would be nothing else to hear or see until the morning.

Dennis Weisser met with the warden hunting teams and park managers early the next day. The forestry man was on hand with his forward-looking infrared (FLIR) camera, which could detect from a helicopter thermal energy on the ground and assemble an image of the source on a video screen. He was eager to demonstrate the superiority of technology over animal tracking. The wardens, feeling discouraged after many days of slogging through the wetlands, were willing to be convinced. Weisser was not. He'd seen the equipment tried on bears before, and it had not worked. (This problem may be related to the insulation values of the bear's thick coat of fur, or the screening effect of forest cover.) But he suggested that young Taggart should go along on the flight; that way they could check the snares from the air while they were searching the area. Weisser didn't mind missing a slog through Whiskey Creek. He preferred doing his hiking on horseback. "If God wanted us to walk," he often said, "he would have given us four legs."

When Taggart showed up, Weisser said, "John, you're to go along with the camera and check the snares."

"Did they ask for me?" The young apprentice was thrilled. The older men exchanged grins.

"Yes," said Weisser; it was but a small white lie. "And Johnny, if you find that bear, check and see if anything registers on that camera." Taggart was pleased until he realized he might miss the action on the ground. Weisser said "Don't worry about it. We will wait for you to get back before we go in."

"I drew the short straw being the rookie, I guess," Taggart recalled. "So I got on the helicopter and we went and checked a couple of sites first. I said, 'Let's go down to [Dodge's mauling site]' 'cause I thought that's where we're going to catch the bear. The forestry guy is in the back of the helicopter, he's got his face in his screen. I'm holding this radar gun out the window and it's attached to this dude's monitor in the back." When they came in over the last snare set, Taggart looked down and saw the head of a large, dark grizzly bear staring up at him from the base of the anchor tree. "'We got the bear!' I said. The forestry guy said, 'No, there's nothing there.'"

Geoff Palmer brought the machine into hover mode over the site. "I said, 'Yes, he is. He's right there.' And the forestry guy says, 'I can't see anything on the screen.' And I said, 'Get your face out of the screen and look out the window!' And, sure enough, the bear was there [in the snare], a big black grizzly bear. And it was so surprising: that FLIR unit did pick up heat from the trucks, it might have even picked up people, but it didn't pick up the bear. And we were at treetop level, and you'd think the bear would have been giving off all kinds of heat, fighting the snare. And the bear had dug a grave, eh? He had dug a grave at least five, six feet long and about three feet wide, right in that cobble, the creek substrate. And he was lying there waiting, he was in ambush. Anyway I got on the blower to Dennis. I said the bear has been caught, it's a large black grizzly bear. He's at the mauling site and I'm coming back in."

Those listening on the radio were electrified by the news; the in-house bear experts who had been saying there were no black grizzly bears in Banff National Park now had some crow to eat. Chief Warden Andy Anderson must have chewed on his pipestem a bit while digesting this new revelation. He had to set aside the implications this revelation might have on his previous decision to reopen the area, and concentrate on current realities. Taking the bear alive and relocating it somewhere far from Banff would be a more popular move with bear conservationists, but from Parks Canada's perspective in 1980 it was not a viable option. Even if no rabies tests or necropsy were required, where would he relocate the bear? What were the legal implications if the bear mauled somebody else? Was there a zoo out there where this king of bears, used to roaming over hundreds of square miles of mountains, could spend the rest of its days pacing inside a steel enclosure? The need for tests made other speculation academic. No, the bear had to go, the sooner the better.

His orders were to use lead.

A grim-faced crew assembled at the Banff recreation centre, hoping that this time they really had the right bear, hoping this nightmare was now about to end.

Rick Kunelius remembers that morning. There was not enough day light for taking photographs for the record, as they walked up the creek to the last mauling site with their guns at the ready. With him were Dennis Weisser, Lance Cooper, John Taggart, and Monte Rose. Cooper summed up the mood: "That's something you want to take a long shot at," but Weisser explained to the crew that, from his experience, they should form a line and move in close before shooting. The sightlines in the bush precluded shooting at a distance; it was dangerous for the crew, and might result in poorly placed shots and unnecessary suffering for the bear. The two provincial officers had their rifles along, but Weisser took Taggart aside and told him they were there for backup only. "Let the wardens do the shooting, John. We've done our job, it's up to them to finish it."

They came at last to a spot within distant sight of the tree where the snare trap was anchored, and they stopped. The bear heard them coming and it roared out its warning as they approached. They could not see it. It had dug an ambush pit out with his free front paw, and as they came a bit closer and peered through the trees, all they could see were its ears, turned toward them and poking up behind the edge of the pit.

The crew spread out, Weisser and Taggart in the rear. Weisser had advised: "He will charge you for sure, and that's when you open up with the shotguns." Weisser had his reservations about shotguns, but the wardens thought highly of them. Rose and Kunelius had

12-gauges, Cooper had his .270 rifle. They all cycled live rounds into the chambers, checked their safeties to make sure they were on, and moved forward again with their fingers outside the trigger guards. They could hear the bear's heavy breathing as it waited them out. Up came the weapons to the shoulder as they stepped slowly forward. The range decreased, 30 yards, 20 yards, 15 yards. Lance Cooper said to himself, "This can't be good." Was this bear on the snare still, or not? Now they were close enough to see that the bear had chewed through and knocked over several small trees (six inches in diameter) in its efforts to be free. It had blazed its epitaph with his teeth on the anchor tree nearly seven feet from the ground and painted it with its blood.

When they were 30 feet away (according to Lance Cooper), the grizzly came up out of the pit with a roar. It seemed as if it would just keep going up to the top of the tree, but its arc was toward the hunters, and the leap closed another six feet off the distance between them before the quarter-inch cable on its left front foot (for it was the left in the case of this most singular bear) stopped it with a bowstring *whang* and a jerk that made the tree shake as if frightened. The grizzly hung there against the cable for a heartbeat, reaching for them with the free paw, talons outstretched as if in supplication, as if beckoning for them to come just a little closer to meet its embrace. The crew were frozen on the spot, too astounded by the creature's might, agility, and majesty to shoot.

Then that heartbeat passed, and the first shotgun boomed. A round hit the black grizzly as it leaned against the cable and knocked it back down into the ambush pit. The first rounds in the shotguns were the 8 mm buck so highly touted in those days; next in line were solid slugs. But they found out later that the 8 mm balls just circled around under the bear's hide without penetrating through the under-lying four inches of fat. It was knocked over, true, but that just made it angrier than ever as it came back up for more, shaking its head and roaring at the insult of being taunted with bee stings. The men opened up again in a volley of shots. The bear rolled over, got back up again. Then Taggart heard Lance Cooper say, "That's enough!" And the .270 spoke, the bullet struck below the ear and cut the big black grizzly down. It slumped and rolled down the bank as if it had suddenly called a truce and now only wanted to reach the water of Forty Mile, the mountain water that tasted of home and of open spaces and ozone. The vanquished grizzly lay with one arm suspended in the snare above its head. It died half sitting, hind feet in the water, while the echoes of the guns rolled from peak to peak and tolled out the news of its passing.

He had almost learned to trust the light, the light mediated by a canopy of forest, but in the end they had come limned in shards of light, the enemy. His body shivered in a spasm of released nervous energy and he was still; he was staring across the water into a dark opening in the forest as the gleam of life faded from his pupils. He had found the winter den at last, and he slipped away into its welcome. With his last breath, he drew in the all-encompassing odour of the Motherdark, and so he died and was born into her protective arms again, with his eyes fixed on the shadows of the trees across the wild and rippling water.

— SEVENTEEN —

NECROPSIES AND RECKONINGS

Exit, pursued by a bear.

WILLIAM SHAKESPEARE
The Winter's Tale

ON THE MORNING OF September 4, Alan Westhaver heard the first gunshot echoing back from Mount Norquay. He glanced at his watch: it was 7:57 a.m., and that's how the black grizzly of Whiskey Creek received the name of a legend – 757.

Tim Auger and Perry Jacobsen went into the woods with other wardens to help drag the mighty bear out. They gathered around him where he leaned against the bank, and they talked in hushed tones about the chase he had led them. His colour was mainly black, like the typical American black bear, changing to brown on the underside of his chin and neck. He had a lighter-coloured brown stripe around his shoulders and over his chest, the mark of the biggest bear, the distinguished one the Stoneys call *Wahtonga*. He had few of the silvertip hairs seen on mature grizzlies in the Rockies. The wardens had to smile: why would anyone think this was of the smaller species of bear? But his victims only had a glimpse of him charging in, no time to stare, and there was that black fur and that lighter patch on his chest confusing the issue. Steve Herrero said later he understood why someone might mistake 757 for a black bear under those circumstances.

"We just stood there in awe," Rick Kunelius recalls. "And I remember thinking, why did it have to come to this?"

Weisser unlocked the steel snare from around 757's lower leg. Then they took hold of his fur and waded into the creek; the water turned red and their feet were washed in the blood of the bear. They dragged him down through the deeper channel, half floating him as far as they could before it shoaled out. The tree canopy was open enough there for the helicopter to lift him up on a cable.

The word had spread through the town, and people hurried down to the Parks Canada compound to await events. They leaned against the wire, peering in, where Steve Herrero and Dan Vedova stood waiting for Geoff Palmer to fly the bear in. One of the onlookers was a local woman who spoke for many when she told a reporter she didn't believe the wardens had really killed the bear; she needed to see it for herself.

In the distance the Jet Ranger hovered over the forest above Forty Mile Creek and the noise of its engine echoed over the valley. Then it began to lift upwards with an even mightier roar of power. At his bulk fuel depot near the Caboose, Alden Brososky watched the helicopter come out of the trees, saw the thin line of the cable and then the dark head of a bear rising slowly above the tree tops, and he still remembers that it seemed to take a long time to emerge, growing bigger as it rose into the light. It was harnessed by the neck and by a hind leg, with the other hind leg hanging down, stretched out as if it were still running up that tree into the sky. This magnificent animal was no black bear: this, he realized, was the bear he had seen at the Caboose on August 24, chasing the black bears and raising hell.

The people along the edge of the railroad saw the bear pass just above the treetops, spinning a bit on the cable, one front paw reaching out, not done threatening yet.

As Dan Vedova waited to help stretch 757 out on a flat-deck trailer, the bear loomed closer and closer, swaying on the steel tether. Vedova was shocked to see claws were missing from that free paw, and it was bleeding. The sight distracted him, and when the bear spun one more time Vedova had to duck. Once its bulk was settled on the trailer, the wardens dragged its hind legs out to stretch it on its back. The dead eyes were glazed and fixed on nothing, the mouth was shut in an unfriendly grin, the yellowish tusks of its canines still locked in a last defiant snap. Vedova unhooked the bear and the helicopter lifted and backed into position, to land in front of the nearby hangar.

There were people jumping on the fence now to get a look at the prize. "Killer bear strikes again," the headlines had trumpeted falsely that morning, but that version of the story had died; the "monster killer bear," the "rogue grizzly," was gone almost before the papers hit the streets that day.

The press photographers and TV reporters clamoured to get into the compound, shaking the Frost fence impatiently. Dan Vedova was one of several wardens who wished the ignominious spectacle had been kept out of the public view, but Steve Herrero already had his tape measure out. He pulled back the bear's lips to measure its canine spread, and the cameras clicked like bear's teeth to record the moment. Andy Anderson was anxious to know if the canines matched the holes in Cohoe's waders and the puncture wounds of the more recent victims. Only then could he take a chance on standing down his sentries and calling this case closed. The crowd was yelling at Herrero, "What happened to his paw?" Herrero wrapped it in white muslin to cover the ugly sight. He reported later that the claws had become entangled in the snare cable and had to be cut free. That may be, but Monte Rose told the BBC that he and Kunelius had "got into a little trouble" for removing claws from the bear. They had counted coup on 757.

The black grizzly weighed in at 761 pounds. He was the biggest grizzly bear ever seen in Banff National Park, excepting old Spassky, a good-natured dumpster bear at Lake Louise years ago who weighed (according to Eric Langshaw) over 800 pounds in his prime. "But this was the first *real* bear," said Kunelius. "He stood out alone, far heavier than anything we had handled, or ever will again."[*]Monte Rose, who had led bear control teams at Lake Louise, had never seen the black grizzly before and was at a loss to figure out where he might have come from.

Rose and Kunelius made a plaster cast of the grizzly tracks found at the last mauling site and it matched with the size and the creases of 757's left rear pad. In the end, the mythological size of the bear's hind foot, from the heel to the front of the third toe, shrank under scientific scrutiny to 26.7 cm (10.5 inches). Steve Herrero measured the upper canine spread at 78 mm and the lower at 69 mm. He matched the bear's upper canine spread with the puncture measurements on Joe Dodge's back; at 80 mm, he considered it a good match, especially when combined with the track evidence. As for Remy Tobler, the evidence was a bit more conjectural. Herrero measured the wounds in Tobler's left hip and groin after September 4. The spread on Tobler's hip was 70 mm and 65 mm. "While I find the 70 mm spread a bit small and therefore puzzling," Herrero reported, "I still believe that it was inflicted by the shot grizzly and the discrepancy is within the range of skin distortion and measurement error. The same is true for the 65 mm spread."[46]

Herrero told me he never saw Cohoe's waders. He obtained the measurements from the Mounties around September 5. He believed that the puncture marks were probably made by the big grizzly, since they were 79 mm apart. Allowing for the stretch in the rubber, he felt it was a good match. The punctures were certainly not made by a black bear, since their upper canines seldom exceed 60 mm, according to Dennis Weisser. The black grizzly was about ten years old when he died; neither the grizzly nor the black bear 054 tested positive for rabies. So much for the "crazy bear" theory.

Herrero reported on further suggestive evidence linking 757 to all three attacks: the three incidents were all in the same small area, 757

---

[*] After 1980, with access to garbage cut off, the average weight of grizzly bears decreased by at least a third.

was snared in that same area, and the character of the attacks pointed to the same bear, as bears are individualistic predators. "The bear moved in fast, inflicted injuries centred on the face, and then left within a few minutes."[47]

On September 5, the warden service finally received a necropsy report on B054. Weighing 350 pounds, it was found to be in excellent condition, well muscled with good fat reserves. The RCMP lab found no human blood on its paws, but cautioned that the bear blood present there "may have obliterated the presence of human blood."[48] They found traces of garbage in the stomach, but they also found something disturbing, light brown human scalp and pubic hairs. Ernest Cohoe had light brown hair. However, the bear could easily have ingested the hair among the garbage, and there was no human tissue in its stomach. Herrero was convinced that the black grizzly was responsible for all three attacks.

Superintendent Paul Lange chaired a review board to report on the attacks and make recommendations for the future. Andy Anderson and Steve Herrero sat on that board. Not surprisingly, the board reported, in a decidedly bland press release that December, that "the root cause of bear activity in and around the visitor use areas is garbage availability." It called for visitors, residents, and businesses to accept responsibility for the "proliferation of garbage" and promised that monitoring of the situation by the warden service would be "stepped up." Parks Canada's role in garbage proliferation was not mentioned. The board further found that the black grizzly was responsible for all three attacks.[49] Anderson signed off on the finding very reluctantly at the time, and to this day he believes that bear 054 was responsible for the attack on Ernest Cohoe. "They were basically arguing that the grizzly was the guilty one and the black bear was a mistake. And Lange jumped in there very strongly. Whatever the experts said was going to be it, he didn't want to lose them as supporters, you might say. I said, 'Well, that's fine,' but you know the evidence just wasn't there, and I still had a lot of doubts."

What bothers Andy Anderson to this day is the lack of grizzly bear tracks in the area during the first attack, and even during the second. He can't believe the bear could have been in the area without being seen by one of his men. The bear beds found in the area were made by black bears. He was unwilling to grant real significance to the sighting made by Alden Brososky on August 24, which the wardens finally learned about on September 11.

"That put the grizzly on the scene – possibly," said Anderson. "But it still didn't make the grizzly responsible for the first mauling, because of the pecking order aspect of this thing. The black bear goes out and lays down where we found the bedding areas; along come some people shouting and hollering, and it's in an ugly mood after getting beat up. It stands to reason that it goes after the next intruder. So to me it didn't verify either way, and anyway, the information was not available to us at the time. The final reason for my belief that the black bear was the one that mauled Cohoe," he says, "is that I cannot believe Muskett could look up from a prone position at that huge monster of a grizzly and then mistakenly describe and verify the black, which was half as big, as the perpetrator."

Superintendent Lange retired and moved to Calgary 25 years ago. When I interviewed him, he was 86 years old but still sharp as a tack. He told me that the plans for bear-proof bins were on the books back in 1977, before he got to Banff. As for the delayed implementation, it was basically an operational problem, something he was not in a position to influence as an administrator. The subject of Eric Langshaw's lawsuit against CP Hotels came up, and after all these years he told me something that he did not reveal back in 1979–1980. "I felt we should get our own house in order before we charged anybody else," he opined. Langshaw aside, Paul Lange was right. Charges laid on September 10, 1980, against the Caboose and other businesses for failing to store garbage in approved containers were all dismissed; the defence lawyers took great delight in showing the judge pictures of the spilled garbage in Parks Canada's own campgrounds.

Remy Tobler launched a lawsuit for "damages in negligence" against Parks Canada, which finally made it to the federal court in Calgary in 1990, presided over by the Hon. Mr. Justice Cullen. I interviewed Bradley G. Nemetz, Q.C., Tobler's solicitor, who believes he had the case against the Crown neatly sewn up, based on the premature reopening of the danger zone, and on the fact that Parks Canada had, in his view, drawn dangerous bears to the town by closing down the landfill site and not cleaning up the garbage problem first. It was a strong case from the outset, and then helicopter pilot Geoff Palmer made it a slam dunk.

To get the full story, I met Palmer at the Starbucks on Pico Boulevard in Los Angeles in February 2007. As I pulled up to park the car, a white kid with rasta braids skateboarded past, his lips, nose and ears adorned with metal jewellery. He looked as if he had fallen face first into a fishing tackle box. Geoff Palmer sauntered across the street, wearing a T-shirt, jeans, and cowboy boots. His five-foot-seven-inch frame was still trim enough for the cockpit of an A-Star or Huey helicopter, and his fine-featured face held a friendly smile. Today he is 56 and owns a company called Productions Helicopters, based in Los Angeles. As we sipped our dark-roast coffees, he let his mind drift back to Canmore in 1980. "I was at Craig's Way Station having breakfast. I grabbed a newspaper and I was reading about this bear mauling case, and I realized it was the same bear mauling that I had flown in. And I was saying to myself, that's not accurate, that's wrong, that's bullshit. I just saw there were discrepancies." Palmer felt compelled to address these discrepancies for the record.

His sudden appearance in the fall of 1990 startled the court, and the judge called a recess. Nemetz sat down with Palmer; what the pilot told him was something no one had mentioned before. Palmer claimed he had seen a grizzly bear during his flight with Bill Vroom on August 24, 1980, after the Cohoe mauling. Nemetz knew what Vroom and Everts had seen, but he was struck by a possibility he had missed up till now. He asked himself: "Why did we all assume that it was the same bear?" Who was to say that the bear spotted by Palmer was the same bear spotted by Warden Everts, as it darted out of the swamp and crossed the road? Chagrined at this failure of logic, an essential tool of trial lawyers, Nemetz concluded that Palmer would clinch his case against the federal government. A grizzly had been in the swamp in 1980, and Parks Canada had been warned about it, according to Palmer.

Palmer described that moment for me. "Basically I was flying in transition just ahead of the downwash at 20 miles per hour, and proceeded to pull into a hover. I could see that the bear was digging something. The downwash behind us caught up and was now below us. I kicked in the pedal to move the machine around, and looked over my right shoulder. I said, 'It's a fucking griz!' I could see the bear for something like five to 15 seconds. I was waiting to hear the report of the shot."

But the shot was never fired. Palmer's explanation? "I guess I had not used enough pedal because Bill couldn't see it." At the trial, Palmer testified that Vroom made no response to his exclamation about the "griz." In our interview, I asked Palmer about this. His answer: "My conversation about it being a grizzly was on the interior intercom. They had headphones on and doors off. We were communicating constantly, so if they didn't hear it maybe it was when they were leaning out of the doors and in the downwash."

Vroom testified that he did not remember if he heard Palmer's voice when the bear was spotted. "He didn't remember if he had on earphones or not," noted Justice Cullen in his judgement. "He didn't remember where he was sitting." Justice Cullen underlined Palmer's "big griz" statement in his reasons for judging in favour of the plaintiff, Remy Tobler.[50]

Yet what Vroom basically said was consistent with what he reported in 1980. "I just saw the back end of a dark-coloured bear disappear under the limb of an evergreen tree."[51] The lapses in Vroom's memory in 1990, however, did not impress Justice Cullen, whereas Palmer, in the following excerpt from his testimony, was very definite about what he had seen 10 years earlier: "I thought it was a grizzly bear because of the size of the animal, the bulk of the animal around the shoulders. The face of the animal when it turned to look at me had a pan shape to it, and just its size; it was huge."[52]

This would have been a very convincing description, if Chief Warden Anderson had ever actually heard it, especially since at that moment in the hunt he still suspected he was dealing with a grizzly bear. It would have confirmed his suspicions. Anderson testified that "after the helicopter got back no one told him it was a black bear but rather a 'black-coloured bear,'" which, once again, is consistent with what Vroom saw. The Crown's lawyer, in rebuttal, pointed out that Palmer had a duty to his employer to report more officially on what he had seen, and questioned why it had taken him 10 years to come forward with his information about the grizzly bear. He accused Palmer of "building up his participation in his own imagination to the point where it has much more significance than it had at the time."[53] Justice Cullen was not moved by this argument.

The most telling evidence against the Crown, however, was Palmer's description of a meeting between himself and the chief warden after the black bear was shot. It allegedly took place on August 28, just after the meeting where Anderson had decided to reopen the area and announce the shooting of bear 057. He was coming down the steps of the warden office, probably feeling relieved at having the problem solved. The judgement transcript reads "Because Palmer had identified the killer bear as a grizzly, he allegedly was invited by Anderson to go over and have a look at it."

Palmer testified that he told Anderson that the bear dead on the floor was the wrong colour (not dark enough) and the wrong species and not the bear Palmer had seen from the helicopter.

Anderson remembers no such conversation to this day, but Justice Cullen judged that "Palmer's evidence is credible and I believe he advised . . . Anderson that they had the wrong bear and he told him why. Anderson's duty was not to ignore Palmer but rather to check out what Palmer told him."[54]

One of the things that frustrates Anderson is the fact that the human hairs found in black bear 054's stomach could not be entered as evidence to support his belief that 054 was responsible for one or more maulings that summer. One of the main points in Tobler's case was his contention that the area had been opened to the public too quickly after the first mauling. (Tobler was attacked on September 1.) In an e-mail I received from Anderson, he wrote that Tobler's lawyer "based the negligence charge on the basis that the hunt [for the first attacker] should have continued; and anything subsequent to that was not relevant." The hairs were never compared to Cohoe's hair, but Anderson conceded that the hair "was not necessarily conclusive, as it was a garbage-eating bear."

In his decision, Justice Cullen chastised Banff residents for not cooperating with Parks Canada to control garbage "even when they received notices to do so," and for not taking the issue seriously before September 1980, but it was Parks Canada he held responsible for Tobler's mauling. In his conclusion, Cullen wrote, "It is clear that the Parks people, the servants of the Crown, were guilty of careless acts and negligent misstatements. They did not . . . meet the duty to take such care in these circumstances as was reasonable to see that visitors would be reasonably safe. The process they followed for garbage management, if anything, made the area of the attack more dangerous. The follow-up procedures followed after the bear attack were too hasty; sufficient preventative action was not taken; experts were not called; the site of the attack was not properly examined for clues of identification of the bear; test results that were sought from a forensic laboratory were not waited for; nor were adequate signs erected as a caution to future users of the area. Statements obviously made by Preston and other Parks people gave the visitor a false sense of security, which ultimately led to the bear attack."[55]

Remy Tobler was awarded $134,617.39 for damages and also received his costs. He told the *Calgary Herald* he felt "very happy" that the Canadian justice system sided with him and added, "I think Parks

Canada learned a lot from this case." I would have to agree. Bear management in the national parks has definitely changed for the better since 1980.

The Whiskey Creek maulings sent a shockwave through Parks Canada and several young wardens, former students of famed bear biologist Chuck Jonkel at the University of Montana, at Missoula, were detailed to pick up the slack and write new plans for bear management in the mountain national parks. Alan Westhaver was assigned to straighten out garbage storage in Banff. Along with engineer Bob Cross, Steve Herrero, and a Lethbridge, Alberta, manufacturer, Jacob Neufeldt, he laboured to ensure that bear-proof bins and approved commercial enclosures became the new normal in Banff. Today, those Haul-All Waste and Transfer bear-proof bins are found in bear country from Canada to Mexico. Wardens Westhaver, Kunelius, and Terry Skjonsberg (son of Earle Skjonsberg), and others rewrote a more humane protocol on bear handling and immobilization; they updated the bear management plan, which is still in use today. Warden Mike Gibeau, who worked with Bill Vroom in Whiskey Creek, went on to obtain his Ph.D. with Steve Herrero as his advisor. Today he is the carnivore specialist for the Mountain District National Parks, a position that was unheard of in 1980. Also unheard of then are the wildlife overpasses and underpasses that enable bears and other game to safely cross the Trans-Canada Highway.

Alan Westhaver saw the post-Whiskey Creek years as a time of great satisfaction and accomplishment. "It wasn't five years after Whiskey Creek that we went from between 65 and 80 tranquilizations and relocations a year down to four or five a year in Banff. Now it's hard to keep people in practice; even our bear specialists do very few immobilizations these days. Now we try to protect carnivores and their role in the trophic pyramid. So that was really a turning point, a beginning point. It was Andy Anderson and Peter Whyte who brought us guys on board and turned us loose on these problems, to find some better ways of doing things."

They seldom use lead on a bear in Banff park today; there is usually a veterinarian on hand any time a bear or other animal has to be immobilized or put down. In the seventies, management actions by the warden service to remove dangerous bears were the number one cause of bear mortalities. Today, the number one cause, according to Steve Herrero, is the Canadian Pacific Railway. In the past six years, trains in Banff park have killed four female grizzlies. Five cubs were orphaned, none of them made it to adulthood. The bears died while feeding on grain spilled from CP boxcars. In May 2007, CP announced it would repair 6,000 hopper cars in the next five years to try and stop the leaks.

Sixty grizzly bears are thought to have their home ranges in Banff National Park. Only 20 are thought to be female. A bear's reproductive rate is tied closely to nutrition. The females in Banff, now cut off from the rich calories once available in garbage, have difficulty getting enough fat these days. Mike Gibeau describes them as "food-stressed bears." These bears spend much of their time actively avoiding people, so chance encounters are rare. During berry season, they feed by "visual cues" (they need to see the berries in order to feed) so they have to feed in daylight, when people are abroad. When they are displaced by people, they are not feeding. According to Gibeau, Banff park has some of the smallest grizzlies around. "These days," he told me, "the biggest bear we've seen was 615 pounds. The average male is only 400 pounds, the average female 250 pounds. We've got adult females here that are 20 years old that only weigh 200 pounds sopping wet, and 15-year-old males that only weigh 450 pounds. These are skinny bears."

These food-stressed bears take longer to become sexually mature and they have the lowest reproductive rate in North America, so the loss of even one of these bears has long-term implications for the population. As a result, the warden service dedicates more money and manpower than ever before to monitoring grizzlies, especially the females, trying to keep them off the railroad tracks and away from the highway, hazing them with noisemakers or even rubber bullets, to keep them from straying into harm's way. Parks Canada currently supports wildlife managers when they want to close areas so bears can feed on berries and other rich foods without being harassed by hikers and mountain bikers.

Bob Muskett told me that after the death of his friend Ernest Cohoe he was not able to go fishing for a long time with his son, Kelly, unless they had a shotgun along. "Even though I knew on that particular day a shotgun would not have been any value to us, it made us feel a bit more comfortable. But I was okay as long as there was no dense bush like where the bear came out of."

Steven Cohoe's attitude toward bears these days is both humane and inspiring: "I don't have a hatred for them. I watch out, carry bear bells and pepper spray." He is a hunter and fisherman, but says, "Let's not forget, that's the bear's home." What upsets him is not the presence of bears, but the fact that every year when he goes out to fish and hunt he finds new roads slashed and bulldozed through our provincial forests, cutting the game habitat into ever small fragments. "There's a reason why states like Montana and Wyoming have more game than us and that's because they don't allow all these roads down there," Cohoe states.

Andreas Leuthold, like Muskett, was scared for a time, about five years in his case. "But I forced myself to go out," he said. "Every noise made me jump – it was very scary.

"I saw Remy last about 1992. He was over in Switzerland. There are no bears there, so he got over the fear of going out walking. Remy had a very positive outlook on life. Last time I saw him he was riding a mountain bike. He'd bought a house outside Zurich."

Remy Tobler got married and had children, Leuthold told me, but endured many operations on his disfigured face. There was a point where the doctors wanted to do more operations and he said, "Don't bother with it anymore." For people who didn't know him before, his appearance was not so strange, said Leuthold. "It was just those who knew him before who noticed the difference."

Joe Dodge recovered from his injuries and had the cheek, according to Andy Anderson, to show up in Banff to ask for the hide of the black grizzly. It was only then that Anderson had second thoughts about interceding with the RCMP on Dodge's behalf.

The origins of the Whiskey Creek mauler remain a mystery, but Steve Herrero told me that he believes, though he cannot prove, that a bear he observed being relocated in 1977 was the black grizzly of Whiskey Creek. The story of that relocation is in Herrero's book, *Bear Attacks*. Herrero got a very good look at the bear after it charged out of the trap much faster than he anticipated and climbed part way up on the hood of his truck, and stared through the windshield into his eyes. In his field observation book, Herrero wrote at the time, "He looks like he could be trouble on the move."

That black grizzly, captured at the Cascade landfill, and trailered out to Tyrrell Creek, never returned, unlike most other dump bears. It appears to have simply blinked out up Tyrrell Creek that day and dropped off the radar screen. Steve Herrero does not remember whether any conversations about the 1977 bear came up in 1980 before 757 was shot, although he said the incident was fresh in his mind at the time of the September 3 meeting.

But a few days later Herrero, pondering 757's carcass and fur colour, definitely had his memory jogged and dug out his old field notes. He had written, "This aggressive bear charged the trap door and as a result, injured its face." Bear 757 had a scar on his face. Furthermore, Dennis Weisser asked me if I remembered the old Moose Horn Bear; this was a grizzly that had been poached near Rock Lake, Alberta, when I was a seasonal warden in Jasper National Park in the early seventies. I said I did; I'd published a poem about him called "The Death of Mustahyah." Weisser reminded me how that bear had a scar on its head where it had been nicked by a bullet. He said the Whiskey Creek grizzly had the same kind of scar on its forehead. "You'll never tell me that bear didn't know what firearms were. The guys had been all through that swamp back and forth, the bear was in there, but it didn't attack them. It knew they had firearms. The people that were attacked didn't have firearms, so wherever it came from, it had experience with firearms."

On September 4, 1980, at the Canadian Wildlife Service field station near the warden office, Herrero's assistants removed the black grizzly's brain for rabies testing. They pulled a premolar tooth and sectioned it to age the bear. They checked his dentition (his incisors were well worn) and they hoisted him on a beam scale and recorded his weight. Then they opened up the carcass with knives and bone saws and dissected the internal organs, looking for parasites and disease processes – looking for explanations.

Steve Herrero had attributed 757's massive weight to feeding on garbage, but there was no sign of garbage in the bear's gut, and no evidence of human hair, tissue, or clothing to link him to the attacks. The only flesh in his stomach was the elk meat they had set out for bait; the only hair was elk hair. The rest of the material in his guts was fir tree needles.

They discussed the carcass, its scars and injuries, referring to the bullet holes as entrance wounds and exit wounds. They measured the four-inch-thick layer of fat 757 had worked so hard to accumulate, to sustain him through the winter, to keep him fit to spread his genes to receptive females in the spring. By trying to understand him, they would reduce the mystery, make him part of their expertise and knowledge.

The bear's tongue, a red banner lolling from between the massive teeth, defied them, defied us. He declined to be summed up, he would be a clown now he was dead if he could not be himself. Even when the bear was reduced to bones, a single fragment, one of those long claws or a sliver of white skull cracked by a bullet, would be there as mute and uncompromising on the shelf in a university laboratory as it was in the flesh when the heart still faintly pulsed. The head was empty now, the brain frozen; its innocent and terrible violence drained; the purpose had fled and left nothing but the evidence.

We had made this lord of bears seek out the most inaccessible hiding places: when great emotions stirred in him to roar out defiance, our presence had caused him to retreat into silence. We had roused him to fury, but we could never make him lower his head in homage to our overwhelming weapons, or confine his spirit with our instruments of science. In the end, he had escaped: he had eluded our determination to understand and explain him.

All that remains of the Whiskey Creek Bear is his time-faded pelt. It is on display (though all of his claws are missing) on the wall of the Banff National Park Museum.

NOTES

1. Darcy Henton, "Icon of the Wilds' Fate in Our Hands," *Edmonton Journal*, October 16, 2007.
2. "Hunter Remembers Attack," *Great Falls Tribune*, October 17, 2007.
3. Julius Strauss, "Ursine Town-crashers Get Bearish Reception," *Globe and Mail*, September 28, 2005.
4. Paul Matheus, "Pleistocene Brown Bears in the Mid-Continent of North America," *Science*, November 12, 2004.
5. James W. Whillans, *First in the West: The Story of Henry Kelsey. Discoverer of the Canadian Prairies* (Edmonton: Applied Art Products, 1955), p. 137.
6. David Thompson, *Travels in Western North America 1784–1812*, Ed. Victor G. Hopwood (Toronto: Macmillan of Canada, 1971), p. 269.
7. Henry Kelsey, *The Kelsey Papers* (Regina: Canadian Plains Research Centre, University of Regina, 1994), p. 2.
8. Parks Canada, untitled report, known locally as the *Whiskey Creek Report*, compiled by Park Warden Peter Perren (November 5, 1980), p. 4.
9. Ibid., p. 99.
10. Stephen Herrero, *Bear Attacks: Their Causes and Avoidance*, Rev. Ed. (Toronto: McClelland and Stewart, 2003), pp. 53–54.
11. For this exposition on diet and dentition I am indebted to Herrero (op. cit.) and to Bjorn Kurtén, *The Cave Bear Story* (New York: Columbia University Press, 1976).
12. Sid Marty, *Men for the Mountains* (Toronto: McClelland and Stewart, 1978), p. 212.
13. Stephen Herrero, "Grizzly Bears and People in the National Parks," *Alberta Wilderness Association Newsletter* (1976), p. 10.

14. Further explained in author's book *Switchbacks: True Stories of the Canadian Rockies* (Toronto: McClelland and Stewart, 1999), pp. 225–237.

15. Frank C. Craighead. Jr., *Track of the Grizzly* (San Francisco: Sierra Club Books, 1979), p. 146.

16. Herrero, *Bear Attacks*, p. 244.

17. Craighead, pp. 212–214.

18. "Claims Versus the Crown – Muser Bear Mauling." Parks Canada, Record Group 84, Acc. E-2003-00300-1, box 29, file C1617/W2/77/ 07/01 Vol. 1., Federal Records Centre, Prairies – Northwest Region, National Archives Canada.

19. Robert G. Kaye, "Interactions Between Bears and Humans. A Background Paper for the Four Mountain Parks Planning Program" (Gatineau, Quebec: Parks Canada, no date), pp. 16–17.

20. Kenneth M. Phillips, Dog Bite Law. http://www.dogbitelaw.com (accessed December 11, 2006).

21. United States Geological Survey, "Mount St. Helens." www.usgs.gov (accessed 2005). Distances based on measuring scales in *National Geographic Atlas of the World*, Washington, D.C.: National Geographic Society, 1981), p. 75.

22. M.J. Rose and A. Westhaver, "Bear Summary Report 1980: Banff National Park Area #1" (Author's collection), p. 39.

23. R.J. Cook et al., "Impact on Agriculture of the Mount St. Helens Eruptions," *Science*, Vol. 211. no. 4477 (January 1981), pp. 16–22.

24. Canada. Atmospheric Environment Service fonds, 1929–1933, 1955–1980. Archives, Whyte Museum of the Canadian Rockies.

25. Rose and Westhaver, pp. 56–57.

26. In the Provincial Court of Alberta, Her Majesty the Queen against the Caboose Company Ltd., trial transcript (Author's collection), February 9, 1981, p. 9.

27. Parks Canada communiqué (Author's collection), Dec. 18, 1980.

28. Personal statement of Robert L.C. Muskett, "Events on August 24, 1980, Regarding Bear Attack to Ernest Cohoe of Calgary." (Typescript 3 pages, September 11, 1980.) Copy provided by Robert (Bob) Muskett.

29. Herrero, *Bear Attacks*, p. 91–107.

30. Tribal Elders John and Nora Stevens (Author interview, Morley, Alberta, 2005).

31. The Hon. Mr. Justice Cullen, "Judgment, Remy Tobler and Her Majesty the Queen in Right of the Government of Canada as Represented by the Minister of the Environment" (December 18, 1990), p. 22.

32. James Gary Shelton, Recent Activities. www.direct.ca/cabc/6ReAc.html (accessed December 3, 2007). See also James Gary Shelton, *Bear Attacks II: Myth and Reality* (Hagensborg, BC: Pallister Publishing, 2001), pp. 55–74.

33. W.F. Lothian, *A History of Canada's National Parks*, Vol. 3 (Ottawa: Minister of Supply and Services Canada, 1979), p. 22.

34. Parks Canada, *Whisky Creek Report*, p. 132.

35. Letter, Andy Anderson to Peter Whyte, September 3, 1985. Submitted to the Federal Court of Canada, Trial Division. Remy Tobler, Plaintiff and Her Majesty the Queen in Right of Canada as Represented by the Minister of the Environment, Defendant. Examination for Discovery of Remy Victor Tobler, September 15 and 16, 1983, p. 34.

36. Barbara Trueman, "Banff Bear Trial," CBC Calgary video library, tape E110.

37. Published by Minister of Supply and Services Canada, 1979.

38. Examination for Discovery of Remy Victor Tobler, September 15 and 16, 1983, p. 34.

39. Ibid., p. 35.

40. Ibid.

41. Ibid.

42. BBC Radio 4, *Run up a Tree and Other Bad Advice*. Radio Documentary (September 4, 1995).

43. Her Majesty the Queen against The Caboose Company Limited, p. 24.

44. Michael Jamison, "Neurosurgeon, Griz Are Sniffing Champs of the Wild," *The Missoulian*, missoulian.com (accessed September 22, 2007).

45. Parks Canada, *Whisky Creek Report*, p. 101.

46. Ibid., pp. 173–176.

47. Ibid.

48. Ibid., p. 206.

49. Parks Canada communiqué, December 16, 1980.

50. The Honourable Mr. Justice Cullen, Judgment, Federal Court of Canada, Trial Division. Remy Tobler and Her Majesty the Queen in Right of Canada as Represented by the Minister of the Environment. December 18, 1990. p. 23.

51. Proceedings before the Hon. Justice Cullen, in the Federal Court of Canada Trial Division, Remy Tobler and Her Majesty the Queen in Right of Canada, November 27, 1990. p. 861.
52. Cullen, Judgment, p. 22.
53. Ibid., p. 24.
54. Ibid., p. 26.
55. Ibid., p. 29.

ACKNOWLEDGEMENTS

A nonfiction book that attempts to cover events that occurred nearly three decades ago could not approach accuracy without involving the memories of others. I wish to extend thanks and recognition to Parks Canada, to Park Superintendent (Ret.) Paul Lange, to Regional Biologist (Ret.) Bruce Leeson and former public relations officer Ken Preston. I want to thank the following active and former members of the Park Warden Service: Chief Park Warden Ian Syme, and retired chief park wardens Andy Anderson, Perry Jacobsen, Peter Whyte, and Paul Kutzer. Park wardens of other rank who helped in my efforts are Tim Auger, Lance Cooper, Keith Everts, Halle Flygare, Mike Gibeau, Larry Gilmar, Clair Israelson, Rick Kunelius, Tim Laboucane, Eric Langshaw, Doug Martin, Don Mickle, Ian Pengelly, Monte Rose, Earle Skjonsberg, Dan Vedova, Bill Vroom, John Wackerle, Alan Westhaver and Jack Willman. Thanks also to former warden dispatcher Helen Kennedy for recalling a painful event in detail, and to former head dispatcher Maureen Vroom for access to the diary of her late husband, Bill. For the RCMP's insight on events, I am grateful to Sandro Parillo, Dennis Krill, and Geri Friesen. John Taggart and Dennis Weisser explained much of the background on the use of snares in the live capture of bears. Geoff Palmer shed additional light on helicopter operations in 1980.

Thank you to the following informants: Alden Brososky, Stoney Indian tribal Elders John and Nora Stevens, Bruce Patterson, Louis

Kovacik, and Dick Russell. Thanks also go to Terry Milewski and Nancy Walters of the Canadian Broadcasting Corporation for helping me to find video coverage of the Whiskey Creek maulings. Noah Richler kindly gave me a copy of his radio documentary "Run Up a Tree and Other Bad Advice," BBC Radio 4, September 4, 1995; E.J. Hart of the Whyte Museum and Archives of the Canadian Rockies cheerfully provided me with facts on Banff weather records. Mike Madel of Montana Fish, Wildlife and Parks provided information on bear maulings in his state.

The events in this book would not ring true without the valuable information and documents made available to me by Remy Tobler via his former solicitor, Bradley Nemetz, Q.C. Thank you also to Mr. Nemetz for his personal insights so graciously shared on the Whiskey Creek incident and his approach to Tobler vs. the Crown. Andreas Leuthold was a mauling victim who offered essential insights on the events that occurred that summer, while Bob Muskett shared both documents and memories and Steven Cohoe generously recalled events about the mauling of his father, Ernest, and its effect on the Cohoe family. I have been greatly aided by my association over the years with biologists and bear experts Mike Gibeau and Steven Herrero. They have answered countless questions with regard to Whiskey Creek in particular and bear behaviour and habitat in general.

Thank you to my editor, Elizabeth Kribs, who made many suggestions that strengthened this book; she deserves a Governor General's Award for patience. Thank you also to my copy editor, Anne Holloway, and to my former editor, Jonathan Webb, who championed the book at the beginning, and thanks to all the devoted people at McClelland and Stewart for caring about books and authors. The person who has sacrificed the most to help me complete this book is my wife, Myrna, to whom I say again, with all my heart, thank you.